PC Repair and Maintenance: A Practical Guide

PC REPAIR AND MAINTENANCE: A PRACTICAL GUIDE

JOEL ROSENTHAL
KEVIN IRWIN

CHARLES RIVER MEDIA, INC.
Hingham, Massachusetts

Editor: David Pallai
Production: DataPage Technologies, Inc.
Cover Design: The Printed Image

CHARLES RIVER MEDIA, INC.
10 Downer Avenue
Hingham, Massachusetts 02043
781-740-0400
781-740-8816 (FAX)
info@charlesriver.com
www.charlesriver.com

This book is printed on acid-free paper.

Joel Rosenthal and Kevin Irwin. *PC Repair and Maintenance: A Practical Guide.*
ISBN: 1-58450-266-5

All brand names and product names mentioned in this book are trademarks or service marks of their respective companies. Any omission or misuse (of any kind) of service marks or trademarks should not be regarded as intent to infringe on the property of others. The publisher recognizes and respects all marks used by companies, manufacturers, and developers as a means to distinguish their products.

Library of Congress Cataloging-in-Publication Data
Rosenthal, Joel.
  PC repair and maintenance : a practical guide / Joel Rosenthal and
Kevin Irwin.
     p. cm.
  ISBN 1-58450-266-5 (Paperback with CD-ROM : alk. paper)
  1. Microcomputers—Maintenance and repair. I. Irwin, Kevin. II.
Title.
  TK7887.R665 2003
  004.165—dc22
                        2003016398

Printed in the United States of America
03 7 6 5 4 3 2

CHARLES RIVER MEDIA titles are available for site license or bulk purchase by institutions, user groups, corporations, etc. For additional information, please contact the Special Sales Department at 781-740-0400.

Contents

Dedication

To our families—Risë, Laura, Karen, Olivia, and Lincoln.

Acknowledgments

We'd like to thank Dave Pallai, not the least for suggesting that Joel write his own book. We'd also like to thank Bryan Davidson and Beth Roberts; Steve Irwin, for advising us along the way; Michael Rosenthal, for steering Joel in the direction of computers; Rina Youngner and Ann Doris Weiss, Joel's high school English teachers who helped turned Joel into a good writer; Laura Rosenthal for helping to make sure the cross references were valid; Max Hersch, Roman Martynenko, Kelman Khersonsky, and Brian O'Connor for technical advice; and Steve Zelicoff, for keeping Kevin in shape enough to be able to work on the book.

This book wouldn't have been possible without you.

Introduction

Personal computers are, at once, horrendously complicated yet simpler than one might expect. How can this be? Computer professionals spend years working on computers, but never learning all there is to know. There's just too much information for one human being to absorb in a lifetime, especially because the technology changes continually and there are so many different types of each component. However, it is not necessary to know anything close to "everything" to be able to repair or even build computers. Because the parts are all modular, most technicians rarely, if ever, use a soldering iron. When a component such as a modem has a hardware problem, you wouldn't spend hours trying to repair it. You simply replace it—a procedure that normally takes a few minutes. Other problems can be corrected through software. So, while it cannot be said that repairing computers is "simple," it is nowhere near as complicated as the complexity of the computer would suggest.

PC Repair and Maintenance: A Practical Guide is designed to enable the reader to repair personal computers running Microsoft® Windows®, primarily Windows 9x (which includes 95, 98, and Millennium Edition, or "Me"), 2000 (mainly 2000 Professional), and XP. This book gives you hints and tricks that few other books provide. Many actions that Microsoft documentation would seem to suggest are impossible are often quite possible with software that is available for download, sometimes even at no charge, from the Internet. These kinds of tips might help you succeed in repairing a computer, or at least saving data, when other technicians might fail.

We don't believe it is necessary to have a deep understanding of every facet of how a computer works in order to diagnose and repair computer problems, so we explain only as much as necessary for each scenario. Furthermore, it is impossible for any book to cover all computer issues. Our goal with this book is to give you the basic information needed to make common repairs and to help you to be able to find information necessary to make other repairs. We decided not to spend much time with monitors, printers, imaging devices, or networking; repairing these devices takes highly specialized skills. Moreover, the software that comes with these devices often modifies the Windows interface from the standard, so configuration screens can differ from one computer to another. Additionally, there are many different types of these devices, each requiring different skill sets. In fact, there are entire books on some of these and on networking, so we don't feel that mere chapters can do them justice. We will limit our coverage to some common issues regarding these devices.

One theme evident throughout the book can be summed up in the phrase "Quality in, performance out." We explain how to select quality replacement and expansion components—even some relatively unknown manufacturers make satisfactory components. Moreover, it is often not necessary to pay top dollar to get quality components. Additionally, we want to make it clear that there's no shame in asking for advice from manufacturers and other experts. Getting appropriate advice can prevent serious problems and save huge amounts of time and money.

This book and accompanying CD-ROM contain many photographs, diagrams, and videos showing the right and wrong ways to perform various tasks, even to the level of physically connecting connectors.

SPECIAL NOTES

1. Due to version and configuration differences, some computers might not have items described in tutorials. In this case, please use Windows Help if you can't find what you're looking for.
2. This book often uses greater-than signs (>) to indicate the next step in a software command. For example, Start > Settings > Control Panel > System.
3. Windows versions are usually referred to by the following designations:

   9x: Windows 95, 98, and Me. These versions are sometimes referred to individually.

   2000: Windows 2000 Professional. Much of the information also covers Windows 2000 Server and Advanced Server.

   XP: Windows XP Home and Professional Editions. These are also referred to individually in places.
4. We use URLs in this book to direct you to helpful Web sites. We leave out the "http://www." from each URL that starts that way. URLs without "www" are shown in full.

   Just as telephone directories are out of date by the time they are printed, some of these URLs won't be in service by the time you read this book. However, there is little or no exclusivity on this type of information, and we encourage you to look up any information you need.
5. Most changes in 2000 and XP require that the user be logged on as an administrator. We don't point that out in subsequent chapters.

1 Overview

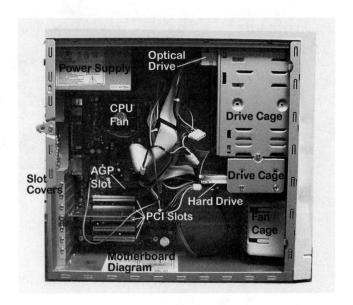

T his chapter describes the basic structure of a personal computer, along with a list of tools needed by a PC technician, and some general advice on computer repair.

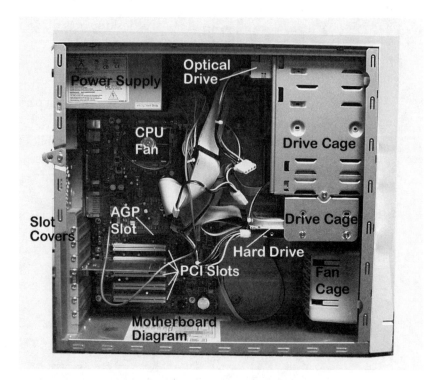

FIGURE 1.1   A typical PC system.

THE PC

Figure 1.1 shows a typical personal computer.

Proper Terminology

Some terms are commonly misused. The most basic of these is the computer itself, which is the box containing all the main components. All peripherals are connected to the computer. The computer is not the modem, hard drive, or CPU. These three terms represent individual components that are part of the computer. They, along with other terms, are defined here.

Case: The cabinet that holds the main components of a computer.

Power supply: A box-shaped device that converts wall-outlet AC power to low-voltage DC used to power the devices in the computer.

Motherboard (system board, main board, desktop board): The large printed-circuit board to which all other parts are connected.

Expansion slots: Slot connectors on the motherboard for attaching various components. Motherboards typically have several expansion slots.

Central processing unit (CPU, or processor): The chip that performs all of the calculations necessary for the computer to do its job.

Random access memory (memory, or RAM): Chip assemblies that store data for very quick recall. The main memory in a computer requires constant power to be able to hold data. Every task performed by a computer requires the program and data to be loaded into memory.

Hard drive (hard disk drive, HDD): A device that stores data on permanently enclosed magnetic disks. The vast majority of computers have at least one hard drive. Data stored on a hard drive remains after the power is disconnected. The *operating system* (OS) (such as Windows), along with programs and data, are almost always stored on a hard drive.

Basic Input Output System (BIOS): A program that works as soon as the computer is powered on to test hardware, locate the OS startup files on the hard drive in order to start the OS, and support the transfer of data among hardware devices. The BIOS is usually stored on a *Complementary Metal Oxide Semiconductor* (CMOS) flash memory chip. *Flash memory* is expensive memory that holds its data indefinitely after the power has been disconnected, but the data can be changed. See Chapter 2, "System Configuration and Computer Hygiene," and Chapter 3, "Motherboards and Their Components," for more information.

Optical drives: Including CD-ROM, CD-RW, DVD-ROM, and various writable DVD drives, optical drives are devices that read, or read *and* write data from or onto discs using laser beams.

Floppy disk drives (floppy drives, FDD, diskette drives): Devices that store data on removable magnetic disks. Virtually all floppy drives sold since the mid-1990s have been of the 3.5" variety. These floppy disks are enclosed in a thin, hard, plastic shell. Because of this, they are sometimes confused with hard drives. However, because of their limited capacity, their susceptibility to data loss, and other reasons, floppy disks have become much less useful in recent years. However, as you will see in subsequent chapters, floppy disks can be indispensable for certain repairs.

Ports: Connectors, usually on the back of the computer, to which peripheral devices can be connected.

Modem: A device that allows the computer to access a telephone line for the purpose of faxing, Internet access, data transfer between computers, or other telephone-related uses. Internal modems plug into expansion slots, while an external modem connects to a port on the computer.

Monitor (display): A device resembling a television that displays the computer's video images.

Sound card (multimedia device): A device whose primary function is to allow a computer to play and record sound. A sound card can either be a separate card that plugs into an expansion slot, or a component built into the motherboard.

Video card (video adapter, graphics adapter, display adapter): A device whose primary function is to generate a video signal ("picture") to be shown on the monitor. A video card can either be a separate card that plugs into a slot on the motherboard, or a device built into the motherboard.

Network card (network adapter, network interface card, NIC): A device that connects the computer to the network. A *network* is a group of computers connected together so that they can communicate with each other. Network cards either come as a separate card or are built into the motherboard.

COMPUTER REPAIR TOOLS

Table 1.1 lists various PC repair tools and the importance of each.

TABLE 1.1   PC Repair Tools

Tool	Comments
Standard screwdrivers (not magnetic)	High-quality Phillips screwdrivers are indispensable. At the very least, you'll need small and larger Phillips screwdrivers with various shaft lengths. A few different sized flat-head screwdrivers are very helpful to have. *Do not use magnetic screwdrivers inside computers.*
Cordless rechargeable screwdriver	Saves time and effort; especially useful when fixing multiple computers.
Paper clips	An unbent paper clip makes a perfect tool for releasing the drawer of an optical disc drive (see Chapter 7, "CD and DVD Drives").

TABLE 1.1   PC Repair Tools *(continued)*

Tool	Comments
Multitester/voltmeter	Essential. A multitester has many uses, the most common of which is testing power supplies. It can test voltage, continuity, resistance, and more. Unlike a multitester, a voltmeter's only function is to measure voltage.
ATX power supply tester	A simple tool that indicates whether the power supply is indeed outputting power, and provides convenient terminals that allow you to easily test the voltage using a voltmeter or multitester.
Cable testers	Testers are available for most types of cables used with a computer. While there are other ways to test cables, such as swapping them with known good cables, cable testers save time and trouble.
Port-testing software	Used to determine whether various ports are working correctly.
Breakout boxes	Another device used for testing cables and ports. Allows complete flexibility in changing the electrical configuration of cables and ports for testing purposes.
Loopback adapters	Available for serial and parallel ports, loopback adapters simulate signals that are input into a computer. Works with port-testing software, described earlier.
Anti-static (ESD) wristbands or anklebands	Tool to protect computer circuits against the damage even carpet shocks can cause.
Anti-static (ESD) spray	Very effective in reducing static electricity on fabric and carpet.
Anti-static (ESD) mats	Provides a static-free surface. Can be used with anti-static wristbands. Includes anti-static floor mats.
POST card	A card that can be plugged into an expansion slot and contains a small display to a show a problem code, POST cards are timesavers that provide accurate and specific diagnoses.
Diagnostic software such as Micro-Scope and PC Certify	A worthwhile investment. These products can significantly reduce the time needed to diagnose all sorts of computer problems.

TABLE 1.1   PC Repair Tools *(continued)*

Tool	Comments
Disk drive installation software	Software utilities that are provided by the drive manufacturers and from other sources, many of which are available at no charge. These sometimes come with the drives, but can also be downloaded.
BIOS flashing utilities (by companies such as MR BIOS®)	Use these to flash BIOSs and to perform other rescue operations on BIOSs and CMOS chips with problems. See Chapter 3.
USB network adapter	Allows for easy network access on a computer that has USB ports but no internal network adapter. Used for data transfer and Internet access on networks set up for it.
Internet access	Allows access to Web-based virus-scanning software and other utilities, and easy downloads of device drivers. See Chapter 2. It is also essential for obtaining technical support. See Chapter 11, "Troubleshooting."
Data transfer cables	Cables of various types such as serial (null-modem), parallel, and USB that allow for different methods of data transfer. Very often, the best solution for a computer with serious OS trouble is to format the hard drives (which erases all content), and reinstall the OS and all software. Data transfer is often the most efficient method of saving data that will be erased by formatting the drive. Various software utilities, some of which are supplied with Windows, allow for data transfer through these cables.
Cleaning and maintenance tools: vacuums and dust-cleaning sprays	Computers get dusty inside, and dust build-up interferes with proper cooling. Use sprays such as Blow Off™ while vacuuming to clean out the dust. See Chapter 2 for details. In addition, the accompanying CD-ROM has a visual presentation of the proper cleaning methods.
CD/DVD scratch repair kits	These can often save damaged software and data discs.
Uninterruptible Power Supply (UPS)	These provide continuous power to a computer when there is a power failure. Indispensable when making changes to a computer's BIOS, because a power failure during these operations will render a computer useless unless a replacement BIOS chip is obtained, which isn't always possible.

TABLE 1.1   PC Repair Tools *(continued)*

Tool	Comments
Data-recovery software	Software that can often recover data from damaged hard drives.
Data-recovery companies (such as Ontrack)	When a hard drive crashes and the data on the drive is extremely valuable, these companies can often recover data from these drives for a substantial fee.
Problem-solving software	Various software programs such as Norton Utilities™ and McAfee® Clinic that solve many different computer problems and optimize performance.
Infrared temperature sensor	Available from companies such as Raytek (*raytek.com*), this uses a laser to point at an object such as a CPU to detect its temperature. Can be very helpful in detecting bad connections or heat-related problems.

GENERAL ADVICE

There are some basic recommendations that will make repairs run as smoothly as possible and ensure good post-repair performance.

Quality In, Performance Out

Obviously, the quality of replacement parts is one factor in determining performance after the repair. When it comes to selecting replacement parts, there can be dozens or even hundreds of choices, and naturally, there are wide variations in quality and price. For example, while most computer-literate people can differentiate hard drives solely by their data-storage capacity, overall computer performance is affected by differences in hard drives such as rotation speed and whether the manufacturer uses quality components and quality production methods.

How to Spot Quality Components

How do you determine which parts are high quality? It's not necessarily a matter of selecting the most expensive components. There are many clues to help guide you in this matter. The most obvious are that the components come with some type of manual or guide, and the company supplies you with a way of contacting them for support or warranty needs. The manual might be in the form of a file on the installation CD, and the contact might be an address, a telephone number, or more likely these days just a Web site or e-mail address. You want to be able to reach customer service and tech support. Some vendors have excellent customer service and tech support, but other vendors are virtually impossible to reach. Often, you can't reach the company unless you can provide the product's serial number.

Additionally, look at the packaging and the actual components themselves. If they look cheap and shoddy, you should be wary. Moreover, if the price is so low that it seems too good to be true, then most times it is. However, that doesn't mean that real bargains aren't available. Let common sense be your guide.

Be Careful with Components

While hardware components are not extremely delicate, they aren't indestructible either, or else you wouldn't need to replace them. They are susceptible to physical and electrical damage due to mishandling and power surges. Follow these guidelines to minimize the risk of damage:

Make sure the power supply is set to the correct voltage: In North America, electric utilities provide 110–120 volts AC to wall outlets. In much of the rest of the world, the standard is 220–240 volts. Check the power supply at the back of the computer. Most have switches labeled 120/240. Make sure the voltage setting matches the actual voltage, or you could face catastrophic results.

Use surge suppressors and UPSs whenever possible: Power surges and undervoltages can damage or even destroy components. See Chapter 2 for more information.

Don't force components: Connectors should be pushed in directly, not at an angle, and most go in only one way. Match up the pins with the holes. If you try to force a connector in the wrong way, you can bend or push in pins, damaging the connector and most likely causing the device to malfunction. In the case of a device with a permanently connected cable, which is common with monitors, damaging the connector requires that a qualified monitor technician repair the monitor.

There are different procedures for inserting expansion cards, memory chips, and CPUs, although the same "no-force" warning applies. See Chapter 3 for more information.

Prevent static damage: Discharge as much static as possible by touching a ground—any large metal object. Avoid carpet. Use anti-static floor mats, surface mats, and wrist ground straps. Make sure all circuits are wired correctly, including grounding.

Wire organizing tip: Do not use rubber bands or metal twist-ties inside a computer. Use plastic wire ties and snip off the ends to avoid scratching your hands and arms.

Document all changes: Keep a record of every change you make; you might have to undo certain changes. Mark all jumper and wire positions, before changing them, with a fine-tipped permanent marker. Make notes and diagrams of wire and jumper positions, and keep a record of all software configuration changes.

IT'S NO SHAME TO SEEK ASSISTANCE

Obtain the correct information before starting or continuing with a repair. This saves not only time but even damage that can sometimes be caused by doing something wrong. In addition to the information found in this and other books, a vast amount of information is available on the Internet from manufacturer's Web sites and from sites dedicated to assisting computer technicians. See Chapter 11 for information on finding assistance. The Industry Contacts document on the accompanying CD-ROM has contact information for many hardware and software providers, along with helpful Web sites.

ON THE CD

2 System Configuration and Computer Hygiene

BIOS OVERVIEW

When a computer is first started, it needs some direction as to what to do. It needs to know where to find the OS's startup files, how hardware is to be accessed by the OS, what hardware is installed on the system, among other things. It is the job of the BIOS to perform these tasks. BIOSs are made by a number of different companies, often customized by the motherboard manufacturers or system builders for a particular motherboard or computer. Some common BIOS brand names are Phoenix™, AMIBIOS®, Award™, IBM®, and MR BIOS®. They are in the form of CMOS chips that store the information.

Power On Self Test (POST)

The first event that happens when a computer is powered on is the POST, performed by the BIOS. The POST consists of a quick series of diagnostic tests, mostly to make certain that essential hardware is present and operating. The most essential hardware is the BIOS itself, processor, memory, video system, and a source of OS startup files (almost always a hard drive). The POST first checks the BIOS, and then the other items. If any of these are not operating correctly, the computer might not start or run correctly. As long as the BIOS program is not set to "Quiet Boot," the POST will give a single beep to let you know that all the tests were successful. If the POST detects problems, it will give a beep code and/or a text message to let you know what is wrong. You can find a list of common beep codes on the accompa-
ON THE CD nying CD-ROM.

Setup Program

The program run by the BIOS is usually called the setup program. Different motherboard manufacturers vary as to how to access the setup program. The most common method is to press a given key just after the first information appears on the screen after the computer is powered on. Often, the screen will give a prompt such as "Press Delete to access Setup." <Delete> is the most common key. Others include <F2> on Dells and Hewlett-Packards, <F10> on Compaqs, and <F1> on some Gateways. Setup screens vary widely, so we will cover the most common and important BIOS settings.

Before you go into a setup program, make sure that you are ready to write down any changes you make. Some setting changes can render a computer unbootable, and if you don't know which changes you made, you'll have a difficult time finding the change that caused the problem.

NOTE

To help prevent changes from causing serious problems, BIOS manufacturers offer a way out. After you have changed BIOS settings, setup programs offer you a choice to accept or discard changes as you exit the program. Use this function if you are unsure of any changes you have made, or if you haven't recorded those changes on paper. You can always go back and make the changes again. Figures 2.1 and 2.2 show examples of setup screens.

Important BIOS Settings and Information

Because there is so much variability among setup programs on different BIOSs, we will cover common and important items only.

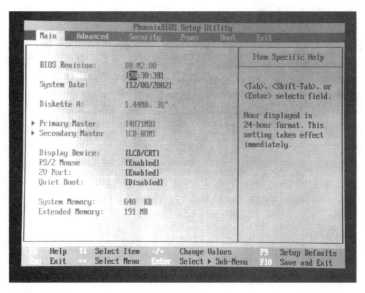

FIGURE 2.1   A sample setup screen.

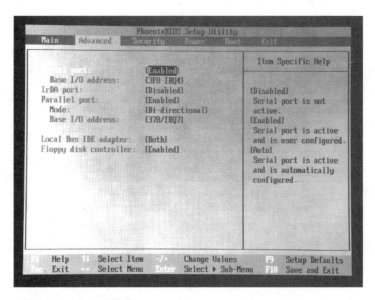

FIGURE 2.2   Another setup screen.

System Date and Time: This can also be set in Windows.

BIOS version number: Sometimes it is necessary to update the BIOS. BIOS programs are delineated by version numbers; if the motherboard or computer manufacturer's Web page shows a download with a higher number, that means a more recent BIOS is available. See Chapter 3, "Motherboards and their Components," for more information on updating BIOSs.

Port assignments: If the computer has ports (serial, parallel, etc.) that are not being used, and it is necessary to free up their resources, you can disable them in the setup program. Conversely, if you need to use them and they are disabled, you can re-enable them in Setup.

Supervisor and user passwords: You can set passwords for the computer.

If you set a supervisor password and forget what it is, you can also forget about retrieving it, and you might not be able to finish booting the computer. Sometimes, there are steps you can take to reset the password. See Chapter 3 for more information.

Power settings (ACPI, or Advanced Configuration and Power Interface): Contains power use settings including those for hibernation, standby, and in battery-powered computers, power conservation settings. Often, BIOSs contain settings that allow proper shutdown of Windows just by pressing the power button on the computer or keyboard once. Some systems have different levels of standby types.

Boot order: Traditionally, a computer is set to boot first from the floppy drive, and then from the main hard drive (Drive C). This means that the computer will check the floppy drive first for boot files. If there is no disk in the floppy drive, the computer will then go to the hard drive to look for boot files. That is why if you leave a non-bootable floppy disk in the drive and try to boot up, you'll get an error message such as "NTLDR is missing. Press any key to restart." or "Non-system disk or disk error." This can be changed to pretty much any order, including CD and DVD drives. It is useful when installing Windows on a new or just-formatted computer to set the computer to boot first from a CD-ROM drive, and then insert the Windows installation CD-ROM into that drive. This saves you from having to use boot floppies that might or might not come with the Windows CD-ROM.

Memory settings, DRAM Timing: Don't change these unless so instructed by a support technician.

AGP Aperture: Don't change unless you are familiar with troubleshooting techniques and feel comfortable in this area. The main thing to remember here is that the AGP Aperture Size should almost always be set to at least 16MB and never to more than the actual physical RAM installed in the system. This setting will allow a possible increase in graphics (video) performance by permitting the graphics system to share system memory if needed. A higher setting often (but not always) means better graphics performance, so test the results of any change you make here by viewing the graphics performance.

CPU Frequency, Voltage Control, other settings such as frequency (speed): On many BIOSs, this can be set automatically or manually. If you're setting them manually, you have to know the exact settings for your CPU so you don't damage your motherboard or CPU. Settings other than those specified by the CPU manufacturer should be made only by very experienced technicians.

PC Health: These include CPU and system temperatures at which warnings are made and shutdowns occur.

Integrated peripherals: These are items such as sound "cards" and network adapters that are part of the motherboard. The most common use of these settings is to disable these devices when additional peripherals of the same type are installed. For example, if the user installs an expansion sound card on a system that has onboard sound (because the onboard sound device has failed or because the user wants to upgrade to a better sound device), the onboard sound needs to be disabled to prevent problems that can occur with two active sound cards.

Interrupts (IRQs): These settings can also be changed in the Windows Device Manager (we provide more information later in this chapter).

Extended System Configuration Data (ESCD): If this setting is available, it should be enabled every time a new component is installed in the computer. Each time ESCD is enabled, the configuration resets at next boot. If a computer won't boot after installation of a new component, enabling ESCD and rebooting the system can sometimes solve the problem.

IDE Detection: This is normally set to Auto for automatic detection of IDE disk drives. Disabling auto-detection on unused drive channels can speed the boot process. See Chapter 6, "Magnetic Disk Drives," for more information on IDE drives.

Self-Monitoring Analysis and Reporting Technology (S.M.A.R.T.) drives: This technology, incorporated into most modern IDE hard drives, can alert the user of possible impending hard drive failure and most likely allow for data backup before this happens. Because of this, S.M.A.R.T. drive support should always be enabled in the setup program. Interestingly, computers are often delivered from the factory with S.M.A.R.T. drive support disabled.

Plug and Play (PnP) settings: We describe Plug and Play capability later in this chapter. PnP should be enabled in the vast majority of cases. Sometimes in Windows 95, you will have to disable Plug and Play support. There are certain other unusual situations that require you to disable Plug and Play, as you might find when researching certain problems or reading installation manuals.

Load defaults: Setup programs have default settings. Loading default settings is a good way to get your computer back to its original configuration. Do this only if all else fails. Before loading the default settings, *go through each screen and write down every setting.* Some devices might not work with the default settings.

WINDOWS CONTROL PANEL

Control Panel is one of the most important areas in Windows for configuring your computer. Although many of the applets in Control Panel can be accessed from elsewhere, Control Panel is the central location for these tools. There are several ways to access Control Panel, and these vary depending on Windows version and configuration. Tutorial 2.1 explains three ways to access Control Panel. If none of these applies to the computer you're working on, please consult Windows Help.

TUTORIAL 2.1   **ACCESSING CONTROL PANEL**

A. **Windows 9x, 2000, and XP with Classic Start menu:** Go to Start > Settings > Control Panel.
B. **Windows XP with standard Start menu:** Go to Start > Control Panel.
C. **All versions if so configured:** Open My Computer and click or double-click Control Panel.

Applets

In Control Panel, *applets* are small programs that are used to configure individual components of the OS and hardware. Control Panel contains many applets. The applets and their names vary from version to version. Certain third-party programs install additional applets in Control Panel. This section covers pertinent applets not covered elsewhere in the book.

Wizards

A *wizard* is a program that leads the user through various steps of configuring software or hardware by prompting for answers to questions. Wizards facilitate simpler configuration of hardware and software by making sure that all of the necessary components are properly configured and that none are missed. Many of the applets in Control Panel contain wizards. The disadvantage to wizards is that they sometimes can limit options available in traditional configuration screens. However, most components can be configured from traditional screens after the wizard has been completed.

The remainder of this section deals with the more important applets.

For XP users, if you reach Control Panel and find that it shows none of the applets described in the following paragraphs, click the Switch to Classic View link that should appear at the top of the menu on the left side of the screen. The default "Category View" is designed more for end users than for technicians.

Accessibility Options

Accessibility Options are aids for people with various disabilities. They are also available in most versions in Start > Programs > Accessories along with an Accessibility Wizard. This applet is fairly self-explanatory. Check here if you are experiencing unusual keyboard behavior such as ignored brief or repeated keystrokes, sounds such as beeps when certain keys are pressed, exceptionally large or high-contrast video, and so forth. Make sure the user doesn't need these settings before disabling them. If you do need to disable them to work on the machine and the user needs them, make sure to write down all settings and restore them before returning the machine to the user.

Add/Remove Hardware

This goes by different names in the various versions of Windows. Its purpose is to scan the computer for new hardware components and to install the drivers for them. In the event that Windows doesn't automatically detect new hardware, compatible hardware can often be installed by following the wizard. This applet is becoming less important as Windows installs almost all Plug and Play hardware automatically. We cover this and related wizards, plus Plug and Play technology, in greater detail in the upcoming section on device drivers.

Administrative Tools: Computer Management

The Administrative Tools folder is available in 2000 and XP only, although there are versions of a few of the tools in 9x. This is a series of tools, most of which are not intended for the average end user. These tools are accessible by themselves, and many are accessible through one of them: Computer Management. Computer Management is also accessible by right-clicking the My Computer icon and clicking Manage from the menu that appears, and from the programs list in the Start menu if so configured. Computer Management is divided into the following three categories.

System Tools

System Tools comprises a collection of tools allowing you to monitor performance and events, view information about hardware and software, and manage shared folders and user and group accounts.

There is another set of tools in all versions called System Tools. These are accessible from the programs in the Start menu and are discussed later in this chapter.

The pertinent tools in this folder vary between 2000 and XP and are:

Event Viewer: You might be directed by a support technician or article to use Event Viewer. For detailed information on Event Viewer, go to *http://support.microsoft.com*, click the link for searching Knowledge Base articles by number, and enter 308427.

Device Manager: We discuss Device Manager in detail later in this chapter.

Storage

Disk Management: Disk Management is the one very useful program here that isn't readily available elsewhere. It allows you to view a graphical depiction of the condition of all disk drives installed in the computer. Indicators show the type of partition (system, logical, primary, etc.), its condition (healthy, failed, formatting, healthy (at risk), etc.), file system (FAT, FAT32, NTFS), and other information. As long as the system is bootable, Disk Management allows you to repair some types of disk problems (of course, if the system isn't bootable, you won't be able to start Disk Management).

Management of hard drives at this level is rather complicated. To understand more, see reference books on Windows 2000. We discuss some disk restoration techniques in Chapter 6.

Services and Applications

Services: Shown in Figure 2.3, this is the important subcomponent here. It allows management of services on the computer. A *service* is a small program or part of a program whose purpose is to support larger programs or OS components. Many services need to run for Windows and certain installed programs to operate. Some should start automatically with Windows, and some should be started manually only when called on by a program or OS process. If you

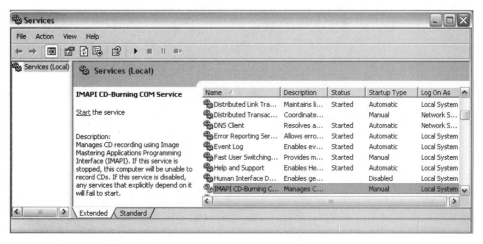

FIGURE 2.3 Services applet.

get a message that says that something isn't working because a needed service isn't started, go to Services. Locate the service (hopefully the error message identified the particular service) and double-click on its line in the list. Here, as shown in Figure 2.4, you'll see controls that allow you to start the service manually, set it to automatic so it starts when Windows starts, set it to manual so it waits for a command to start, or disable it so it never starts. If you attempt to start the service and it won't start, it's time to troubleshoot. See Chapter 11, "Troubleshooting," for general troubleshooting information.

You can also use the XP version of MSConfig to set services to start or stop with Windows. We discuss MSConfig later in this chapter.

Add/Remove Programs

Known as "Add or Remove Programs" in XP, this applet is used most often for uninstalling programs. One mistake many Windows newbies make is to delete program files rather than uninstalling them. This can cause problems with the Windows registry (we discuss the registry in Chapter 11). This applet has several uses:

Installation of programs: This applet is no longer frequently used for installing programs. Usually, to install programs, you can simply insert the program installation disc and follow the prompts, or double-click on a program installation file icon and follow the prompts. If you do decide to use this to install a

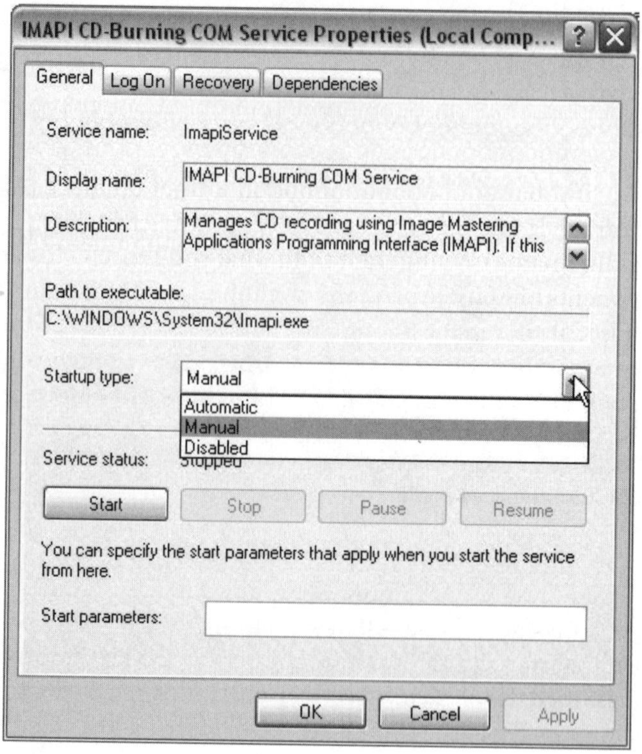

FIGURE 2.4   Configuring a service.

program, click the Install button on 9x or the Add New Programs button on 2000 or XP, and follow the simple prompts.

Uninstallation of programs: The Uninstall wizard is a very useful tool. It is a good idea to uninstall programs that are no longer likely to be used, in order to free up space on the hard drive. One common problem computers have is that their hard drives become nearly full. A computer might run badly or not at all unless the hard drive has enough free space to hold the *swap file* for *virtual memory* (we define these terms later in this chapter). Other reasons to uninstall programs are if they are causing problems on the computer or if installation of a new version of the program requires that the old version be uninstalled first. Click the name of the program in the list and follow the prompts. You might be asked while running this wizard to decide if certain files should be retained or deleted. Usually, your choices will be "Yes" (delete the file), "Yes to all" (delete all such files), "No" (retain the file), and "No to all" (retain all such files). Unless you are certain, it is safest to select "No to all." At the end, you'll usually get the message that not all of the items were deleted and that you should remove the remaining items manually. You can safely forgo doing so, although you might want to delete shortcuts. *Shortcuts* are small files that allow you to access other files. Most of the icons on the desktop are shortcuts, as are the programs listed in Start > Programs. If there are still shortcuts on the desktop for a program you have uninstalled, right-click the shortcut icon and click Delete.

If you absolutely must uninstall a program that doesn't show up in the list, you can locate the program's folder and delete it. First, make sure that the program's name isn't different from what you expect—for example, different components of McAfee products might be called McAfee or Network Associates. If it is truly not in the list, the program's folder is most likely in the root directory (main folder) of the main hard drive, but it could be on the desktop, the Program Files folder, or elsewhere. If you have error messages during boot or other problems after deleting the program folders, you can try to fix the problem using a registry cleaning program (see Chapter 11). If that doesn't solve your problems, reinstalling the program (assuming you have the installation media) might help until you can get assistance in properly uninstalling it. It is generally a good practice, however, not to delete programs unless you know how to deal with the aftermath.

Addition and removal of Windows components: Most people don't need every component that comes with Windows to be installed on their computer. Sometimes, you might need to remove an unused component to free up disk space. Other times, a user will need a Windows component that wasn't installed originally. This is where you make these additions and subtractions. On 9x, click the Windows Setup tab, as shown in Figure 2.5. In 2000 and XP, click the Add/Remove Windows Components button. This calls up a list of installable components, as shown in Figure 2.6. Note the check boxes next to each item. Empty white check boxes mean that none of the components in that category are installed or set to be installed. White check boxes with a check mark mean that all of that category's components are installed or set to be, and gray check boxes with a check mark mean that some of the components are installed or set to be installed. When you have selected a category, clicking the Details button provides a list of items in that category, and a description appears under the list. Make your decisions, click Next, and then follow the remaining prompts. In many cases, you'll be asked for the Windows installation disc. In 9x, rather than using the Windows CD-ROM, you often can navigate to the folder C:\Windows\Options\Cabs, where C: is the hard drive partition where Windows is installed. Cabs refer to Cabinet files. *Cabinet files* are highly compressed files, in this case containing all of the Windows installation files.

Creating an emergency boot disk (9x only): You might recall from Chapter 1, "Overview," that the emergency boot disk is an essential tool when the com-

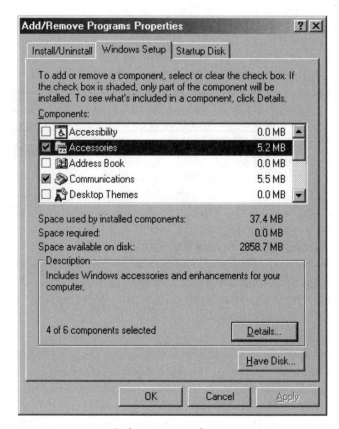

FIGURE 2.5   9x Windows Setup tab.

puter won't boot. This is where you create it; the wizard is straightforward. As we discuss in Chapter 11, 2000 and XP don't have this applet, although it is possible to make an emergency boot disk for these versions. Make sure you have boot disks for each version of Windows 9x you will be working with. See Chapter 11 for more information on boot disks.

Windows Update: Although present on all versions, it is accessible from here on XP only. We discuss Windows Update later in the chapter.

Folder Options

This applet has two useful tabs. The View tab has a list of items with check boxes. To see all folders and files that could be needed for repair, it's be very helpful to clear the following check boxes: "Hide file extensions for known file types," and "Hide protected operating system files [Recommended]." You might also want to

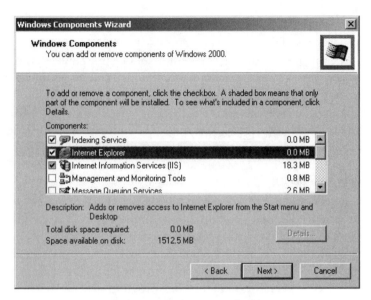

FIGURE 2.6   XP Windows Components Wizard.

select the "Show hidden files and folders" option button. It's probably a good idea to change the latter two settings back to their defaults before returning the machine to the user, however.

The other useful tab is the File Types tab. Have you ever noticed that when you double-click on a data file, Windows starts the correct program to open the file? This is where those file-program associations are stored. One of the best uses for this tab is undoing the unwanted file associations that certain applications, especially media players, make. Select the file extension you want to configure and click Advanced. Click the function in the Action list (usually "open" and/or "play," in the case of a media file). Click Edit, and browse for the program you want to perform this function. You might want to change the icon as well. Then, click OK. With a lot of luck, your file-program associations will remain the way you set them. Unfortunately, programs have a tendency to change these settings without your knowledge.

To select the program to play audio CDs automatically when you insert a CD in the drive, edit both the file type called Audio CD (with no file extension), and the file type described as "CD Audio Track," bearing the CDA extension. If you want to use the basic Windows CD player rather than Windows Media Player, you can usually find the program cdplayer.exe in the folder C:\Windows (or Windows NT in 2000)\System32, or C:\Windows.

TIP

Game Controllers

This applet is fairly self-explanatory—it's used to configure game joysticks and other controllers. However, one point about game controllers must be stressed: follow the game controller manufacturer's instructions to the letter, especially if the instructions say to install the software before plugging in the device. Although installation is usually simple, an incorrectly installed game controller can be a nightmare to reinstall correctly. You might find yourself at the manufacturer's Web site or making a toll call for support if directions are not followed carefully.

Power Options

Power options are settings related to A/C and battery power, standby and hibernation, and UPS (battery backup) configuration. *Standby* is the function that shuts off power to almost everything but the memory. When full power is restored, by moving the mouse or using the keyboard in most cases, or pushing the power button on some notebook computers, the computer is left in the same state it was in before it was placed in standby. All of the same programs will be open to the same places. *Hibernation* (also known as *suspend*) is similar to standby, but the entire memory is written to the hard drive and the power is shut off completely. Like standby, when power is restored (usually by pushing the power button), the computer returns to the same state it was in before hibernation. The options that appear in this applet depend on whether the hardware and BIOS support them—if they don't, the functions simply don't appear. For example, if there is no UPS installed on the computer, the UPS tab doesn't appear. Notebook computers tend to have the most functions in this applet because of the data loss that can occur if the battery were to die while files are open. Peruse the available tabs to see all the configurable properties here.

System

System is perhaps the most important applet in Control Panel. Accessible from here and also by right-clicking My Computer and clicking Properties, System has a number of useful components. Figure 2.7 shows the 9x version, Figure 2.8 shows the 2000 version, and Figure 2.9 shows the XP version. The different tabs are as follows:

> **General tab:** The General tabs are nearly identical on all the versions, and contain some helpful information. The exact OS version plus installed service packs are identified. *Service packs* are significant updates to Windows OSs that are offered by Microsoft. We discuss them later in the chapter. Other information on this page are the name the OS is registered to with the registration code number, the general category of CPU and amount of RAM installed on the machine, and sometimes, contact information for the computer's manufacturer.

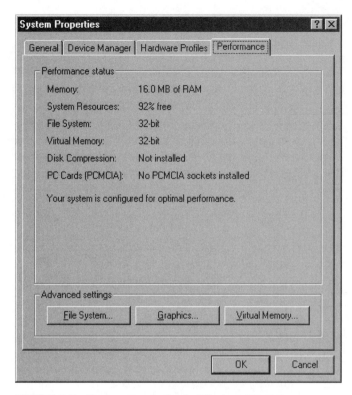

FIGURE 2.7   System Properties in Windows 9x.

Computer Name (XP)/Network Identification (2000): These tabs contain network settings that are beyond the scope of this book, but if you will ever deal with networks, you should familiarize yourself with them.

Hardware (2000 and XP): This tab contains the Add Hardware Wizard (XP) or the Add/Remove Hardware Wizard (2000). They are the same wizards described earlier in this section under Add/Remove Hardware and are covered in detail in the next section. The other important function here is Device Manager, which is also covered in the next section.

Remote (XP only): This tab contains authorization settings for Remote Assistance and Remote Desktop. These should be enabled on any XP computer if you want to be able to view someone's computer screen from a remote location through a network or even over the Internet. Click the Advanced button and select the appropriate check boxes. We discuss Remote Assistance and Remote Desktop in Chapter 11.

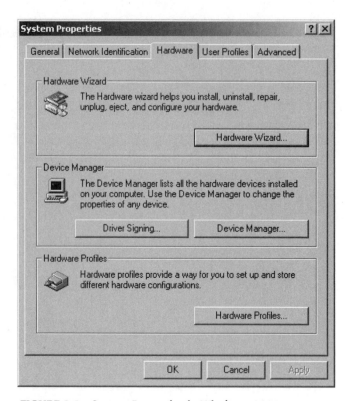

FIGURE 2.8   System Properties in Windows 2000.

Advanced (2000 and XP): The most important function is Startup and Recovery. Click the Startup and Recovery button in 2000, or the third Settings button in XP. The System Failure settings on the bottom part of this dialog box apply to the "blue screen of death." The *blue screen of death*, officially known as a stop error, can happen on XP and 2000 machines when something serious happens. Windows suddenly shuts down and the contents of memory are dumped into a file called memory.dmp located by default in C:\Windows [or Winnt]\System32. It is recommended to clear the "Automatically reboot" check box on 2000; it is important to be able to read the entire blue screen, and automatic rebooting doesn't leave the screen on long enough for anyone to write the entire error code. The error code consists of a cryptic statement such as KMODE_NOT_LESS_OR_EQUAL followed by several long *hex* numbers (we define hex numbers later in this chapter). If you get the dreaded screen, write down the entire error code and search for it either on Google™ or on Microsoft's Knowledge Base. More information on searching for error messages is available in Chapter 11. If you don't get useful information and want to get support from

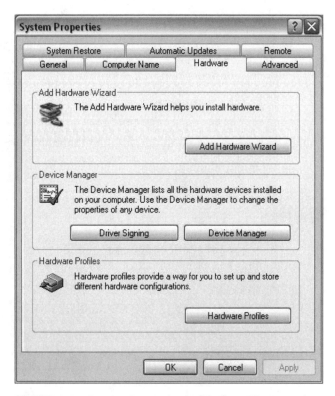

FIGURE 2.9   System Properties in Windows XP.

Microsoft, they'll ask you for the memory.dmp file so they can diagnose the problem by reviewing everything that was in memory at the time the stop error occurred. Note that this file can be very large. Figure 2.10 shows the 2000 Startup and Recovery page.

Performance (9x only): We discuss the Performance tab in the Windows Performance section later in the chapter.

DEVICE DRIVERS (DRIVERS) OVERVIEW

Device drivers are software files that contain instructions that allow the OS to interact with hardware. For example, it takes one or more mouse drivers for the OS to understand what to do when you move the mouse. The printer driver tells the printer what to do when you click Print. Almost all devices need some type of driver in order to operate, so virtually every new device comes with a driver disk or disks. Windows also contains a large selection of drivers for all types of hardware.

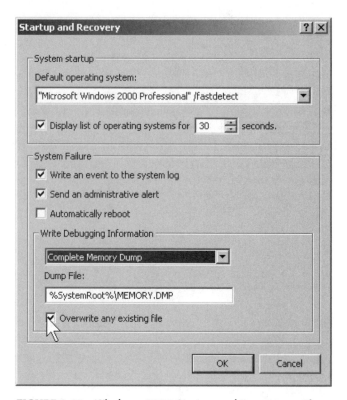

FIGURE 2.10   Windows 2000 Startup and Recovery settings.

Some devices are so important that generic drivers are available immediately after powering on the computer. These are the video and keyboard drivers. Generic drivers for these devices are built into the BIOS. That is because, barring the presence of devices used by those with certain disabilities, a computer is useless without a monitor running at least at some point during its operation, and cannot be controlled without a keyboard. A *generic* driver is a driver that will work with many or all of its class of devices, but will usually not allow for full functionality of a particular device. To illustrate this, you might notice that, while booting, your monitor might display larger text and few colors. Then, toward the end of boot-up, you'll see much better color and smaller, sharper text. That is because the generic drivers that allow for video as soon as the machine is powered on aren't designed to take advantage of the full capabilities of the video card and monitor. Once the device-specific drivers are loaded into memory, later on in the boot process, you should see more colors and greater resolution. You can find more information about video in Chapter 8, "Video, Sound, Modems, and Network Adapters."

Drivers are also usually specific to the OS version, or version group. In many cases, a driver will work in all versions of Windows 9x, while another driver will work with Windows 2000 and XP. In some instances, there is one driver for all of these versions, and in others, there is a separate driver for each version. This all depends on the individual device.

You will notice that many devices come with "software." Usually, this includes both drivers to make the device operational and programs to make them functional. For example, a CD-RW drive with just its device driver installed will work only as a CD-ROM drive. To be able to "burn" (record) CDs, you need a program that will give you controls that allow you to use the device for all of its intended purposes. Often, the software that ships with a hardware device includes one or more third-party programs that are certified by the device manufacturer to be compatible with that device. The drivers to operate the device, and sometimes drivers for competing devices, are included in the program. However, some devices, most notably printers, come with software that is designed by the printer manufacturer solely for that device. And in some cases, Windows will have built-in software components that can be used to perform the tasks of the hardware device. For example, the most recent versions of Windows Media Player™ can be used to burn multimedia CDs on a CD-RW.

Installing Drivers

All of the versions of Windows discussed in this book are PnP OSs. Often disparagingly called "Plug and Pray" when introduced in Windows 95, Plug and Play refers to the capability of a device to be recognized and installed automatically by the OS without the user having to manually configure the resources used by the device. A computer's BIOS, OS, and the device all have to be Plug and Play compatible for Plug and Play to work; nearly every PC BIOS, OS, and virtually every device sold since Windows 95 became common is so compatible. If everything is working as it should, Windows will automatically detect any newly installed Plug and Play device and attempt to install the drivers for it.

NOTE

Manufacturer's installation instructions always supercede the instructions in this chapter in case there are any differences.

Installing a driver is part of installing a device. In fact, when Windows messages refer to "installing or uninstalling a device," they mean primarily installation and uninstallation of the drivers for that device. Here are the most common ways that device drivers are installed on Windows PCs:

Automatically by Windows: Windows detects the device on bootup and installs the drivers for it.

Almost automatically by Windows: Windows detects the device and prompts for the location of the driver. The user supplies the disk or location of the driver files on the hard drive, and answers the prompts.

Manufacturer-supplied installation CD: The installation CD starts automatically upon insertion. The user follows the prompts to install the software. Often, there is more than one program to install in this situation.

Installation program on the hard drive: The user runs the program, usually by double-clicking, and installation proceeds in the same manner as the previous method.

When installing or reinstalling a driver, make sure you know where the drivers are. If they are on a floppy or CD, make sure you know which drive the disk is in along with the path to the driver files. If the drivers are on the hard drive, which is common if you downloaded them from the Internet, make sure you know the path to the files.

TIP

If you download a file from the Internet, make sure to navigate to a folder that you can easily find when prompted for a location. Otherwise, Windows might direct the file to a hidden temporary Internet folder that is almost impossible to find, even if you know where to look and your system is configured to show hidden and system files.

Reinstalling a Driver

One very common problem that occurs with PCs is for a device to stop working correctly or at all. In most cases, there is nothing wrong with the hardware; instead, the driver has become corrupted. Corrupted drivers can sometimes even affect the functioning of the entire computer.

There are various degrees of reinstalling drivers. Try these in order if you haven't solved the problem:

1. Reinstall the existing driver.
2. Uninstall and reinstall the driver.
3. Uninstall the driver from your system and reboot. When Windows restarts, it should detect the new hardware and start to install the drivers again.

If you have the documentation and driver disks from a device, follow the provided directions. For example, corrupted drivers are common with Hewlett-Packard printers. Tutorial 2.2 describes a typical case of reinstalling a printer driver.

TUTORIAL 2.2 **REINSTALLING PRINTER SOFTWARE**

Make sure you have the driver disk or have downloaded the file before proceeding with these steps:

1. In Windows XP with the standard Start menu, go to Start > Printers and Faxes. In all other versions, go to Start > Settings > Printers.
2. Right-click the icon for the printer you want to uninstall and select Delete from the pop-up menu that appears.
3. Follow the prompt to confirm deletion.
4. Insert the driver disk or execute (run) the installation file on the hard drive.
5. Follow the prompts to install the printer software.

In other situations, follow the procedures outlined in Tutorial 2.4a, *Reinstalling a Known Driver in Device Manager*, or Tutorial 2.4b, *Letting Windows Select the Best Driver to Install*. The procedures vary slightly with different versions of Windows.

The one place where all or almost all drivers can be accessed is Device Manager. There are many ways to get to Device Manager, not all of which can be used on every computer, depending on Windows version or configuration. A few methods are described in Tutorial 2.3. If none of these methods applies to the computer you're working on, please search Windows' Help for Device Manager.

TUTORIAL 2.3 **ACCESSING DEVICE MANAGER**

A. **Windows 9x:** Right-click the My Computer icon on the desktop and select Properties from the pop-up menu that appears. Click the Device Manager tab.
B. **Windows 2000 and XP:** Right-click the My Computer icon on the desktop and select Properties from the pop-up menu that appears. Click the Hardware tab, and then the Device Manager button. In XP, you might be able to right-click My Computer in the Start menu to view the pop-up menu.
C. **All versions:** You can access Device Manager through the System applet in Control Panel. See Tutorial 2.1 for instructions for opening Control Panel.

Some computer owners rename My Computer to their own names.

TUTORIAL 2.4A   **REINSTALLING A KNOWN DRIVER IN DEVICE MANAGER**

1. Follow the appropriate procedure described in Tutorial 2.2 to access Device Manager.
2. In Device Manager, click the "+" sign next to the category of hardware whose driver you want to reinstall. One or more devices appear under the category name.
3. Double-click the name of the device. The device's Properties page appears.
4. Click the Driver tab. The driver page appears. You will have various options here, depending on the Windows version.
5. Click the Update Driver button. You'll be prompted to search for a suitable driver or to select a driver from a list, except in XP, which will prompt you to install a driver automatically or to select from a list. If you have a driver disk, insert it now.
6. Follow the instructions for your system:
   A. **Windows 9x and 2000:** Select the "Display a list…" or "No. Select driver from list" option button and click Next.
   B: **Windows XP:** Select the "Don't Search…" option button and click Next.
   A list of drivers might appear in the window.
7. The existing driver usually appears first in this list. If you want to reinstall it, click Next and follow the remaining prompts. If you have inserted a disk, or know where you can find the driver on the hard drive, click Have Disk.
8. If you know the path to the driver, enter it in the text box. To browse for the driver, click Browse, and then locate the driver. In case the driver is on your desktop, know that the default path to the desktop in Windows 9x is C:\Windows\Desktop. In Windows 2000 and XP, the default path is C:\Documents and Settings\[logged-on username]\Desktop. Once you find the file, its name should appear in the text box. Note that only a file with the extension ".inf" will be considered a driver.
9. Click OK and follow the remaining prompts.

If you get warning messages, consider them carefully. Some Windows warning messages are critical (but see the note immediately following Tutorial 2.4b).

TUTORIAL 2.4B   **LETTING WINDOWS SELECT THE BEST DRIVER TO INSTALL**

1. Follow Steps 1 through 5 of Tutorial 2.4a.
2. In the Update Device Driver wizard that appears, select the option button appropriate for your version:
   A. **Windows 95/98:** Select the "Yes (Recommended)" option button that answers the question, "Do you want Windows to search for the driver?"
   B. **Windows Me:** Select the "Automatically search for a better driver (Recommended)" option button.
   C. **Windows 2000:** After clicking Next, select the "Search for a suitable driver for my device (Recommended)" option button.
   D: **Windows XP:** Click the "Install the software automatically (Recommended)" option button.
   Then, click Next.
3. Windows 9x and XP start the search at this point. If Windows doesn't find a driver, it prompts you to search in other locations. Windows 2000 allows you to specify a location here. If you don't, it will search the hard drive only.
4. If you haven't inserted a disk and Windows has found a driver it says will work, follow the prompts to install that driver. If you have inserted a disk, or Windows hasn't located a suitable driver, and you know where the driver is, browse or otherwise specify the location of the file. Then, follow the prompts to install or not install the driver.

If Windows warns you that a driver might not be suitable for your hardware, don't attempt to install it. However, Windows might give you a message that says that the driver is not digitally signed. While a driver with a digital signature will almost certainly work, other drivers intended for the specific Windows version will probably work also. You can ignore this particular warning in the vast majority of cases.

If using one of these methods doesn't solve the problem, the next step is to uninstall the device and then reinstall. The procedure is similar to that in Tutorial 2.4a. In Windows 9x, select the device in Device Manager and click the Remove button. Follow any prompts you see, and then click the Refresh button. In 2000 and XP, right-click the device and click Uninstall from the pop-up menu. Then, close Device Manager. The Hardware tab of the System applet should be visible. Click the Hardware Wizard button and go through the wizard. Follow all the prompts. Then, run Add/Remove Hardware in Control Panel and install the driver following the directions in Tutorial 2.4a.

The last thing to try before suspecting bad hardware is to uninstall the device following the methods just mentioned. Then, restart the computer. Windows should recognize the device as newly installed and start the process to install the driver. If you have an installation program disk, cancel the Windows installation and run the installation program after the computer has finished rebooting.

If you have tried all of these things and the device still doesn't work, there is a good chance that the device is broken. Uninstall the device again, only this time, shut down the computer and physically remove the device. If you have a similar device handy that you know is good, you might want to try to install it. If the newly installed device works, that is more evidence that the previously installed device is defective. Then, obtain a permanent replacement device and install as directed. For more information on installing devices, see the chapter in this book appropriate to the device you want to install.

Rolling Back a Driver

In case there is a new problem with the computer after the installation of a new driver, Windows XP gives you the option of "rolling back the driver." Double-click the device name in Device Manager and click the Rollback Driver button on the property sheet. The previous driver will be reinstalled.

Occasionally Windows will automatically select the wrong driver for the OS. For example, one customer reported that he attempted to install an MPX chipset-based network adapter on a Windows 95 machine, but despite following the directions, the network adapter didn't work. It turned out that Windows pulled drivers for the wrong OS off the network card's installation CD. We fixed the problem by removing the wrong driver, manually selecting the driver in the CD's /drivers/win95 directory, and restarting the computer.

Obtaining Device Drivers

Computer technicians often spend a great deal of time searching for drivers. Many times, the driver disks are lost, and other times, upgrading the OS requires new drivers. Additionally, new drivers can often improve the functionality of existing devices (but sometimes, new drivers can cause problems too).

There are some standard locations to find drivers. The first place to look is the Web site of the device manufacturer. See the Industry Contacts document on the accompanying CD-ROM for a list of manufacturer contact information. Some Web sites make it easier to find driver downloads than others do. Note that a high-speed

Internet connection is extremely valuable when downloading large files. If you don't have access to such a connection, and you need a large file, you might be better off attempting to order a disk from the manufacturer, if available. The cost usually isn't prohibitive, but you'll have to wait for delivery.

Another good source for drivers is Windows itself. For example, an old printer might come with drivers only for 9x and previous versions. If you need that printer to work with 2000 or XP, run the Add Printer Wizard in the Printers folder (see Tutorial 2.2 for instructions on accessing the Printers folder). If Windows doesn't install the device automatically, you will eventually be able to reach a page allowing you to select the device manufacturer and model name/number. Sometimes, you'll need to insert the Windows disc in the drive for Windows to use this driver, unless you browse for the appropriate files. In Windows 9x, these are often in C:\Windows\Options\Cabs. A driver for a close model number might or might not work with your hardware. For example, an HP DeskJet 660 driver will work with an HP DeskJet 672C printer.

This procedure isn't limited to printers. Run the Add Hardware Wizard (or equivalent) from Control Panel to install other types of devices in the same way.

Microsoft also keeps a huge selection of drivers. If you search *Microsoft.com* for "drivers," you'll get a wealth of pages where you can find drivers, including third-party companies that sell drivers.

When you download drivers, there are different types of files you can download. Some downloads are compressed files in .zip form, requiring you to have a program such as WinZip (*winzip.com*) or Stuffit Expander™ (free from *aladdinsys.com*) to expand. More common is the executable file. These files have the .exe extension and must be run, usually by double-clicking the icon. These come in two types: the setup program and the self-extracting zip file. If the file is a setup program, once executed, usually by double-clicking the icon, it will immediately start the process of installing the device driver and perhaps the operating program. If it is a self-extracting zip file using WinZip, you'll see a text box displaying the destination path of the extracted files. Figure 2.11 shows this process. Change the path to a folder that you can easily locate, such as the desktop. Note that you do not need to have WinZip to extract the files from this type of file—a dedicated WinZip program is part of the file.

Occasionally, you'll run a self-extracting file and see a command prompt or MS-DOS prompt window. To be able to locate the extracted files after extraction, create a new folder and put the self-extracting file in this folder before running it. The extracted folders and files will be placed in the new folder as well.

Often when you download files from a self-extracting file, you'll see folders bearing the names of various OSs and versions. You can delete any folders for OSs that you won't be using, such as Windows 3.1, OS/2, Solaris, and so forth. One title you might see is Win32. This refers to 32-bit Windows OSs, which include all of the

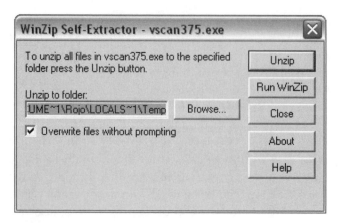

FIGURE 2.11 A WinZip self-extracting file.

versions covered in this book. You install these drivers using the Windows Add/ Remove Programs applet in Control Panel, or by navigating to the drivers when Windows has detected the new hardware on boot.

Chipset Manufacturers

If you searched everywhere else for a driver but had no luck, there is one more place to try: the chipset manufacturer. A chipset is the set of integrated circuits used on a particular device, and is often made by a manufacturer other than the device manufacturer. Look at the device and try to read the name and numbers on the larger chips. If the item is identified in Device Manager, it sometimes is identified by chipset rather than by device manufacturer. If that fails, search on the Internet (we recommend *google.com*) for information about the device; you can often find the chipset manufacturer and model number from the device manufacturer's Web site. You can also run a diagnostic program such as Micro-Scope (*micro2000.com*) or PC Certify (*pccertify.com*) to identify the hardware. This is especially helpful on a laptop, which you will be unlikely to open.

Locating the chipset manufacturer and model number is no guarantee that the manufacturer's Web site will have a driver, and if it does, that the driver will work with your device—but it's certainly worth a try.

Device Status

When you look in Device Manager, you might sometimes see a yellow question mark or exclamation point, or a red "x" next to a device listing (see Figure 2.12). The red "x" or yellow exclamation point indicates a resource conflict (discussed later in this section), a problem with the device and/or its driver, or that the device

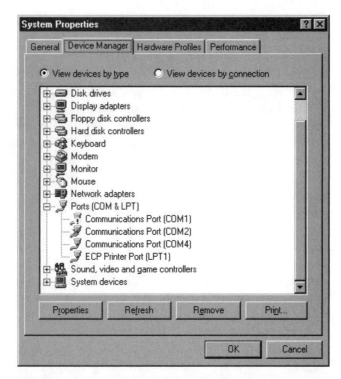

FIGURE 2.12   Device Manager indicating problematic hardware.

has been disabled in Device Manager. The yellow question mark indicates that Windows has detected a newly installed device but cannot determine the nature of that device. Use the procedures described earlier in this section to diagnose and remedy the problem.

If you see the "This device is working properly" comment on a device's property page, don't count on it. The device might or might not be working properly. However, a comment stating that there is a problem with the device will always be correct.

Device Manager Resources

Every device uses some of the computer's resources. *Resources*, in Device Manager, are computer functions that allow devices to operate. More than one device attempting to access the same resource at the same time is called a *resource conflict*, which we discuss later in this section.

There are four types of resources in Device Manager:

IRQ or IRQL (Interrupt ReQuest Line): For a device to operate, it has to "interrupt" whatever the processor is doing to get the processor to do its part in performing the task. An *IRQ* is a channel for the device to use to interrupt the processor. There are a limited number of IRQs built into the motherboard. Each device must be assigned an IRQ on installation to do its job. If more than one device attempts to access the same IRQ at the same time, the computer will *lock up* (freeze and have to be powered down and restarted) because of this resource conflict. This is a rare occurrence with Plug and Play, but it can happen with certain old expansion cards. Older versions of Windows didn't do as good a job preventing resource conflicts as newer ones do. Many older devices have *jumpers* (electrical connectors that can be moved to different places for the purpose of changing configuration), or microswitches (very small mechanical switches that serve the same purpose). Figure 2.13 shows a card with both jumpers and microswitches. Some devices are designed to work only on certain IRQs, so if another device is on that IRQ, it will have to be changed to another

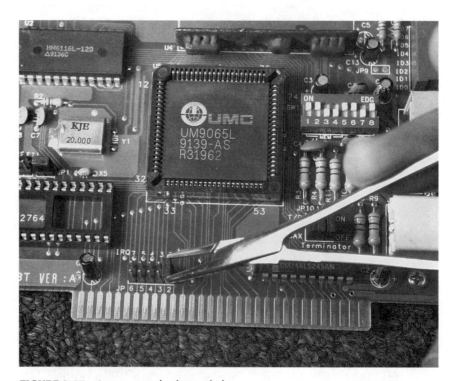

FIGURE 2.13   Jumpers and microswitches.

IRQ. If that is not possible, one of the devices might have to be replaced. For the past three or so years as of this writing, computers have been able to reliably share IRQs to some extent. However, IRQ sharing can occasionally be problematic. Figure 2.14 shows the Resource View in Device Manager.

For many years, usable IRQs were limited to 14, numbered 00 through 15, but with 02 and 09 not available. After all the usual devices were added to the required system devices, very few free IRQs were left. Only recently has the number of IRQs been increased to 24 (see Figure 2.14). Considering the capabilities of the USB and IEEE 1394 (FireWire) interfaces, which can accept a practically limitless number of devices, 24 IRQs should be all a PC will ever need.

Input/Output Address (I/O Address): Every device on a computer needs an address just as every building in a city needs an address. These addresses help locate the devices on a computer, and correspond to actual solder traces on the motherboard. They are often confused with memory addresses, but they are actually not related. They are measured in hexadecimal (hex) numbers, which is a system that makes huge numbers take up less space when displayed or written. If you remember different base numbers in grade school and high school math, such as base 6 or base 2 (binary), you will understand hex numbers, which are base 16. Instead of adding another digit after number 9, hex numbers continue with A through F. For example, F hex is equal to 16 in decimal (base 10); 11 in hex is 17 in decimal. You can use the Windows Calculator, Scientific view, to easily convert hex numbers to decimal, and vice versa, although there's

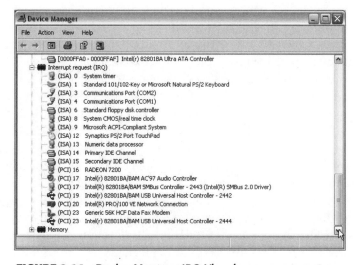

FIGURE 2.14 Device Manager IRQ View in newer computer.

not usually a reason to do so. The main thing you need to know is that, like IRQs, I/O addresses must be unique on a given computer.

Memory Addresses: Memory Addresses are a way to specify the exact location in the system's main memory that a device accesses. They are also measured in hex numbers and cannot be duplicated on the same system.

Direct Memory Access (DMA) Channels: *Direct Memory Access* is a system that allows a device to access memory directly without having the processor manage that memory access. Despite the fact that this saves processing power, this is not widely used, and each computer needs only a few DMA channels, one of which is used by the DMA controller itself. On many systems, only the floppy controller uses DMA, so DMA channel conflicts are rare. However, any hardware that does support DMA should be configured to use it.

Resolving Resource Conflicts

Any time two or more devices are assigned the same resource without being managed by Windows' IRQ sharing, there is a resource conflict. If the devices attempt to access the same resource at the same time, a *lockup* is likely to occur. Lockups are situations in which the computer suddenly stops responding. The first sign of this is usually that the mouse pointer won't move. You'll also notice that the cursors stop blinking, and keys depressed on the keyboard have no effect. These symptoms can sometimes happen temporarily, however, so there is an easy test to determine if the computer is really locked up (as long as your keyboard has a working Num Lock or Caps Lock light): press the <Num Lock> or <Caps Lock> key on the keyboard. If the light doesn't go on or off, you can bet that your computer is locked up. If the Num Lock light responds, wait a minute or two to see if the computer starts responding again, and then try the Num Lock test again. If the computer is truly locked up, the only alternative is to shut off the power to the computer and reboot. You can shut off the power on all newer computers (those with a soft power switch) by pressing and holding the power switch for several seconds until the power goes off. A *soft power switch* is one that activates an electronic circuit to start or stop the computer, as opposed to a mechanical switch that simply shuts power on and off by opening or closing the circuit. On computers with mechanical switches, simply pressing the button once will do the trick. Many computers have a mechanical power supply switch on the back that can be used. If all else fails, turn off the surge suppressor/power strip switch, or pull out the plug.

Reconnect the power, if disconnected, and restart the computer. To avoid another lockup, go into Safe Mode. *Safe Mode* is a mode of Windows in which only essential hardware is activated. This will allow you to resolve many problems with a greatly reduced risk of the computer locking up in the middle of your efforts. Follow the instructions in Tutorial 2.5a or b as applicable to boot into Safe Mode.

TUTORIAL 2.5A **BOOTING INTO SAFE MODE IN WINDOWS 9X**

1. As soon as the computer powers back on, press and hold the <F8> key. This should call up the Windows Startup menu. If this doesn't work, try pressing <F8> repeatedly, or consult the documentation for the computer on the Internet, if available.

2. Enter the number for Safe Mode and press <Enter>. The computer should then boot into Safe Mode. In Windows 9x, ScanDisk will probably run to detect and repair errors on your hard drive that result from powering down the computer without shutting down Windows. Go ahead and wait for ScanDisk to run. If you don't have time, you can cancel Scan-Disk and run it later—the sky won't fall.

If you miss the opportunity and Windows starts to boot into normal mode, press <Ctrl> + <Alt> + <Delete> to restart the computer and try again. To do this, press and hold <Ctrl> and <Alt> simultaneously; then, while they're still depressed, press <Delete>.

TUTORIAL 2.5B **BOOTING INTO SAFE MODE IN WINDOWS 2000 AND XP**

1. After restarting power, watch for a black screen with the message "Starting Windows." Underneath will be a message that says, "For troubleshooting and advanced startup options for Windows ____, press F8." You'll have to press <F8> in the few seconds that the message appears. Once the progress bar starts, it is too late and you'll have to press <Ctrl> + <Alt> + <Delete> as described in Tutorial 2.5a to restart and try again. Some configurations cause systems not to show any of these messages. In this case, repeatedly press <F8> as soon as it starts to boot. Figure 2.15 shows the Windows Startup menu.

Assuming you can successfully boot into Safe Mode, you can then open Device Manager and attempt to resolve the resource conflict. If you can't even boot into Safe Mode, see Chapter 11 for troubleshooting information. You can manually assign resources through Device Manager, but it's generally better to let Windows make resource assignments if possible. If you have legacy expansion cards that work only on one IRQ, or cards that have jumpers or DIP switches to select between only two IRQs, you'll have to do a bit of planning to resolve the conflict. Make the selection to view devices by resource in Device Manager. In 9x, select My Computer

```
Windows 2000 Advanced Options Menu
Please select an option:

    Safe Mode
    Safe Mode with Networking
    Safe Mode with Command Prompt

    Enable Boot Logging
    Enable VGA Mode
    Last Known Good Configuration
    Directory Services Restore Mode (Windows 2000 domain controllers only)
    Debugging Mode

    Boot Normally
    Return to OS Choices Menu

Use ↑ and ↓ to move the highlight to your choice.
Press Enter to choose.
```

FIGURE 2.15 Windows 2000 Startup menu.

in the Device Manager Window and click the Properties button below. Then, make sure the Interrupt Request (IRQ) option button is selected. In 2000 and XP, click "Resources by type" in the View menu. This displays a list of IRQs and the devices assigned to them. Then, make a note (literally—write it down on paper) of all devices in which a yellow exclamation point indicates a problem. By double-clicking each of these devices and then the Resources tab on the dialog box that appears, you'll see which resources the device is using, and a list of conflicts on the bottom of the dialog box. If you don't see the resources used, click the Manual configuration button and the conflict list should appear. Write down all this information. Then, review the list of IRQs for unused numbers, noting that there are certain IRQs that are reserved and cannot be reassigned, and that some devices must have certain IRQs and I/O addresses and can accept no others. Then, write down a list of problem devices and plan for them to use free IRQs and I/O addresses. Configure manually in the Resources tab of the device's Properties dialog box by clearing the "Use automatic settings" check box, highlighting the Resource type in the Resource settings windows, and clicking the Change Setting button, as shown in Figure 2.16. Note that many devices will not let you change settings, and often the Automatic settings check box is dimmed (grayed out). Table 2.1 lists typical resource reservations on a typical 16 IRQ computer.

If you can't seem to get the resource conflict solved, check in the BIOS to make sure that PnP is enabled. Sometimes, PnP can be shut off spontaneously.

TIP

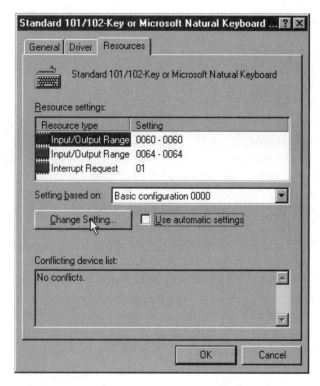

FIGURE 2.16   Changing resources manually.

TABLE 2.1   Common Reserved Resources

IRQ	Device	I/O Address Range
00	System timer	0040 – 0043
01	Keyboard controller	0060 and 0064
02	Unavailable	———
03	COM 2	02F8 – 02FF
03	COM 4	02E8 – 02EF
04	COM 1	03F8 – 03FF
04	COM 3	03E8 – 03EF
07	LPT1	varies
08	Real-Time Clock	0070 – 0071
13	Numeric Data Processor	00F0 – 00FF
14	Primary IDE Controller	01F0 – 01F7, 03F6
15	Secondary IDE Controller	0170 – 0177, 0376

As you can see, there aren't many other available IRQs, and some of the ones not listed might be taken by other devices. If you have taken an A+ course, you probably know that the COM port resource assignments are almost set in stone. However, there are not many devices that use COM ports 1 through 4 these days. Internal modems use internal COM ports, which we discuss in Chapter 8. Certain PDAs, UPSs, and external modems use COM ports, but some of these devices also use USB or other interfaces. Therefore, unless the user has and needs multiple COM ports, they could be disabled in Device Manager or in the BIOS, freeing up their resources. Some machines have multiple parallel (LPT) ports. These are good for many printers and scanners; however, most or all parallel port scanners have pass-throughs allowing you to connect the scanner to the computer's parallel port and a printer to the scanner's pass-through parallel port, while using only one IRQ. Therefore, unless the user needs more than one parallel port, additional LPT ports can be disabled as well. Of course, if there is no IRQ shortage or problem with resource conflicts, it is best to leave the configuration as is. In other words, if it ain't broke, don't fix it.

If you still have resource conflicts, you can remove (uninstall) all Plug and Play devices with conflicts and reboot the computer. Depending on the Windows version, you might be asked to reboot after each device is recognized and reinstalled. Reboot as soon as you are prompted. You might have to try many different configurations until you eliminate all the conflicts.

WINDOWS PERFORMANCE

Performance drains can make even the newest and best computers run more slowly than they should. There are many ways to gauge a computer's performance, and many ways to improve it.

System Properties, Performance Tab (9x Only)

The quickest way to gauge performance of 9x computers is by viewing the Performance tab, shown in Figure 2.17. Notice in Figure 2.17 where it displays "System Resources: 73% free." This is an average of processor time and memory used. Programs that start with the computer, such as antivirus software, have a significant effect on this number. However, a 9x computer that has just booted should have a number ranging from the low 80s to the mid 90s. Lower numbers indicate that something is using too much resources. As you make the performance-enhancing changes described in this section, keep checking this tab for changes. Hopefully, the number will increase.

Note the additional two buttons in this tab. These open a host of other settings that should almost always be set to their defaults. In File System properties, set the

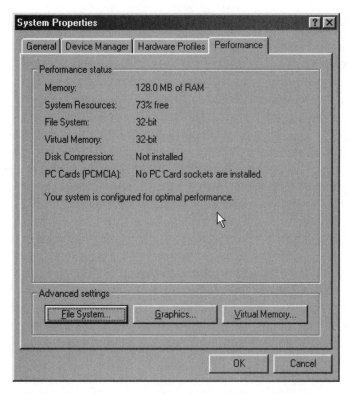

FIGURE 2.17   9x System Properties, Performance tab.

typical role of the computer in the text box. Set Read-ahead optimization to Full, and System Restore disk space use (Me only) to Max unless there is a shortage of hard disk space. In the Floppy Disk tab (Me and 98 only), leave the check box cleared. In the CD-ROM tab, set the Supplemental Cache size to large and, unless the computer actually has a CD-ROM drive that is slower than 4x, set the access pattern to be optimized for quad speed or better. On Removable Disk (Me and 98 only) and in Troubleshooting, leave all check boxes cleared. Close this and the File System tab and click the Graphics button. The Hardware acceleration should be set to Full. Close this and click the Virtual Memory button. *Virtual memory* is the use of disk space to supplement physical memory. Whenever there is not enough physical memory, Windows sends some data to a file on the hard drive in a process called *paging*. Too much paging can come from not enough memory and/or a slow hard drive and cause poor performance and excessive hard drive wear. Additionally, the processor has to manage paging, limiting its availability to other processes. Unless directed by a support technician, make sure that virtual memory is set to be managed by Windows.

Task Manager (2000 and XP)/Close Program (9x)

The biggest drain on resources is the number of programs and services running. You can use these applets to see a list of what is running, and close unimportant or troublesome programs. In all versions, press <Ctrl> + <Alt> + <Delete> to get one of these applets (in Windows 2000, click the Task Manager button on the dialog box that appears). The 9x Close Program applet has limited functionality compared to Task Manager in 2000 and XP, but it is still very helpful. Call it up and look at the list of programs. In 9x, two programs, Explorer and Systray, have to be running for Windows to run. You might see the indication "not responding." Wait for a minute before closing a program so indicated unless you know for certain that the program is crashing—sometimes this is a temporary condition. Close a program by highlighting it in the list and clicking End Task. You'll usually get a box that says, "This program is not responding," prompting you to end the program or return to Windows and wait. This box appears whether or not the program is responding. Click End Program. If you want to close several programs, you don't have to wait for each to close. Keep highlighting them and clicking End Task, and respond to the prompts as they occur. If you can't immediately identify a program by its name in the list, you can try to discover it by searching the computer for a file by that name. Go to Start > Find (or Search) and enter the name of the file exactly as shown in the Close Program box. Then, perform the search. Once the file is found, choose the option to open the containing folder. This should tell you the program the particular file is from, and from that, you can determine if you want to close it.

Application Tab

The 2000 and XP Task Manager provides much more information. The Application page lists all running applications and the status of each. If you need to view information that is covered up, move your mouse pointer to the line between the words *Task* and *Status*, and then click and drag to move the dividing line (this can be done in many Windows dialog boxes).

Processes Tab

The Processes tab shows much more detail than the Applications tab does. Generally, only the System Idle Process should be using a large amount of CPU time for an extended period of time. If you see another process using an extraordinary amount of CPU time or memory for more than several seconds, there might be a problem with that process. Figure 2.18 shows a Windows Task Manager Processes screen with a problematic process. You can highlight the process and click End Process. You will be warned that stopping a process can cause the computer to become unstable. Generally, it is safe to end any process that is running with an actual user listed, although you'll want to save any of that process's open files first, if ap-

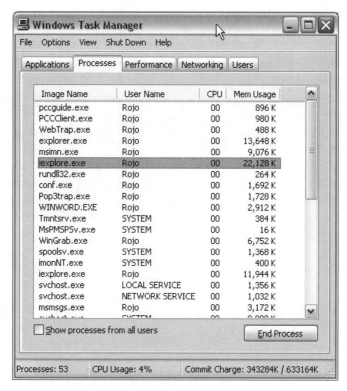

FIGURE 2.18 Processes tab of Windows XP Task Manager.

plicable. If the User column indicates SYSTEM, LOCAL SERVICE, or NETWORK SERVICE, closing the process might cause the system to be shut down. You can right-click a process and change its priority. If you increase its priority, the process you select will get CPU time before others of lower priority. Changing priority to Realtime might cause the computer to stop responding. Change this only if directed to do so by a support technician.

Performance Tab

As shown in Figure 2.19, the Performance tab contains graphical displays related to memory and processor usage. If you watch these graphs while you work on other programs, you'll see processor use and possibly memory use react to certain actions. If processor use is excessive (over 50%) for continued periods of time and there is no obvious explanation for it, you'll have to try to find the culprit. It could be a process or program that's causing the problem, or it could be that the processor is not up to the job. If memory use is also excessive, the problem could be a slow hard drive or

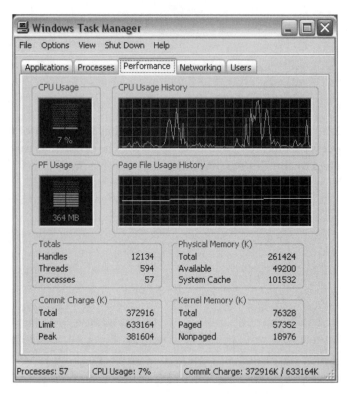

FIGURE 2.19   Performance tab of Windows XP Task Manager.

inadequate memory. However, if the user is running Windows XP Professional on a 300 MHz Celeron machine with 64MB of RAM and a 5400 RPM hard drive with a small cache, and trying to use the computer for video editing or as a network server, you don't have to do any serious troubleshooting to know why it runs slowly. A newer machine might be upgradeable, but in a case like this one, advise the user to find a less demanding use for this computer and to get a new one. Chances are good that it wouldn't pay to upgrade a computer like this one to be able to handle rigorous duty.

System Tray

Now, look at the *system tray* on your computer. By default, it is located in the bottom right-hand corner of the screen, and it usually displays the clock. Then, look at Figure 2.20. If your system tray has that many or more icons, especially just after booting, chances are your computer does not have much resources

FIGURE 2.20   Overloaded system tray.

remaining—the computer this came from has 35%. Most of these icons represent a process that has reserved some memory. The problem is that many programs are designed to constantly remind you that they are there, and thus they place an icon in the system tray. Many of these icons, however, don't serve much of a purpose while they aren't being used. For example, if you have dial-up Internet service and go online for an hour a day, but use the computer for other activities while not online, there is no reason to have an instant messenger (IM) program running in the background. It makes more sense to start the IM program when you go online and turn it off when you go offline. Some video adapter software puts an icon in the tray, but it is rarely necessary. Generally, the only icons that don't use a meaningful amount of resources are the Windows Volume Control, the Power Properties icon that can appear based on a check box in the Power Options applet described earlier in this chapter, the Network Connection icon, and, in notebook computers, the Unplug or Eject Hardware icon. There is one icon, however, that represents a program that uses a lot of resources that should stay in the system tray—antivirus software.

So, how do you prevent a system tray from becoming overloaded? There are a few ways. First, go into the configuration for any program that places an icon there. Look for settings such as "Disable Start Center," "Start program when Windows starts," and so forth. Second is the Startup folder in Start > Programs. If you find an icon for a program that you don't want to start automatically with Windows, right-click the icon and delete it. This can cause no harm, but most startup programs are not found in this folder. In 2000 and XP, you can prevent unnecessary services from starting by using the Services applet in Administrative Tools, as described earlier in this chapter. As a last resort, you can edit the registry. Follow the instructions in Chapter 11, and go to HKEY_LOCAL_MACHINE\Software\Microsoft\Windows\CurrentVersion\Run and delete the values for any service or program you don't want to start with Windows.

Don't edit the registry unless you have backed it up first, because one mistake can render the machine unbootable, requiring you to reinstall Windows. You can find information on backing up the registry in Chapter 11. A better way to remove icons is by using MSConfig.

NOTE

MSConfig (98, Me, and XP, Can Be Added to 2000)

This applet provides a convenient graphical interface to allow you to easily stop a program from loading with Windows. Go to Start > Run and enter *msconfig*. Then, click OK. When the program appears, click the Startup tab. You'll see a list of programs, each with a check box next to it. As you might have guessed, each selected check box indicates that the program will start with Windows. Clear any that you don't want to start, but do so one check box at a time.

Don't clear any check boxes unless you know that the program you are disabling from startup is not necessary for startup. This is not common, but on certain machines with Windows 9x, most notably Sony VAIO computers, files such as config.sys and autoexec.bat must be set to start with Windows or the machine won't boot and Windows might have to be reinstalled. On certain Compaq Presarios, a file called sxgdsenu.exe appears in the startup. Do not disable this from starting, or the computer won't shut down. Other essential programs can be found here as well.

Some notes and tips on MSConfig:

■ Certain versions of MSConfig have a Cleanup command. Do not use it—it can cause problems.
■ If you have XP and 2000 machines, you can copy the msconfig.exe file (C: [the partition where Windows is installed] \Winnt [or Windows]\System32\ msconfig.exe) and install it in the System32 folder in 2000. It will work normally in 2000.

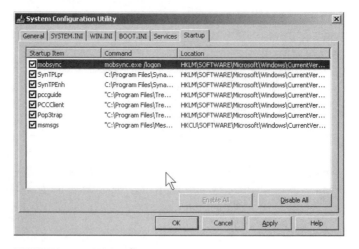

FIGURE 2.21 MSConfig.

■ The Windows XP version of MSConfig also allows you to set services to start or not start with Windows. We discussed services earlier in this chapter.

■ After making changes in MSConfig, you will be prompted to restart your computer. However, there is no need to reboot until you are finished with everything you want to do. After you do reboot, check to see if the changes you made solved the problems you were attempting to resolve.

Sysedit

Sysedit is a helpful tool accessible by typing *sysedit* from the Run dialog. When run, a text editor opens the system startup files autoexec.bat, config.sys, win.ini, system.ini, and sometimes protocol.ini so they can be easily modified. If a support Web site or technician tells you to edit any of these files, using Sysedit is the best method.

AUTOEXEC.BAT

This is where batch files, paths and many other commands are placed to start up and load before Windows. For troubleshooting here, you would remark out the command line by placing "REM" in front of it. This prevents that line from loading on the next boot and makes it easier to reverse the change if needed. Note that MSConfig in 9x has similar functionality. Figure 2.22 shows autoexec.bat on a typical Sysedit screen.

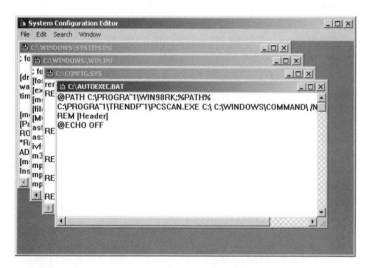

FIGURE 2.22 Sysedit open to AUTOEXEC.BAT.

Config.sys

This is where device drivers such as DOS mouse drivers and CD-ROM drivers as well as the buffers and files command are placed. The "REM" method is used in config.sys as well.

Other INI Files

System.ini: This file tells Windows about your system such as which desktop interface (called a *shell*) will be loaded at boot. Each section has a specific name in brackets with the information below. Unlike the REM statement in autoexec.bat and config.sys, a line is commented out by placing a semicolon ";" as the first character in the line. This is safer than deleting the line, because if you comment out a line and find that it is causing problems you can easily reverse the change by running sysedit again and removing the semicolon.

Win.ini: This is the file that tells Windows about the default settings, window positions, colors, ports, printers, and installed software. Microsoft recommends that the Win.ini file be 32KB or smaller, and it should never be larger than 64KB. Each section has a specific name in brackets with the information below. Unlike the REM statement in autoexec.bat and config.sys, a line is commented out by placing a semicolon ";" just in front of the line. Again, this is safer because if you comment out a line and find that it is causing problems, you can more easily reverse the change by just running sysedit again and removing the semicolon.

Boot.ini: This is used only in 2000 and XP, and tells Windows which hard drive partition contains the boot files. Unless you know how and have a reason to, never edit this file, or your computer won't boot. You can find more information in Chapter 11.

SYSTEM TOOLS

In addition to the system tools available in the Administrative Tools folder, Windows has a series of system tools accessible through Start > Programs > Accessories. Many of these are helpful for the proper operation of a computer.

Backup

This comes with all versions except XP Home. For more information on backing up and restoring data using Backup, see Chapter 11. However, on 2000 and XP Pro, there are more pertinent uses for this program, such as the emergency repair process and the Recovery Console, which we also cover in Chapter 11.

Disk Hygiene

Included in System Tools and in other locations are tools for maintenance and repair of hard drives, including those we discuss next.

Disk Cleanup

Disk Cleanup is a simple applet that facilitates deletion of unnecessary files. Call it up, select the hard drive(s), and let it find files to delete. Temporary Internet files are always good to delete. Make sure that the user doesn't need to save any of the files already in the Recycle Bin before deleting them for good. Run this before running a defragmentation program (covered next).

Disk Defragmenter (Defrag)

As files and folders are added, created, and deleted from a hard drive, they tend to get *fragmented*; that is, they end up in pieces spread out all over the drive. This causes slow performance, because the hard drive heads have to move all over the drive just to read one file. Run this applet to put all fragments back together in order on the disk and increase performance. There is one interface for 9x and another for 2000/XP, but both are user friendly. A badly fragmented drive could take hours to defragment. It is best to run Defrag in Safe Mode, or at least shut off all screen savers and other programs, including those in the system tray. Advise users to run this monthly, or after deleting large amounts of data or uninstalling large programs. Running this more frequently causes unnecessary wear and tear on the drive.

There are also third-party utilities that perform defragmentation. Diskeeper® from Executive Software (*execsoft.com*) claims to defrag drives three to five times faster than "built-ins." It also has the capability of scheduling defrag jobs and performing continuous defragging to prevent a drive from ever becoming fragmented. Executive has a Lite version, which does not have the scheduling or continuous defragging capability, and a full-featured trial version with a limited operating life.

Our tests show that the Windows 2000/NT defrag utility works similarly to Diskeeper, but the 9x defrag utility will arrange files much differently than Diskeeper does, at least when 9x's "Rearrange my files so that my programs start faster" check box is selected.

ScanDisk/Chkdsk/Error-checking

These are applets that can solve certain hard disk problems. Windows 9x comes with ScanDisk. Anyone who has ever had a lockup or a power failure on a Windows 9x machine causing the computer to be powered off without shutting down Windows first will be familiar with ScanDisk, because it starts automatically during boot after such an incident. For general maintenance of Windows, however, you can run ScanDisk from System Tools. There are three check boxes in the interface: Standard, Thorough, and Automatically fix errors. Standard looks for problems with files, and Thorough adds a scan of the disk surfaces for errors. Always leave the "Automatically fix errors" check box selected; it would be pointless to run ScanDisk without it. Running in Thorough mode can take hours.

If a 9x computer won't boot and gives a hard drive-related error message, this often means that a file needed for Windows is on a damaged sector on the drive. Boot to DOS (covered later in this chapter) and run ScanDisk by typing *scandisk* from a command prompt. After it runs its standard file scan, it will prompt you to run a surface (Thorough) scan. Do so, and follow the subsequent prompts to fix the problem.

In 2000 and XP, you have two choices: Chkdsk and Error-checking. To run Chkdsk, open a command prompt or the Run dialog and type *Chkdsk /f /r* (*/f* sets Chkdsk to automatically fix errors it encounters, and */r* sets it to attempt to recover data from bad sectors). To run Error-checking, right-click the drive you want to check, click Properties from the menu that appears, click the Tools tab, and then the Check now button in the Error-checking section. Neither will be able to accomplish much right away if there are open files such as when Windows is running on the disk being checked. In this case, you will be prompted to schedule the program to run the next time you start Windows. Do so, and then reboot. You have 10 seconds to cancel Chkdsk by pressing any key, but if you don't, you'll have to wait for Chkdsk to complete its tasks. When run after rebootings, there is no difference between Chkdsk and Error-checking. In fact, the only difference between the two is that when run in Windows, Error-checking uses a *Graphical User Interface* (GUI), and Chkdsk uses a command prompt.

There is a version of Chkdsk available on Windows 9x, but it's not particularly useful. Use ScanDisk instead.

We discuss other system tools in subsequent chapters.

WINDOWS UPDATE

Microsoft is constantly coming out with updates to virtually all but its oldest software, which it makes available on the *windowsupdate.com* Web page. The purposes of updates are to patch "security holes," improve functionality, fix bugs, update drivers, and so forth. In 95, you'll just have to go to *http://windowsupdate. Microsoft.com*, but in the other versions, you'll almost always find a link to Windows Update in the Start menu. In XP, it will be above the All Programs list and also in Add or Remove Programs in Control Panel. Microsoft divides its updates into three categories: Critical Updates, Windows Updates, and Driver Updates. At some point, you will also be prompted to install software to install these automatically, which is convenient for the end user. Critical updates should usually all be installed, but Windows updates should be chosen—for example, there is no need to install Internet Explorer support for the Danish language if the user doesn't read it. Driver updates aren't necessarily a good idea; if a hardware component is functioning correctly, it is best not to install a Windows driver update for it. There are situations in which the new driver will stop the component from functioning.

It is highly recommended to have a high-speed Internet connection to install updates, because some updates can take hours when using a dial-up connection.

TIP

MS-DOS (DOS) AND THE 2000/XP COMMAND PROMPT

The Microsoft Disk Operating System (MS-DOS) is Microsoft's original OS. It is a variation of the OS used on the original IBM PC back in 1981. It is a 16-bit OS. It is not necessary to understand exactly what the terms *16* and *32 bits* mean in relation to OSs. It is enough to know that 32-bit systems are much more capable and less troublesome than their 16-bit predecessors. The original consumer versions of Windows (1.0–3.11) were 16-bit OSs. They were actually nothing more than graphical interface shells that used DOS as the OS. Windows 9x versions are 32-bit OSs that still make use of DOS, while 2000 and XP are true 32-bit OSs. You'll notice that the command prompts in 9x are called "MS-DOS Prompt," while the other two versions' command prompts are called "Command Prompt." This means that while the 9x command prompts actually use DOS, the 2000/XP command prompts are 32-bit programs that emulate DOS. 2000 and XP can run many 16-bit programs that don't attempt to access hardware directly; they have built-in emulators for DOS and Windows 3.x programs.

In 2000 and XP, when you access the command prompt from Programs (or All Programs) > Accessories, if you type cmd in the Run dialog, you get the 32-bit DOS emulation program. However, if you type command in the Run dialog, in most cases you get actual DOS.

NOTE

There are four different ways to run a 9x computer in DOS:

A. **Reboot to DOS:** Go to Start > Shut Down and select the "Restart the computer in MS-DOS mode" option button (95 and 98 only).

B. **Use the MS-DOS prompt:** Go to Start > Programs > MS-DOS Prompt (95 and 98), or Start > Programs > Accessories > MS-DOS Prompt (Me).

C. **Boot to a DOS disk:** Use the emergency boot disk or a rescue disk from software such as an antivirus program to boot the computer.

D. **Boot to Command Prompt or to Safe Mode, Command Prompt Only:** Safe Mode is described earlier in this chapter. Power on the computer, press F8 repeatedly as soon as it starts to boot, and select either of these options from the boot menu (95 and 98 only).

So, what is the purpose of using text-based commands on Windows machines? There are several uses from a repair standpoint. First, many utilities have no graphical interface so they must be controlled with commands. Second, there are times when it is necessary to boot into DOS to fix problems that can't be fixed in Windows 9x. For example, an earlier section discussed running ScanDisk in DOS when Windows wouldn't boot because of a hard disk problem. Certain procedures, such as restoring damaged Registries, must be done in DOS. Remember, early PCs ran on DOS alone, so DOS has many commands to manipulate files, folders (which it calls *directories*), and disks. A program called FDISK is necessary to view the status of and also format and partition hard disks. We discuss FDISK in Chapter 6. Some DOS files, including config.sys and autoexec.bat among others, are still used to varying extents in all versions.

TIP

You can use an emergency boot disk to start a 2000/XP machine, but the default hard drive file system on those OSs, NTFS, is not compatible with DOS disks. Therefore, you won't normally be able to do anything useful unless at least one of the disk partitions is formatted as FAT or FAT32. However, there is a freeware utility available called Active@ NTFS Reader for DOS *from ntfs.com that will allow you to read but not write files on an NTFS partition while in DOS. You can copy this utility to any 9x boot disk and use it to boot the computer. Then, you can start the utility and use it to read files. If there is a FAT partition available on the machine, or if there is room on the boot disk, you can copy a file to it. You can also run this utility from Windows 9x in the event you have a 9x machine with an NTFS partition.*

Paths

The system of paths used by all versions of Windows originated in DOS. A typical path looks like the following:

```
C:\Documents and Settings\User\Documents\long file name A.tiff
```

where C:\ represents the C partition on the hard drive, Documents and Settings is the top-level folder, User and Documents are subfolders, and long file name A.tiff is a file. Note, however, that this path is *not* a valid DOS path. In DOS, all file and directory names must fit the *8.3* standard. 8.3 means that directory names have a maximum of eight characters, and filenames have a maximum of eight characters followed by a maximum three-character extension. The sample path, converted to 8.3, might look like this:

```
C:\DOCUME~1\USER\DOCUME~1\LONGFI~1.TIF
```

For more information on 8.3 conversion, go to *http://support.microsoft.com*, click the link for searching the Knowledge Base by article number, and enter the article number KB142982 into the search box.

Using DOS and Command Prompt Commands

Most DOS and Command prompt commands are simple to use. Unfortunately, most articles and the help files in DOS and command prompts describe these commands using excessive punctuation to delineate the portions that require substitution by actual information. Consequently, if you are not proficient in these commands and you are following one of these articles, you will likely type in punctuation that wasn't intended to be there, resulting in nothing but error messages. Moreover, the instructions might not work, even when typed correctly. Here is an example of a badly described command, the ATTRIB command, which is used to view and set the read-only, archive, system, and hidden attributes of a file or folder/directory:

```
ATTRIB [+R|-R] [+A|-A] [+S|-S] [+H|-H]
[[d:][drive:][path]filename][/S[/D]]
```

This is a typical description of a DOS command—too bad it doesn't work as described. The actual command works only by first navigating to the file or directory you want to configure by typing *CD SYSTEM* after the opening C:\WINDOWS prompt where CD is the Change Directory command, and SYSTEM is the folder you want to navigate to. To use it to remove the Read Only, Hidden, and System attributes of the file ccapi.dll in C:\WINDOWS\SYSTEM, you would type the following after the C:\WINDOWS\SYSTEM prompt:

```
attrib -r -h -s ccapi.dll
```

For more information on using DOS and command prompts, see Appendix C. You can also search the Internet for DOS tutorials or command-line tutorials.

There is a good page at *glue.umd.edu/~nsw/ench250/dostutor.htm#2a*. Another good one is *pcnet-online.com/content/general.htm*. Select the appropriate articles from the list.

OVERVIEW OF VIRUSES AND OTHER HAZARDOUS PROGRAMS

Unfortunately, there are many conscience-free people out there with nothing better to do than write and circulate programs designed to harm computer data, software, and even hardware. Many of today's computer problems come from viruses and could have been prevented by proper use of good antivirus software. The virus situation is so bad that any unprotected computer that has been connected to the Internet for a while is likely to have some kind of virus. Simply avoiding opening e-mails from unknown senders and not opening attachments is nowhere near enough. Besides that, people who do delete such messages and attachments probably end up deleting important messages and attachments. Yet many people either don't install antivirus software or never update the program they have. People need to realize that, to be effective, antivirus software needs a file written to deal with nearly every different virus. Virus developers are at work 24/7. That is why antivirus program developers offer "pattern updates" from their Web sites as often as several times a week. Most of these programs offer some type of automatic updates—they check to make sure programs are up to date every day the user logs on to the Web, and prompt the user to accept the update if available. Just follow the instructions supplied with the program.

The program will also prompt the user to scan for viruses regularly. In fact, any prompts from antivirus programs should be heeded as soon as possible. This doesn't mean that you should let a program start a routine scan or some other time-consuming process while you're in the middle of an important task, but you should let it scan as soon as you're finished.

If the program finds a virus, it will probably attempt to clean, quarantine, or delete the file(s) and prompt you to scan the entire system for additional infection. This should be done as soon as possible to avoid further contamination. These programs also offer virus encyclopedias both in their user interface and on their Web pages. If the program tells you it cannot effectively deal with the virus, search your program's encyclopedia for instructions and follow them if possible. If your program's encyclopedia doesn't have helpful information, you can search the encyclopedia of one of its competitors.

If you have a spare computer with a good virus scanning program, a great way to scan for viruses is by removing the hard drive to be scanned and connecting it to the spare as an additional hard drive (see Chapter 6 for information on installing hard drives). For ease in connection, the spare should have a hard drive cable connected by itself to the secondary IDE controller, and a power connector, both coming out of a space on the front of the computer. Find something stable to prop up the hard drive and run the virus scan. There are several advantages to doing it this way. First, you know that no files will be in use on the scanned hard drive. Error messages are much less likely and rebooting is unnecessary to clean infected files. Use 2000 or XP so that Windows will recognize any file system. A computer like this is also good for backing up data. Figure 2.23 shows an example of such a spare computer.

Sometimes, virus scan programs report infected files in the hidden _Restore folder in Me, 2000, or XP, but cannot clean or delete the files. While the file can be safely deleted in DOS in Me, it might not be possible to delete the individual file in 2000 or XP. It is easier to disable System Restore, reboot the computer, and re-enable System Restore to delete the entire _Restore folder. See Chapter 11 for instructions on disabling and enabling System Restore.

FIGURE 2.23   A computer dedicated to virus scanning and data backup.

Popular Anti-Virus Programs

Here are four effective antivirus programs:

McAfee® Virus Scan® by Network Associates: This is available in both a CD-ROM version and an online version. The online version can be part of the McAfee Online Clinic, which offers many other valuable services for computers. Web page: *mcafee.com*

Norton Antivirus™ by Symantec: This is one of many antivirus and other helpful products available from Symantec. Web pages: *symantec.com* and *norton.com*

PC-Cillin™ by Trend Micro™: Trend Micro has a wide range of antivirus and other security-related products in its line. Web page: *antivirus.com*

AVG Anti-Virus by Grisoft: This one leaves no excuses not to have antivirus protection—one version is available free of charge! Web page: *grisoft.com*

Spyware, Malware, and Other Malicious Programs

Spyware consists of programs that do things such as steal your private information. Malware is programs that can cause harm to a computer, yet they aren't considered viruses. There are other types of problematic programs as well. These programs often end up on the computer from the user visiting, and especially downloading from, two types of Web sites: porn sites (adult sites), and the ones most likely to be installed when teenagers get to the computer, such as:

- Bonzi Buddy
- Comet Cursor
- Date Manager
- Gator
- Gnutella
- Kazaa Desktop
- Weather Bug
- Xupiter
- Any dialer.exe program the user didn't install on purpose

Although some of these provide valuable services, it is still better not to have them. Some of these don't show up in installed program lists in Add/Remove Programs. If that is the case, you'll have to go into Program Files and delete their folders, and then use a registry cleaner to delete their entries (see Chapter 11 for information on the registry).

Another way to deal with them is to install and run a program called Ad-Aware™ from Lavasoft (*lavasoft.nu* or *lavasoft.de*). There is a free version and an inexpensive version; both are worth the weight of a hard drive in gold (there are also other programs for this purpose). Download the latest version and install it (make sure to read and comply with the terms of the license). Then, run the program. You'll most probably discover many junk programs even if you have no idea how they got there. Make the choice to remove everything unless you find something you know you need. Instruct the user to update the signature file and run Ad-Aware regularly—once a month or more will be advisable, depending on the frequency of surfing and the types of Web sites visited.

SURGE SUPPRESSORS AND UPSs

Every computer should be connected to a good surge suppressor, and preferably a UPS. A *surge suppressor* is a device that absorbs abnormally high voltages that can damage a computer. You plug the surge suppressor into a wall outlet and plug the computer and other peripherals such as monitor and printer into it. A *UPS* is a device that provides a battery backup to keep your computer running for a few minutes in case of a power failure. Except for very expensive models, UPSs provide power just long enough to allow the user to save work and shut down the computer—most can do this automatically. The advantage to this is the prevention of lost data, and the capability of allowing users to work uninterrupted in the event of very brief power failures. Most or all UPSs provide surge suppression, so you don't need a separate surge suppressor. Most or all UPSs also provide *brownout* protection—that is, they take over from the wall outlet and supply power when the wall voltage dips below a minimum acceptable level.

Selecting a Quality Surge Suppressor or UPS

There are hundreds of outlet strips available for less than $10, even as low as $2 or $3. Except in very rare instances, these provide little or no protection. When selecting a surge suppressor and/or UPS, there are many things to consider.

For both UPSs and surge suppressors:

■ The needed number of regular outlets and, for transformers, widely spaced outlets.

■ The necessary specifications. For an instructive article, go to *howstuffworks.com/ surge-protector.htm*.

For UPSs only:

■ The amount of time you need the system to continue to run after the power fails.

- Add up the total wattage of the computer, monitor, and other essential peripherals, and make sure the UPS is designed to work with at least that amount of wattage.
- In most UPSs, some outlets have battery backup and some have surge suppression only. Make sure that you have enough backed-up outlets to serve your purposes.

Lightning Protection

It is nearly impossible to protect against a direct lightning strike. By having a good computer grade surge protector installed between all equipment and the outlets including the telephone and network connections, you will minimize your risk of loss. If you are going to be leaving the computer equipment unused for an extended period, it is safest to unplug everything from the outlets, thus eliminating the risk altogether.

HARDWARE HYGIENE

Computers can get dirty inside. While even computers in particularly clean environments get dusty inside, computers in dirty environments, such as industrial settings or homes of people who smoke, get extraordinarily dirty. This dirt and dust can interfere with cooling and even electrical connections inside a computer.

Vacuuming and Spray Cleaning

This dirt and dust should be cleaned out periodically using compressed air sprays of the non-flammable and non-CFC type, and by vacuuming. Mini Shop Vac® vacuums are particularly good for this task. It is best to spray and vacuum simultaneously. Spray in cooling fans and in any spot where you see dust buildup. One place dust seems to accumulate is behind the front panel. If you are cleaning a computer whose front panel can be removed, doing so allows easier access to the dust. There are a few precautions to consider:

- Turn off the computer first before vacuuming to prevent damage from flying debris or rapid cooling.
- Make sure the vacuum doesn't pull cables off their connectors.
- Do not rub the nozzle or brush directly on components.
- Do not invert the spray can. Doing so can emit harmful freezing gas.

For a video demonstration of how to vacuum the dust from computers, see the video entitled *Vacuuming and Cleaning Computers* on the accompanying CD-ROM. The file is called *vacuuming.mpg*.

ON THE CD

3 Motherboards and Their Components

MOTHERBOARD (MAIN BOARD, SYSTEM BOARD, DESKTOP BOARD) OVERVIEW

The motherboard is the part of the computer to which every other component is connected. It contains the processor socket(s), memory slots, expansion card slots, ports for mouse, keyboard, printer, et cetera, and electronic parts, known as the *chipset*, to make everything run. Most motherboards contain some built-in components such as video, sound, network adapter, and others, and they therefore have ports for whatever built-in components they have. For example, if a motherboard has built-in sound, it will have built-in audio connectors as well.

Laptop/notebook motherboards are not covered in this chapter unless otherwise noted.

Form Factors

Since the first PC was introduced, several types of motherboards have been used; the types referred to as *form factors*. What differentiates form factors of motherboards is their size, arrangement of components on the boards, and other details. Cases and power supplies are also classified into the same form factors; they all have to match to some extent for the components to fit properly into the case. The following form factors of motherboards are among those that have been used for PCs: AT, ATX, LPX, Micro ATX, NLX, and Flex ATX, in addition to proprietary boards by Dell, Compaq, Gateway, Hewlett-Packard, IBM, and others. Newer proprietary boards are based on the aforementioned standards, so some substitution is possible. Many sites on the Web explain the differences among form factors, such as *motherboards.org* and *formfactors.org*. Search *Google.com* for "motherboard form factors."

Motherboard Components

It is important for technicians to be able to identify the parts of any motherboard. Figure 3.1 shows an ATX motherboard.

While there are wide differences among the various brands and form factors, all motherboards have certain components in common:

CPU slot/socket: We discuss CPUs in detail later in this chapter.

Memory slots: Physical configurations of memory chips have changed over the years, but the industry seems to have settled on *dual inline memory modules*

FIGURE 3.1   ATX motherboard.

FIGURE 3.2 DIMM slots.

(DIMMs). These chips have 72 or more pins per side, although the two sides are so close to each other that it is not readily apparent that there are two sets of pins. Memory slots can accept one type of memory chip. Board design further limits the compatible memory chips. See Chapter 5, "Memory (RAM)," for more information on memory. Figure 3.2 shows DIMM slots.

BIOS chip: We discuss BIOS chips in greater detail later in this chapter.

Chipset: Every motherboard has a number of *integrated circuits* (chips or ICs) permanently installed on different parts of the board. Each chip has a separate function. It is most common for these chips to all be from a single manufacturer. You might see ASUS® brand motherboards, for example, with chipsets from Intel® or Via. Some companies such as Intel make their own motherboards in addition to chipsets for competitors' products. Manufacturers such as these virtually always use their own chipsets in their motherboards.

AGP slot: All motherboards made in the last several years that don't have built-in video, and some that do, have an *accelerated graphics port* (*AGP*) slot. This is the slot for a video adapter. Figure 3.3 shows an AGP slot. See Chapter 8, "Video, Sound, Modems, and Network Adapters," for more information on video adapters.

FIGURE 3.3   AGP video slot.

DVO connector: Some motherboards have header connectors for digital video adapters. The connectors are called *DVO* and the adapters are called *DVI*. Figure 3.4 shows a DVO connector.

Expansion slots (ISA and PCI): Expansion devices in card form, such as modems and network adapters, go into these slots. Newer motherboards have only *Peripheral Component Interconnect (PCI)* slots, while some middle-aged boards have a combination of PCI and the older *Industry Standard Architecture (ISA)* slots. Some boards have expansion slots that give a choice between the two, as shown in Figure 3.5. In this case, ISA cards have to be inserted upside down (with the soldered-on components facing the bottom of the computer) as compared to PCI cards. As you can see in Figure 3.6, ISA slots are often dark colored, and PCI slots are usually white or off-white. The cards are also easy to differentiate; compared with ISA pins, PCI pins are much smaller and closer together, as shown in Figure 3.6. This is important, as the slots can accept only cards of the same type.

FIGURE 3.4   DVO video header connector.

FIGURE 3.5   A combination ISA/PCI slot.

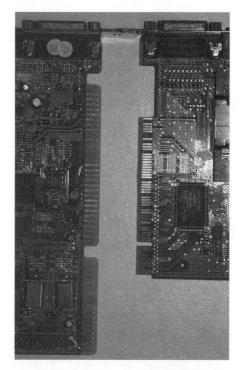

FIGURE 3.6   ISA cards' pins are much bigger and farther apart than PCI cards' pins.

PCI slot and card standards are constantly being reviewed and updated. Several new versions of PCI slots are out or coming out soon. Low Profile PCI devices, for example, are designed to fit in newer small computers. The first iterations of these cards will fit in the original PCI slots, but future versions might not. Also changing is the cards' operating voltage. Newer devices are running at 3.3 volts rather than

FIGURE 3.7 ATX power connector.

the older standard 5 volts. Moreover, 64-bit computers are available, although very expensive as of this writing, and there are necessarily 64-bit PCI cards to fit them. All of these new standards will be important to keep up with, as compatibility between cards and slots will become more of an issue. For more information on the PCI standards, see *pcisig.com/news_room/faqs*.

ON THE CD

See the video "Removal and Replacement of Expansion Cards" on the accompanying CD-ROM for more information. The filename is Removal_and_Replacement_of_Expansion_Cards.mpg.

> **Power connectors:** Every motherboard has power connectors that look something like the one shown in Figure 3.7. Those of you who have taken A+ courses might know this as P-8 and P-9, although the actual designations vary from board to board. Some newer boards have a 12-volt connector like the one in Figure 3.8. The one in Figure 3.8 must be connected to the proper connector on the power supply for the motherboard to receive power. If the board has a 12-volt connector, it must be connected to the power supply to avoid damage to the board.
>
> Note that an AT (form factor) motherboard power connector is different from an ATX connector. The AT connector has two parts, each with black wires on one end. They must be installed with the black wires next to each other at the center of the motherboard's connector, as shown in Figure 3.9.
>
> **Battery:** We discuss the motherboard battery later in this chapter.
>
> **Disk drive connectors:** Virtually every motherboard has two IDE connectors for up to four IDE devices, usually one or two hard drives and one or two optical (CD or DVD) drives. With the proper cables, each connector can support two drives. In addition, there is a connector for the floppy drive. See Chapter 6, "Magnetic Disk Drives," and Chapter 7, "CD and DVD Drives," for more information on disk drives. Figure 3.10 shows IDE connectors.

FIGURE 3.8   If the motherboard has this 12-volt connector, it must be connected. The connector from the power supply is in the inset.

Header connectors: These are multi-pin connectors that are similar to but smaller than the disk drive connectors for ports such as serial, parallel, USB, audio, case speaker, and so forth. If you can't locate the connection instructions on a sticker on the board or in the case, refer to the motherboard documentation in hard-copy form or on the manufacturer's Web site.

Ports: Motherboards have some or all of the following ports: serial, parallel, game, PS/2 mouse, PS/2 or AT keyboard, and USB. We discuss these later in this chapter.

Identifying a Motherboard

While many motherboards are easily identifiable, a few aren't. Here are some identification methods:

■   Look for the brand name, model number, and revision number printed on the circuit board.

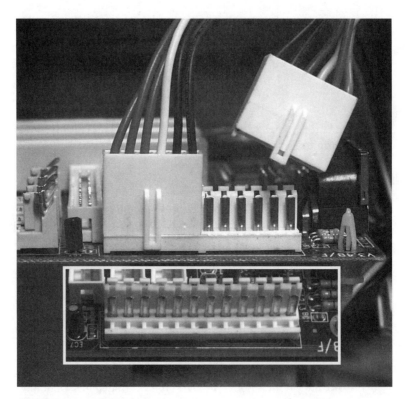

FIGURE 3.9   AT power connector.

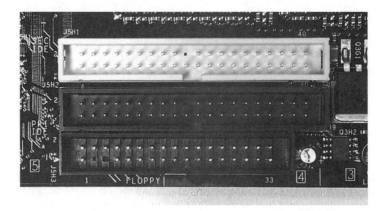

FIGURE 3.10   IDE and floppy disk drive connectors.

■ Look for a sticker underneath the lowest expansion slot. It might not be visible without disassembling the computer and removing the board, or at least by using a small mirror on a handle (preferably nonconductive).

■ On bootup, look on the first screen—if the information does appear, you won't have long to see it unless you press the Scroll Lock key.

■ The information might appear somewhere in the BIOS.

■ If the computer is a brand-name computer, you can often find the board used by going to the computer manufacturer's Web site.

Selecting a Quality Motherboard

While the chipset manufacturer can make a difference in the quality of a mother-board, the manufacturer of the board itself makes the most difference. To select the best, most appropriate board, first decide on the features the user needs such as type and number of expansion slots plus the needed built-in components. Also note that motherboards take only one type of memory. Generally, the faster the memory, the more expensive it is. Therefore, decide on the best memory you can afford and se-lect the motherboard accordingly. See Chapter 4, "Cases and Power Supplies," for more information on memory.

Next, evaluate the manufacturer based on its available technical support and its Web site. Live technical support should be available without long waits. Web sites should have technical specifications and information, plus driver and BIOS down-loads, and these should be easy to find and download, if needed. Then, consider warranty and cost.

Another useful method is to go to the processor manufacturer's Web sites for recommendations of motherboards (*intel.com, amd.com*). Note that Intel doesn't limit recommendations to Intel motherboards and that AMD doesn't make moth-erboards. There are also customer reviews and professional evaluations of mother-boards on Web sites such as *tomshardware.com* and *motherboards.com*.

Built-In (Onboard) Components

Just about all motherboards these days have some built-in components that were available only on expansion cards on earlier PCs. The most common of these are video, sound, network adapters, and modems. It is easy to tell when a board has these systems built in—just look for the appropriate connectors. If the computer is fully assembled, look at the back to determine the functions that are built in. The computer shown in Figure 3.11, for example, has built-in video and sound. This is apparent because these connectors are closer to the top of the computer. Other connectors are lower down, in the stack of expansion cards. By the way, the shiny metal plate surrounding the ports for the built-in components is called the I/O shield. Although this comes with a new motherboard, we'll cover this in Chapter 4.

FIGURE 3.11   A computer with built-in sound and video.

Certain instances call for replacement of a built-in component, usually when that component fails or when the user desires a better component or one with more features. It is practically impossible to replace the individual parts on the motherboard, so the answer is to add an expansion card with the desired function. For example, if the built-in video system becomes troublesome, you can add a PCI or AGP video card. On some boards, you can add a video card and still use the built-in video in order to use two monitors. In the case of a sound card especially, if you add one you should go into the BIOS setup program (see Chapter 2, "System Configuration and Computer Hygiene") and disable the built-in sound device to prevent any conflicts.

Modem Riser

Some motherboards have modems that are not quite built in. You will see a slot that appears to be a very short PCI slot with a small modem attached. The slot is called a *modem riser*. The modem will not work on any non-identical mother-boards. Replace a bad modem of this type by removing the card and installing a new modem in an unused expansion slot.

REMOVAL AND REPLACEMENT OF MOTHERBOARDS

When would you need to replace a motherboard? There are a few situations when doing so makes sense; for example, when the board fails while under warranty, or the user wants to upgrade a good quality computer but the motherboard won't support a faster processor or more memory.

Unless the new motherboard is identical to the old one, most or all drivers will be different. For this reason, you'll want to back up data on the hard drive containing Windows, if necessary, and format (erase) the hard drive before going any further. When you have installed a new board, be prepared to install Windows and all programs from scratch and to restore data from the backup. Although it is possible to replace the motherboard without following this procedure, you can expect the computer to run poorly if you do.

When replacing a motherboard, there are some general precautions to take and procedures to follow.

Removing the Existing Motherboard

This is a fairly simple matter. First, with the power off, disconnect *every* cable from the outside of the computer. After opening the case (see Chapter 4 and the accompanying CD-ROM for more information on opening cases), make sure to use a grounding strap and perhaps other anti-static devices as described in Chapter 1, "Overview." Then, disconnect all cables you can access from inside the computer, including the disk drive cables and small audio cables. You will most probably have to remove the drive cage (see Chapters 4 and 6). Remove any remaining cables and all cards in expansion (PCI, ISA, AGP, etc.) slots and place them on an anti-static surface. It is probably best to leave the processor and memory in their places for now. Now, remove the screws holding the motherboard to the case, and carefully remove the board. If it is still usable and/or the CPU and memory is still in place, place it on the anti-static surface.

See the "Motherboard_Installation" video on the accompanying CD-ROM for an example of installing a motherboard.

Installing the New Motherboard

First, make sure that the new motherboard is the same form factor as the case. Then, make absolutely certain that the power supply is set for the correct voltage to avoid zapping the new board. Look at the back of the case for a small switch that says 115V and 230V, or something similar, as shown in Figure 3.12. This should be set to the voltage available in the country in which it is used; in North America, this voltage is 115.

FIGURE 3.12   Power supply voltage switch.

Next, make sure that no conductive surface comes in contact with any metal parts of the case. While some cases have elevated mounting holes that hold the board away from the case wall (see Figure 3.13), other cases call for standoffs. *Standoffs* are small spacers that go between the board's and the case's mounting holes (see Figure 3.14).

After screwing in the screws, you need to install the power connectors and then follow the manufacturer's instructions for setup, which we discuss next. After you've done this, reinstall all of the compatible peripheral devices (if any) that were connected to the old motherboard. For more information on installing peripherals, see the rest of this chapter, Chapter 2, and the chapter appropriate for the type of device in question.

Motherboard Setup

There are certain things you must do to the motherboard to get everything working together. Some boards have stickers indicating the proper positions of DIP switches and jumpers, but in most cases, the documentation (manual) is essential. If you don't have the manual, you can usually find information on the manufacturer's Web site.

FIGURE 3.13 Elevated mounting holes.

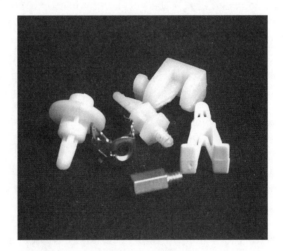

FIGURE 3.14 Standoff assortment.

In some cases, the board was manufactured by one company but sold by another under a different trade name. In this case, you might be able to find the actual brand and model number by peeling off a brand/model-number sticker on the board to reveal the actual manufacturer's sticker. Make sure the board is not under warranty when you do this; peeling off the sticker might void an active warranty.

TIP

See the Industry Contacts document on the accompanying CD-ROM for man-
ON THE CD ufacturer contact information.

DIP Switches and Jumpers

All boards have DIP switches and/or jumpers (see Chapter 2 for general information on these). Depending on the board, these are used to select such settings as the speed and family of the processor, and there might also jumpers to reset the CMOS, redirect the sound from the rear to front connectors, select the type of memory to install, and others.

DIAGNOSING MOTHERBOARD PROBLEMS

The most obvious sign of a damaged motherboard is a burnt or otherwise visibly damaged part. Naturally, motherboards can die without any visual signs. If you are sure the power supply works and is turned on, set for the correct voltage, and is connected correctly, and the CPU is good, but you attempt to boot and absolutely nothing happens, it is likely that the motherboard is dead. In this situation, a POST card such as Micro 2000's Micro-Scope (see Chapter 11, Troubleshooting") might not show anything. The only answer here is to try to replace the board with one that is compatible with the case, CPU, power supply, memory, and peripherals. If this is not feasible, a new computer can often be built with at least some of the existing parts.

Motherboard Batteries

Motherboards come with batteries, usually replaceable lithium coin cells. These batteries are in place primarily to keep the time/date clock running and maintain BIOS setup program settings. The batteries usually last at least six years. If a computer loses its BIOS settings and time/date memory every time it is shut down, you'll need to replace the battery, if possible. The POST (see Chapter 2) might show an error message if the battery has died. Moreover, if someone has set a supervisor password in the setup program, and now has forgotten it, and the computer cannot boot, the only way to reset or cancel the password is to remove and replace the battery. You might be able to use a battery tester to test the voltage of the battery without removing it. Make sure the polarity of the probes matches the polarity of the battery, and check to see if the battery is still good. Double-check the motherboard documentation to make sure the battery is the right type.

Battery Replacement

If the BIOS settings are still valid and you need to replace the battery, know that the motherboard *might* have a capacitor that will hold a charge just long enough for you to replace the battery without losing your settings. However, whether or not it has such a capacitor, it is recommended to write down all non-default BIOS settings

FIGURE 3.15 Replacing a lithium coin cell battery.

before changing the battery. Changing a replaceable battery is a simple but delicate operation. Carefully remove the old battery and insert the new one, as shown in Figure 3.15. Just make sure that the new one is of the correct type and that it outputs the correct voltage.

There is a long thin tab on some battery holders that at first glance looks as though it should be pulled up to remove the lithium coin cell. It is really just a spring tab, and if pulled up will permanently lose its ability to hold the battery down and make contact, thus almost always ruining the board. In this case, slide the battery to the open side and remove it, as shown in Figure 3.15.

Some motherboards have batteries soldered in place. Many of these boards have terminals for connection of a replacement battery; in these cases, the dead battery is left in place, as shown in Figure 3.16.

BIOS OVERVIEW

We discussed the BIOS setup program Chapter 2. Here we cover the physical BIOS chip and the updating of the BIOS.

FIGURE 3.16 Permanently installed battery and replacement battery terminals (four pins).

Updating (Flashing) the BIOS

While the BIOS seems permanent, it can almost always be updated. That is why the BIOS is called *firmware*, rather than software or hardware. The process of replacing firmware is called *flashing*. It is often a simple, albeit delicate, matter to flash the BIOS.

Why Update the BIOS?

There are three main reasons to update a BIOS:

- The motherboard manufacturer might release an updated BIOS to correct bugs in the original. For example, a BIOS update might reduce the operating temperature of the computer.
- BIOS updates sometimes allow the computer to use hardware or software that wasn't available when the original BIOS was released. Examples are a new version of Windows, a hard drive with greater storage capacity than the previous BIOS allowed for, or a processor that didn't exist at the time the BIOS was written.
- BIOS updates can enable new features, such as Plug & Play technology or hibernation (storing the contents of the memory on the hard drive and shutting off the power so that when the user restarts the computer, the session is left as if the computer had not been shut down).

A Reason *Not* to Update the BIOS

If everything is working well, then in most cases you should leave the BIOS alone and not update it. Updating the BIOS for no reason other than the fact that there is a new version available could actually *cause* problems.

Determining Your Current BIOS

There are various ways to view your current BIOS version number. If you have access to your computer or motherboard manual in hard copy, disk, or on the Web, you might be able to find the recommended method. Otherwise, try these until you have found it:

■ Go to Start > Programs > Accessories > System Tools > System Information, and with System Summary highlighted, find BIOS Version/Date in the right-hand pane.

■ Run an information-gathering utility (see Chapter 11 for more information) and look at the BIOS information under Main Circuit Board.

■ Boot or reboot the computer. When you see the BIOS information on the screen, early in the boot process, press the Scroll Lock key as soon as you can to pause the boot process. Then, write down the number and date.

■ While the computer is booting up, press the appropriate key for your system and enter the BIOS setup program (see Chapter 2). Usually, the current BIOS version number will appear on the very first screen you will see.

■ Go to *unicore.com* and run the BIOS Agent. *Unicore.com* is covered next.

Obtaining an Updated BIOS

The first place to look for a BIOS update is on the computer or motherboard manufacturer's Web site. Check the update's date and the version number. If the date is later and the version number is higher than on the existing BIOS, you might want to update. If the manufacturer doesn't have an updated BIOS, *and you have a compelling reason to update it*, the next step is to go to the BIOS manufacturer's Web site. With most BIOSs, doing so will take you eventually to *unicore.com*. This site provides a free utility to find the existing BIOS version on your computer and direct you to the latest upgrade, which is not free. The upgrade might be downloadable, or might be available only by purchasing a new BIOS chip.

Wherever you obtain your update, follow the instructions on the Web page. If there is a downloadable update, it will probably be accompanied by a BIOS *flash* utility (program) such as awdflash.exe or the Intel Express BIOS update utility (which runs in Windows). Download the BIOS update and the flash utility and follow the instructions. The traditional flash utility runs only in DOS, so you'll need a DOS boot disk with the flash utility and the BIOS BIN file copied onto it. Interestingly, a Windows Me boot disk won't work. Use either a Windows 95 or 98 boot disk to start the computer, regardless of the OS. If you don't have access to a 95/98 boot disk, any DOS disk will work. Particularly useful is DrDflash, available free from *bootdisk.com*. The advantage to DrDflash is that there are no drivers on the disk to get in the way. Follow the directions, paying close attention to these warnings:

Use a UPS or else: *UPS* stands for *Uninterruptible Power Supply*; it is also known as a battery backup. If power is interrupted during the updating of the BIOS, your computer will likely be rendered unbootable, and the only solution will be to get a replacement BIOS chip, if replacement is even possible with your motherboard. Make sure that the UPS is working properly, and that the battery is fully charged.

If you are updating a laptop's BIOS, a UPS is unnecessary as long as the laptop's battery is working properly and the laptop is plugged in to AC power.

Back up the current BIOS first: Many BIOS update utilities allow for backing up the original BIOS. Do this if possible; you should be able to go back to the original BIOS if there is a problem with the new one.

Follow the directions exactly: Updating the BIOS is probably the most delicate operation you can perform on a computer. Make sure that you read *all* of the instructions before starting. If you are typing commands, make sure that the syntax of every command is exactly as written in the instructions.

What to Do about a Failed BIOS Update

Unfortunately, sometimes BIOS updates are not successful. If you saved the original BIOS, you can usually run the flash utility to restore it. If this doesn't work, you will probably have to replace the chip. Some Gigabyte™ brand motherboards have a backup BIOS that automatically takes over in the event of a primary BIOS failure, but this feature is not common. In other boards, if the chip is permanently attached to the motherboard, you'll either have to send the motherboard back to its manufacturer for chip replacement, or buy a new board.

If you have a replaceable BIOS chip, then you can hopefully find a replacement. First, try the motherboard or computer manufacturer for a replacement. If they cannot supply one, try *unicore.com*. You'll also need a chip puller to remove the chip, as shown in Figure 3.17.

CENTRAL PROCESSING UNITS (CPUs, PROCESSORS)

Often called the brains of the computer, the CPU is the device that performs the calculations that make computing possible. Although there are several CPU manufacturers, Intel and Advanced Micro Devices (AMD) make the vast majority of processors used in Windows-based PCs, so we will limit our discussion mostly to Intel Celeron and Pentium II, III, and 4 processors, and AMD K6-2, K6-3, Athlon, and Duron processors. For more information, go to *intel.com* or *amd.com*. One

FIGURE 3.17 Removing a BIOS chip.

other processor family worth mentioning is the very inexpensive VIA C3 family from VIA Technologies (*via.com.tw*), which has started to show up in some similarly inexpensive systems. Time will tell if the quality will match that of Intel or AMD.

Selecting an Appropriate Processor

When selecting a processor, the first consideration is compatibility with the motherboard.

Motherboard-CPU Compatibility

A given motherboard can accept certain CPUs. The most obvious limitation is whether the motherboard has a CPU socket or slot, and which type of either it has (we discuss sockets and slots later in this chapter). Of the two most popular CPU brands, Intel and AMD, some boards can accept one and some can accept both. CPU compatibility is further limited by design elements of the board that require certain models and speed (gigahertz, or GHz) ratings. The motherboard manual will specify the processors that are compatible with it. However, you should check the board manufacturer's Web site for updated information. Sometimes a motherboard will accept a processor version that didn't exist when the manual was printed.

CPU Terminology

For you to be able to select the most appropriate CPU, it will be helpful to understand some terminology:

Front Side Bus (FSB): Measured in megahertz (MHz), the FSB is the channel that connects the processor with main memory. The faster this is, the better the performance will be. This number will range between 33 and 800 MHz.

Cache (pronounced "cash"): All new CPUs have cache memory. *Cache*, as it pertains to CPUs, is expensive high-speed memory used for storing frequently used instructions. This saves the time needed for the CPU to get all of its instructions from slower main memory. All other things being equal, the more cache a CPU has, the better its performance will be. The less expensive CPU lines, Intel Celeron and AMD Duron, have less cache than their otherwise equivalent Pentium and Athlon cousins. L2 Cache, the most variable number, ranges from 128 to 512 KB on relatively recent processor models.

Sockets and slots: As discussed in the motherboard section, processors either fit in a socket or slot, depending on their construction. There are quite a few different socket and slot types.

For more information on slots and sockets, see *itp-journals.com/ sasample/T1053.pdf*. There is also a very helpful presentation available at *ccc. commnet.edu/DL/~moriber/pc_3e_03b.ppt*.

Pins: Within the categories of sockets and slots, there are different types of each. The types vary by size, and number and configuration of pins.

Fans and heat sinks: All processors made in the recent past require heat sinks and fans. *Heat sinks* are little radiators used to radiate the heat away from the processor. Heat sinks are crucial; remove the heat sink from some processors while they're running and they will melt, or even catch fire almost immediately. Some Intel processors have built-in temperature protection; they will shut down if the temperature gets too high, but they could still sustain damage. The heat sink and fan work together to keep the processor's temperature within a safe range. It is necessary to use a thermal pad, thermal grease, or silver thermal compound between a processor and the heat sink, which not only helps to transfer heat from the processor but also evens out the surface to reduce the possibility of cracking the processor. Use the compound sparingly. The silver thermal compound has the highest heat transfer capacity of all of these. Figure 3.18 shows the thermal pad on the bottom of the heat sink.

A very helpful article on these heat-transfer materials appears at antec-inc. com/info_DIYArticle2.html. *We highly recommend that you read it.*

FIGURE 3.18 The thermal pad goes on the bottom of the heat sink.

CPU families: CPU manufacturers create *families* of processors for both technical and marketing purposes. Examples of family names are Intel's Pentium 4 and Celeron, and AMD's Athlon and Duron. Generally, each member of a family has the same internal design with the only differences being speed and perhaps some less-publicized specifications. Celerons don't fit that definition exactly, however; all of Intel's lower priced processors since Pentium IIs were current have been called Celerons. Therefore, Celerons have the same general internal design as other Celerons of the same particular generation and form (socket, slot, etc.). Celerons and Durons are less expensive than Pentiums and Athlons of the same speed and form. The differences are in such specifications as cache memory and front side bus speed. They are suitable for basic computing.

Selecting a Replacement CPU

When building or buying a new computer, it might make more sense to select the CPU first, and then select a motherboard to accommodate it. However, in the context of repair, you'll usually have to find a CPU that matches an existing motherboard. Therefore, the first consideration is to review the motherboard documentation to see which processors are compatible with it, as discussed earlier in the chapter. You'll then want to select the best of the compatible processors you can afford. "Best" is usually defined as fastest with the most cache. However, you should also consider the usage of the computer. A computer used primarily for e-mail, to read news on the Web, and to write letters does not need as good a processor as one used for heavy-duty number crunching or video production, for example.

CPU Removal and Replacement

CPUs are often very easy to remove and replace. Currently used sockets are called *zero insertion force (ZIF)* sockets. The processor can be gently placed in the socket, and then a lever is lowered and locked to hold the CPU in place. Slot processors should be gently inserted in their slots. Make sure to use proper grounding protection and be careful not to touch the pins.

ON THE CD   See the "Installing CPUs" video on the accompanying CD-ROM to see examples of installing a slot-type and a socket-type CPU.

There are three ways to set motherboards for the processor in use: automatically, manually with jumpers or micro DIP switches, or in the BIOS setup program. Some motherboards offer more than one of these methods. With the boards with jumpers to set processor parameters, the manuals have charts to show the jumper settings for the processors it takes.

Diagnosing CPU Problems

CPUs are generally trouble-free. The most likely problem is heat damage that can happen when the fan wears out. The most common symptom of heat damage is a computer that starts out working normally, but after awhile performs erratically. Eventually, the computer will lock up. When hearing a report like this, with the power disconnected, open the case and check to make sure that the fan and heat sink are in place—put them in place if they aren't. Attempt to spin the processor fan by hand. The fan should spin freely and continue spinning when you let go, and not make any noise. If you encounter resistance and/or hear noise, replace the fan.

If the fan blades spin freely, the next step is to power on the computer and see if the fan actually spins. Some BIOS setup programs have CPU temperature gauges, and some motherboard manufacturers provide Windows programs to monitor the CPU temperature, among other things. If the fan does spin, you can check these gauges, if present, to determine if the processor's temperature is in the safe zone, which will be indicated on the gauge. Another way to measure the processor temperature is to use a laser temperature gauge. While the computer is running, aim the laser at the space between the processor and heat. Compare your result to the processor documentation's temperature specifications. If the temperature is too high, the processor isn't being cooled properly.

If there is any problem with the fan spinning, shut down the computer immediately and replace the fan. Then, start up the computer and let it run for at least two hours. Next, open some programs and try to use them. If the computer works normally, you can be reasonably sure that the processor didn't sustain any major damage. If you still have problems, it is possible that the processor has been damaged, or that the computer has other problems. If you have a used replacement available, and you are sure that the CPU is now being properly cooled, temporarily replace the CPU. If the problems go away, there's a very good chance that the old CPU has sustained damage and will need to be replaced. Products such as Micro-Scope and its POST card can give you accurate diagnoses.

If the power supply fan spins, but the computer won't otherwise power on, the problem could be a dead or disconnected CPU or motherboard. If everything is connected, the only way to diagnose the problem, after ruling out a bad power supply (see Chapter 4), is to swap a known good CPU or motherboard, one at a time, with the original items. If the replacement device causes the system to work, then you have found the problem.

CPU Fan Replacement Tips

When replacing a fan on a socket processor, you might need to press hard on the retaining clip. Make sure you don't slip and damage the motherboard. Figure 3.19 shows the steps of installing a processor, fan, and heat sink.

FIGURE 3.19 Installing a processor.

FIGURE 3.20   3-pin processor fan connectors.

Fans can have 2- or 3-pin power connectors. Figure 3.20 shows the 3-pin connector. The two basic types are the 3-pin that connects to a connector on the motherboard, and the 4-pin type that connects to any of the 4-pin connectors from the power supply. Adapters are available to connect one to the other.

Socket to Slot Adapters

There are adapters available that allow you to use a Socket 370 processor in a motherboard that otherwise would accept only a slot processor. These can work well when they are first installed, but we have found that they are often the cause of lockups as time goes on. If you are troubleshooting lockups on a machine with one of these adapters, it is a good idea to reseat the adapter in the slot, making sure the slot processor retention mechanism is properly secured and holding the assembly securely in place. If the problem persists, the solution is to get a compatible slot-type processor and install it in place of the socket processor with the adapter.

SOME COOL-LOOKING FANS DON'T COOL ANY BETTER

A few computer owners seem concerned about the appearance of the inside of their computer case. This is fine if the components both work well and look good, but many cool-looking fans don't cool any better than lower cost models. Rather than worrying about the appearance of a fan, check to see if it is approved by the processor manufacturer.

EXPANSION SLOTS

As stated earlier, expansion slots consist of AGP video slots and DVI video header connectors, and PCI and ISA slots. PCI and ISA slots are used primarily for modems, network adapters, sound cards, additional ports (such as USB or parallel), and video cards. You will likely encounter other types of cards as well.

Removal and Installation of Expansion Cards

Removal and replacement of expansion cards is usually simple. You might want to use an anti-static wristband for this. With the computer powered off and disconnected, open the case and remove the screw (if present) holding the card in place, as shown in Figure 3.21.

Next, pull out the card, using only as much force as necessary. Do not bend the card. After removing the card, if you plan on reinstalling it or installing another card, you are ready. However, if you plan to leave the slot empty, you'll want to install a slot cover, as shown in Figure 3.22.

To install another card, just follow the procedure in reverse.

This procedure works for the vast majority of tower and desktop computers. However, if you encounter a computer for which this doesn't, you might need to seek assistance from the computer manufacturer's Web site. Certain Sony VAIO towers require removal of a single panel on the outside back of the computer to unlock all of the cards.

PORTS (INPUT/OUTPUT, OR I/O) OVERVIEW

Ports, for the purpose of this chapter, are physical connectors and their corresponding software that conduct signals into and out of computers. Figure 3.23 shows the most common ports, and some are described in the upcoming list. These are often built into the motherboard, but are also on expansion cards.

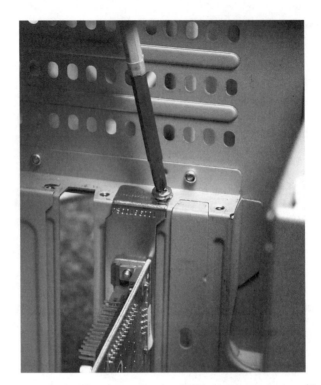

FIGURE 3.21   Removing the screw that holds an expansion card in place.

Serial: 9-pin serial ports carry electrical pulses one at a time and therefore tend to be slow. They are used for older pointing devices (mice), connections to UPSs, *Personal Data Devices* (*PDAs*), digital cameras, and external modems. Serial ports are associated with software COM ports (see the *Device Manager* discussion in Chapter 2). Serial devices can be plugged in and unplugged without risking damage to the device or the computer.

Parallel: Used mostly for printers and scanners, 25-pin parallel ports carry eight electrical signals at one time. Associated with LPT ports in Device Manager and printer software, parallel devices can be plugged in and unplugged without risking damage to the device or the computer.

Universal Serial Bus (USB): USB ports are very versatile. Unlike serial and parallel devices, which require a separate IRQ per device, USB ports can be expanded through the use of USB hubs (adapters that convert one USB port to several), yet all devices connected to a single USB port on the computer safely share one IRQ. USB 2.0 is a newer standard for faster USB devices. Most USB

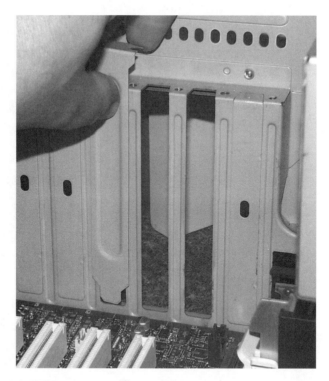

FIGURE 3.22   Installing a slot cover.

2.0 devices run if connected to older USB 1.1 ports, although they will be limited to the speed of the slower port. USB 1.0 devices work normally in USB 2.0 ports. Additionally, USB provides power to devices that don't use a lot of it. Another advantage to USB is that it is hot-pluggable or hot-swappable, meaning that devices can be plugged in and removed while powered on, without risking damage to the device or the computer. Although later versions of Windows 95 might support USB, most USB devices don't support Windows 95.

Video Graphics Adapter (VGA) ports: VGA is the standard for all analog monitors used since the early 1990s. VGA connectors have 15 pins and can be plugged and unplugged without risk of damage.

DVI ports: These are for digital monitors and also can be plugged and unplugged without risk of damage.

FireWire (IEEE 1394): Similar to USB, but much faster than USB 1.1. Used for all the types of peripherals as USB, plus digital audio and video cameras and other devices that require high-speed data transfer.

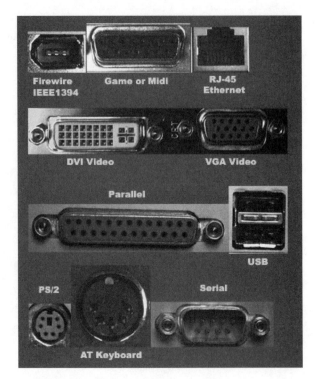

FIGURE 3.23 Common ports.

PS/2: Mouse and keyboard connectors. Plug and unplug only with computer power off.

DIN AT keyboard connectors: Used in older PCs.

PCMCIA (PC Card): Used almost exclusively in laptops, these are used mainly for modems, network adapters, and for tiny hard drives. These cards can usually be inserted in their slots without any special steps, but they should be stopped in Windows Control Panel, PCMCIA or PC Card applet before removing to prevent Windows problems such as lockups, or possible damage to the card.

Game Controller/MIDI port: These are 15-pin ports used for older game controllers and MIDI musical instrument devices.

SCSI (pronounced *scuzzy*): There are no fewer than seven different types of SCSI connectors, so chances are good that if you see a connector not covered here, it's a SCSI.

RJ-45 (Ethernet): This is a connector for a network cable.

4 ▮ Cases and Power Supplies

CASES

A computer's case is more than a box. The case includes the *drive cage*, the internal compartment that holds disk drives, and almost always the power supply, among other features, all of which we discuss in this chapter. As discussed in Chapter 3, "Motherboards and Their Components," cases come in various types called form factors, which differ in layout of components. The case's form factor needs to match that of the motherboard and the power supply. Just as with motherboards, some cases are proprietary and require proprietary power supplies and motherboards.

FIGURE 4.1   A typical ATX case.

Case Components

Cases come with various components, as shown in Figure 4.1.

Most of these components are self-explanatory. Drive bays are areas in the front for installation of removable media (CD, DVD, floppy, Zip, etc.). The 5 1/4-inch bays are for all but the floppy drives. Cases usually come with small speakers, which are there to provide very basic sounds to the user. About all these speakers play are warning beeps and the sound of a modem connecting. These speakers are very important, because multimedia speakers don't work before Windows has booted, if Windows is in Safe Mode (see Chapter 2, "System Configuration and Computer Hygiene"), or if there is a problem with the sound card.

Some motherboards have extremely small speakers soldered onto the board. These are little black plastic cylinders with a hole at the top. These boards don't use case speakers.

While many older PCs had key locks, few newer ones do. Locking a computer prevents it from being powered on. The most important indicator lights are the ones that show that power is on and that the main hard drive is active. The hard drive indicator is helpful to show if the hard drive is running too much (churning), or if the computer is locked up (the light does not go on even though the computer is running). On recent cases, the only button is the power button. Older cases might have a Reset button, which simply turns power off and on, and a "Turbo" button. Leave the Turbo button in the On position unless a tech support technician tells you to turn it off.

I/O Shields

I/O shields are the metal plates that surround the ports that are built into the motherboard. These snap in place, as shown in Figure 4.2. They are used to shield these ports from radio frequency interference (RFI) and to provide openings in the case in the correct size and configuration for the motherboard's built-in ports.

Case Quality

A good quality case can have a big impact on the performance and durability of the computer. Cases sold have to meet requirements for shielding against both external RFI and interference to external devices that is generated by the computer. Good cases are designed to provide for proper airflow to keep the components from overheating. Well made cases do not have a thin tinny feel or sound when you

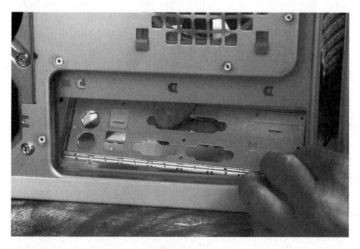

FIGURE 4.2 Attaching an I/O shield.

tap on them. They have rolled edges to prevent injury. Panels should fit together well without requiring excessive effort. When the computer is running, a good case does not make excessive vibration noises. Other attributes of good cases include ease in opening and ease in accessing internal components (we discuss opening cases later in this chapter).

ON THE CD   See the video "Opening Different Types of Cases and Accessing Internal Parts" on the accompanying CD-ROM. The file is called opening_the_Case.mpg.

Case Form Factors and Styles

Cases come in many form factors, the most common being AT, ATX, and Micro ATX. For more information on case form factors, see *formfactor.org*. Available styles include mid-tower, small footprint, desktop (horizontal), and those cases integrated with a monitor.

Opening Different Types of Cases

Cases also vary in the difficulty of opening and accessing internal components. While most cases open easily after removing screws from the back, you will undoubtedly come across cases whose method of opening is not the least bit apparent. Some require removal of the plastic faceplate to access screws behind it, and others are so unusual that you could look at the case for an hour and not figure out how to open it. A few manuals tell you how to open the case, but the problem with that is that in many difficult-to-open cases, the manufacturer is unidentifiable.

One common style of case requires you to remove the left-side panel only (as you are looking at the front of the computer (as shown in Figure 4.3), while many other styles combine the left, right, and top panels into one piece, as shown in Figure 4.4.

Accessing Components

Once you have opened the case, you might be stumped about how to access blocked parts, particularly the processor and disk drives. Some cases are extraordinarily difficult in this respect. These often require you to remove the drive cage. Sometimes you have to disassemble the case, while others, even ones the same size on the outside, need only to be opened in order to reach all the components. In a majority of cases, all you have to do is remove the left panel. However, you might find some cases that require you to remove both the left and right panels to access the screws holding the drive cage, while others allow the drive cage to be easily removed or swung out without removing any screws. Once you remove the drive cage, if necessary, all parts should be accessible.

FIGURE 4.3   Removing a side panel.

FIGURE 4.4   One-piece case cover.

ON THE CD   See the video "Opening Different Types of Cases and Accessing Internal Parts" on the accompanying CD-ROM. The file is called opening_the_Case.mpg.

Choosing a Case

If you decide to replace a case, simply match the form factor to the motherboard and make sure it has the needed number of internal and external drive bays, physical size, power supply capacity (in watts), and front-panel ports. In addition, check the processor and motherboard documentation. There very well might be further limitations on the type of case that can be used.

POWER SUPPLIES

The *power supply* connects to an AC outlet and provides power to the components of the computer through a gaggle of DC connectors. AC is connected through a standard CEE three-pronged power cord (see Figure 4.5), which is used with almost all PCs, including Macs, some laptop power supplies, and many other devices, com-

FIGURE 4.5 The ubiquitous CEE AC power cord.

puter-related and otherwise. New cases come with power supplies, but power supplies often wear out and need to be replaced.

DC Power Output Connectors

The DC power connectors vary somewhat between AT, ATX, and proprietary form factors. While the disk drive connectors are all the same, the motherboard connectors are different and incompatible between major form factors, although subversions of ATX have the same connectors. Figure 4.6 shows different ATX DC power connectors.

In addition to the power connector variants, different cases require power supplies of different shapes and sizes, or they won't fit in the case.

Determining Power Supply Power Requirements

Common power supplies come in a range of about 80 watts to 600 watts. How do you determine how much you need? First, determine the number of drives, the processor, number of expansion cards, and so forth. Know that it never hurts to have more capacity than you need. Check the motherboard and processor documentation. Some power supplies are overrated. For example, if you find a 300-watt

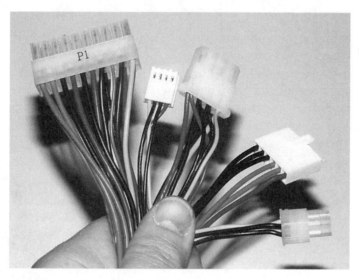

FIGURE 4.6   ATX DC power connectors.

power supply at a very low price, and you notice that it is physically light in weight, it is likely to fail under load.

Proprietary Power Supplies

Many brand-name computers require special power supplies in order to fit in the case or properly power the computer. These power supplies might or might not be more expensive than generic supplies. For example, certain Dell power supplies have an extra connector that fits into a connector on a proprietary Dell motherboard. Unfortunately, this connector matches a connector found on standard ATX power supplies, but the wiring differs. Therefore, don't try to plug in a generic power supply in a Dell motherboard unless you want to fry the board. The good news is that Dell sells replacement power supplies on its Web site for a very reasonable price. However, a particular Hewlett-Packard computer takes a power supply available only from Hewlett-Packard at a rather high price. Sometimes you can get proprietary power supplies from generic manufacturers. Just make sure to do all

FIGURE 4.7 Power supply assortment.

your homework before connecting a power supply to a motherboard on a brand name computer. Figure 4.7 shows an assortment of power supplies.

Diagnosing Power Supply Problems

The most obvious symptoms of a failed power supply occur when you turn your computer on and hear a loud noise, smell something burning, and/or see smoke, and the computer won't power on. Shut off the power immediately; you likely have a blown power supply. If there is smoke, you'll want to ventilate the room—it is toxic. Usually, however, the symptoms of a blown power supply aren't nearly so dramatic; you turn on the computer and nothing happens.

Always Check the Voltage Switch!

We've said it before and we'll say it again: Make sure the power supply is set for the correct voltage.

Unusual Noises

If you hear a grinding noise, or there is excessive vibration, the power supply fan might be going bad. Visually check the rotation of the fan. Don't try to replace the fan, replace the power supply. A loud hum that changes pitch while you're doing different things usually indicates a bad power supply.

Testing the Power Supply

Testing a power supply is straightforward. Antec (*Antec-inc.com*) offers a simple, inexpensive ATX power supply tester, although it is helpful to have a voltmeter or multitester to use with it. Simply connect the tester to the power connector and view the LED. If green, the power supply is working. For a better reading, while the tester is in place, touch a voltmeter's or multimeter's probes to the tester's leads to read the voltage. Voltage should be 12v, 5v, or 3.3v, depending on the connector. Tested voltage should be very close to the rated number.

Removal and Replacement

This is usually straightforward. Make sure the power cord is disconnected. With most tower or desktop case, you'll have to open the case and remove the screws from the back around the power supply. Because some manufacturers have special connectors attached to the motherboard and other devices inside the system, you should draw a diagram of the colors of the wires and positions of the connectors as you are disconnecting them so you can match the power supply and connect it or a new one properly. Then, remove all of the power connectors. The power supply should then come right out. In some computers, the power supply is mounted to a bracket. You'll have to remove the power supply from the bracket. Replacing the power supply, or installing a new one is done the same way, in reverse.

For a useful discussion on PC power supplies, go to http://computer.howstuff-works.com/power-supply.htm.

5 Memory (RAM)

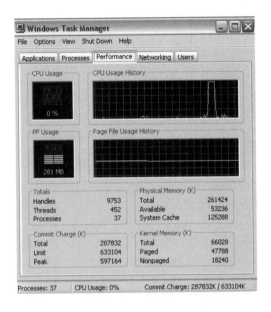

MEMORY OVERVIEW

Computer *memory* is electronic circuitry that holds binary data. It does this by set-ting the positions of microscopic electronic switches to on or off. The on position represents the binary 1, and the off position represents the binary 0. Each 0 and 1 is called a *bit*. The switches are divided into groups of eight bits, called *bytes*. A byte is an 8-bit number that can equal any decimal number between 0 (all 0s) and 255 (all 1s), and is the basis of all computer data. For more information on binary numbers, go to *http://computer.howstuffworks.com/bytes.htm*.

Main memory in computers comes in modules, often called *sticks*, which can contain billions of switches. Memory sticks are measured in megabytes (MB), and soon, gigabytes (GB). One MB equals, oddly enough, 1,048,576 bytes. One GB equals 1,1,073,824 bytes.

The acronym *RAM* stands for random access memory. This means that any part of memory can be accessed directly, as opposed to data stored on tape, which requires fast winding to the appropriate segment.

When selecting memory for a computer, there are several items to consider:

Type: Motherboards can accept certain types of memory, such as SDRAM, DDR SDRAM, Rambus, EDO RAM, and burst-EDO RAM. Check the motherboard documentation or the motherboard manufacturer's Web site. We discuss these types later in this chapter.

Speed: Motherboards can accept memory modules in certain ranges of speed; for example, 100 or 133 MHz. The faster the memory, the faster the performance of the computer. As in memory type, all memory installed in a single computer should be the same speed. If you install two different speeds of memory on the same motherboard, all chips will run at the slower speed.

Quantity (as measured in megabytes): Unlike medication, with memory, more is better, although you can reach a point of diminishing return. The motherboard documentation will specify the maximum amount of memory it can accept. We discuss how to determine the optimum amount of memory later in this chapter.

Quality: Memory rarely fails unless it is exposed to static electricity. The most common problem with memory is when brand new modules are bad—so a good warranty is essential. Kingston, Crucial, and PNY are all good brands.

Error detection: Memory comes in ECC or parity, or non-ECC or non-parity. *ECC* and *parity* are systems for detecting and correcting memory errors. Parity memory can compensate for single-bit errors. This parameter is specified by the motherboard manufacturer, but is changeable in some BIOSs. If the BIOS is set for ECC/parity memory, only ECC/parity memory will work. Again, even if the motherboard will accept either, it likely will accept only one of these at a time. If you have a DIMM (see the next item in this list) and you want to determine if it is ECC/parity or non-ECC/parity, simply count the number of black chips soldered to the module. If the number of chips is evenly divisible by three or five, then the module contains ECC or parity memory. If the number of chips is *not* evenly divisible by three or five, you have non-ECC/parity memory.

Physical module size and pin layout: Almost all currently used memory comes in Dual Inline Memory Module (DIMM) form (see Figure 5.1). However, size and number of pins vary. This parameter must match that of the motherboard. Rambus memory comes in Rambus Inline Memory Modules (RIMMS), which are Rambus' version of DIMMs. Prior to DIMMs, Single Inline Memory

FIGURE 5.1   A 184-pin DIMM.

Modules (SIMMs) were prevalent. Notebook computers take very small DIMMs, called SODIMMs.

CAS Latency: Measured in numbers such as CL2 and CL3; make sure these match the requirements of the motherboard.

Serial Presence Detect (SPD): This is memory with an additional chip that contains information used by some motherboards to set certain memory parameters. This can be used on any motherboard, but if the motherboard requires this type of memory and non-SPD memory is used, the computer will display an error message when attempting to boot. We discuss the error message later in this chapter.

Single- or double-sided module: Some motherboards take either kind, but with a restriction. The Intel D815EEA motherboard, for example, has four memory slots. You can use up to four single-sided modules, but the motherboard will recognize only two double-sided modules. If you install two double-sided modules on slots 0 and 1, any modules in slots 2 or 3 will be ignored. Interestingly, you might not be able to determine this parameter by looking at the module. For more information, go to *kingston.com* and use the Memory Search function to search for memory for the Intel D815EEA motherboard.

Memory Types

There are many types of memory used today. They differ mainly in available speeds and cost. Motherboards are limited to one type of memory. Common memory types include SDRAM, DDR SDRAM, Rambus, EDO RAM, and burst-EDO RAM.

How to Determine the Optimum Amount of Memory

More memory, up to the maximum specified by the motherboard manufacturer, can never hurt a system. More memory allows the computer to keep more programs and processes running simultaneously. Additional memory is usually the easiest way to boost performance of a computer. With the price of memory being so low as of this writing, there is little reason to skimp, except in older computers getting limited use. For example, a Windows 95 computer used mainly to check e-mail, or a Windows 95 computer used only to run a business program designed for the OS version installed on that machine, probably doesn't need more than 32MB of RAM. Once a computer is used for more activity, especially running several programs at the same time, it will definitely need more. The most obvious factor is the performance of the computer. If it runs just fine, there is little or no reason to upgrade it. If performance or booting is sluggish, especially after new programs have been installed, this is a good time to add more memory.

Microsoft sets minimum and recommended amounts of memory for all its Windows versions, and developers set minimum levels for their programs. Recognize that Microsoft's minimums are absolute minimums; computers with this amount of RAM can pretty much run the OS and little else. Even recommended levels are on the low side. Minimum RAM levels for programs are often based on only the OS, that program, and other background processes, such as virus protection running. With current computers running Windows 2000 or XP, as of this writing, 128MB is the minimum amount of memory needed to provide adequate performance—256MB or more is recommended. If the computer is being used for memory-intensive programs such as video editing or multimedia, or if it is a busy server, 512MB to 1024MB (1GB) would be advisable. Again, any time a computer runs slowly, adding memory is a very safe bet. See software boxes or developers' Web sites for minimum hardware requirements.

Windows Virtual Memory Settings

Computers often temporarily need more memory than they have. For this reason, Windows manages virtual memory. *Virtual memory* is the use of a *swap file* on the hard drive for extra memory when needed. The action of moving data between physical RAM and the swap file is called *paging*. If there is not enough physical memory for the normal use of the computer, paging will increase, adding stress to the hard drive containing the swap file, and reducing the overall performance of the computer. Also note that the processor has to manage all the paging, so it doesn't have as much time to perform its other duties when there is too much paging. Therefore, if you run into a situation in which the hard drive is *thrashing* or *churning*, which is visible when the hard drive indicator light is on continuously for extended periods of time, it is possible that the computer needs more memory. It is also possible, however, that the problem is a cheap hard drive. A hard drive without an adequate built-in buffer (2MB or more of cache memory), or one that skimps on other performance-related elements could be inadequate for the job of paging. Therefore, it is best to make sure that the computer has a good hard drive and enough memory. If, however, you need to test the system to see which one is the culprit, use Windows System Monitor (9x), Performance (2000), or Performance Monitor (XP). For more information about these utilities, go to *support.microsoft.com*, select Advanced Search and Exact Phrase, and search for "Chapter 27 - Overview of Performance Monitoring." Make sure to type the phrase exactly as shown.

Finding the Right Memory for a Computer

The usual methods apply to determining the memory specifications that will work in a given computer: check the computer or motherboard manual, the manufacturer's Web site, or call the manufacturer. Where memory is concerned, however, there is an extraordinarily simple method in addition to these. Go to a memory manufacturer's Web site such as Crucial's (*crucial.com*), Kingston's (*kingston.com*), or PNY's (*pny.com*), access the memory upgrade, memory search, or "configurator" program on the home page, and enter the requested information (computer or motherboard brand, model number, etc.). The program will list all of the different memory modules that will work in the computer or specified motherboard. You can purchase memory from some of these sites, or you can go to a bricks-and-mortar retail store to buy them.

Determining the Amount of Memory Installed

There are several ways to see how much physical memory is installed in a computer:

- On Windows 9x, right-click My Computer and click the Performance tab. The amount of physical memory should be displayed.
- In any Windows menu, select Help > About.
- On bootup, before Windows starts, many BIOSs will test the memory and display it.
- Open the BIOS setup program and go to the page with memory settings.
- In Windows 2000 and XP, start the Task Manager (<Ctrl>+<Alt>+<Delete>). The Performance tab shows the amount of physical memory (see Figure 5.2).

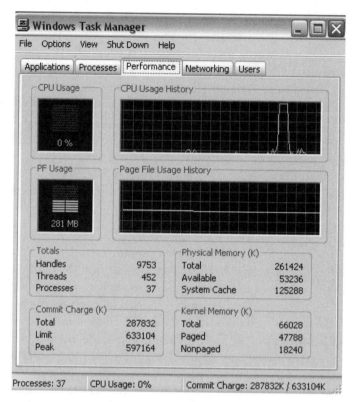

FIGURE 5.2 This computer has 261,424 KB of physical memory.

The Computer Reports the Wrong Amount of Memory

There are several reasons that a computer might report an amount of memory that doesn't match the actual amount installed.

- On some computers, the on-board video uses a portion of the main memory, so the computer indicates the amount minus the memory reserved for video. In some of these cases, the amount reserved for video can be changed in the BIOS Setup program.
- In the event that the number seems just a bit off, remember that one kilobyte is 1024 bytes, and that one megabyte is 1024 kilobytes. Therefore, if your computer shows 262,144 KB of memory, that is actually 256MB of RAM.
- If the amount of memory is off by the size of a whole memory module or large portion of one, there is a problem. Check to make sure the modules are installed correctly, the memory is of a type compatible with the motherboard, and that it matches the other memory installed. Some memory on certain

FIGURE 5.3 Numbered DIMM slots.

motherboards has to be installed in pairs. On some boards, the memory modules have to be installed starting with the lowest numbered slot; in other words, the lowest numbered slot must have a module in it. While you're checking for this, check to see if your slots are numbered starting at 0 or 1. In still other cases, the memory must be installed in capacity order. For example, if you have three modules of 128MB, 64MB and 32MB, the 128 would have to be in slot 0, the 64 in slot 1, and the 32 in slot 2. Even if a motherboard doesn't have these restrictions, it can't hurt to follow them anyway as a matter of course. Figure 5.3 shows numbered DIMM slots. Moreover, if you install more memory than the motherboard allows, your computer will likely show only the maximum amount of memory allowed by the motherboard.

■ If all else fails, you might have a bad memory module. If your computer boots, a diagnostic program such as Micro-Scope or PC Certify will test the memory. Also, some brand-name computers come with their own diagnostic programs such as Hewlett-Packard's HP Diagtools. If the computer won't boot, a POST card can diagnose the memory problem. We discuss these testing methods later in the chapter. Naturally, if you determine that a new memory module is bad, you'll want to contact the manufacturer for warranty replacement. The companies mentioned in this chapter are very good about honoring their warranties as long as the customer has handled the module properly.

MEMORY INSTALLATION

Memory isn't hard to install. First, make sure to take the usual static-avoidance measures, including wearing an anti-static wrist strap. Touch a piece of bare metal on the case before proceeding. With DIMMs, insert the module straight in the slot, taking care to match up the indentation in the module with the notch in the slot (see Figure 5.4). Then, make sure the plastic clips are closed as shown in Figure 5.5.

In old computers that take SIMMs, insert at an angle, and then straighten out. Do this very carefully, as old-style memory modules are exceptionally delicate.

Notebook Computer Memory Installation

Check the documentation for the notebook to find the memory slot. They are usually on the bottom—with the power off, remove the screw(s) to access the slot. Insert the modules at an angle and then straighten out, as shown in Figure 5.6.

General Rules for Memory Installation

- Use the correct memory for the motherboard.
- Follow all instructions from the computer/motherboard and memory manufacturers.
- Make sure all the memory modules match as described earlier in the chapter.
- Start at the lowest number memory slot, either 0 or 1.
- Insert the memory in capacity order starting with the highest-capacity module in the lowest number slot.
- After you have installed the memory, boot the computer and check the memory. If you don't have a diagnostic program, run some memory-intensive programs such as office programs, photo or video, or games with a lot of graphics.

For more help with memory installation, go to *kingston.com* and select Install Guides from the Support menu.

FIGURE 5.4 Match the indentation with the notch.

FIGURE 5.5   An installed module.

FIGURE 5.6   Inserting a SODIMM in a notebook computer.

Motherboards with the Intel 875 and 876 chipsets take DDR SDRAM in a dual channel configuration. There are two channels of memory, A and B, and two slots for each channel, 0 and 1. For best performance, make sure to follow the motherboard manufacturer's instructions. This means that chips in channel A, slot 0, and channel B, slot 0, should match exactly. The same goes for the DIMMs in the two slots 1. The best advice is to follow the instructions in the motherboard manual.

See the video "Installing Memory" on the accompanying CD-ROM.

TROUBLESHOOTING MEMORY PROBLEMS

So, how do you know when memory is a problem? First, if a problem occurs just after you installed new memory, you know that memory is a possible culprit. Other signs of a memory problem include frequent *lockups* (when the mouse pointer won't move and the Num Lock light on the keyboard is stuck on or off), or there is suddenly no video. Of course, neither of these symptoms is a certain indication of memory problems. There can be many reasons why these things could happen, such as viruses or corrupted Windows files. For more information, see Chapter 11, "Troubleshooting."

This applies only to old SIMMs: don't install SIMMs with tin contacts in slots with gold contacts, or gold contacts into tin slots. These two metals react and lose conductivity, resulting in memory failure.

If you get memory error messages, especially early in the boot process, you might have a memory problem.

Many memory error messages are misleading and don't indicate a problem with the memory. Before you attempt to troubleshoot any memory error messages, make sure to read the next section.

Memory Error Messages

Error messages are not always useful. Many are vague or cryptic, and some don't even represent a problem, while others are right on the money. It is also not always apparent whether the error message comes from Windows or from a program. This section will help you interpret memory error messages.

One type of error message that you'll be forced to heed is the type that appears early in the boot process and often prevents the computer from booting. Examples of these are the memory mismatch or memory parity error. They usually mean that the wrong type of memory is installed in the computer, incompatible modules are combined in the same machine, or that a module is faulty or not correctly installed.

If you see the following error message when attempting to boot the computer, the motherboard requires SPD memory for normal operation:

> *SERIAL PRESENCE DETECT (SPD) device data missing or inconclusive.*
> Properly programmed SPD device data is required for reliable operation.
> Do you wish to attempt to boot at XXXMHz bus speed? *Y/N [Y] Type [N] to shut down*

Either non-SPD memory is installed, or the data in the SPD chip has been corrupted. You can continue to operate the computer, but you risk data loss. It is best to replace the module(s).

Sometimes, on Windows NT, 2000, and XP, you'll get a stop error, better known as "the blue screen of death." See Chapter 2, "System Configuration and Computer Hygiene," and Chapter 10, "Troubleshooting Internet Connections," for more information about these errors. There are other types of errors as well. Some of these can be memory related. In the case of stop errors, copy the exact text of the message (encompassing the long hexadecimal numbers at the top of the screen). Regardless of the type, copy the entire error message exactly and search Microsoft's Knowledge Base (*http://support.microsoft.com*) or on *google.com* for the problem. Make sure to either use quotation marks around the error message, or use the Advanced Search function to search for the exact phrase—and don't make any typos.

One common error message category is the out-of-memory error. A message might warn you to save a document because the system is almost out of memory. Often, these messages occur on systems with lots of memory and few programs running. These messages usually indicate a program error, not a problem with memory. If this happens, close the program. The error messages should disappear. Reopen the program and see if the problem returns. If the error messages recur, go to the developer's Web site or contact tech support (if possible) to see if there are any fixes for the problem.

Memory Testing Hardware

Available from companies such as CST (*simmtester.com*), these devices are the quickest, most efficient way to accurately test memory. They can usually tell you quickly exactly what is wrong and also locate the offending module. However, because they are priced in the thousands of dollars, they are cost-effective only if you are testing large amounts of memory every day. For this reason, small repair shops are unlikely to have them. If you need to have memory tested with one of these devices, you might be able to find a business, such as your memory supplier, that has one and will test the memory for you for a fee. Just make sure you transport the memory in an anti-static container and have the container marked to identify whose memory is in it.

Memory Testing Software

Memory-testing software doesn't have all the capabilities of the hardware testing devices, but the price is right.

Also from CST (*simmtester.com*) is a program called DocMemory. As of this writing, this can be downloaded and used free, although the Web site warns that this offer is for a limited time only. Make sure to download the user guide in *PDF* form, and then read it before attempting to use the software. If you don't read it and configure it correctly, the memory test could go on for hours, even days. This is a highly professional program, but note that the Web site might indicate that it does not work with all versions of Windows, although our tests indicate that it does work.

Memtest86 (*memtest86.com*) is also freeware, and is a little rougher around the edges than MemoryDoc, although it too will give you valid results. Read the readme file that comes with the zipped download before using.

Both of these are used in the same way: download and expand the *zip* file, and run the install program to install the memory test program onto a floppy. Then, making sure that the BIOS boot order is set to boot first from a floppy, restart the computer and run the program.

A diagnostic kit such as Micro-Scope (*micro2000.com*) and PC Certify (*pccer-tify.com)* is a great investment because it can not only test memory, but virtually everything on a PC that needs testing. Additionally, the available POST Card can be used to test the system even if the system won't power on. We discuss Micro-Scope and PC Certify in detail in Chapter 11.

Resolving Memory Problems

When you try any of the following, do so with the power off. If you change anything, test the system each time to see if the problem is resolved. Keep a list of each change you make so you don't have to repeat them.

First, make sure that each module is installed correctly. Then, remove the modules one at a time, making sure to continue to follow the rules of memory installation listed earlier in this chapter. If you are using DIMMs, try cleaning the memory contacts (pins) with a pencil eraser. Then, use compressed air, such as Blow Off to blow the dust out of the slot. Reinsert the module and try again. If none of these procedures helps, or if a memory test indicates a bad module, replace the module with a new one, and then test the system to make sure the problem doesn't recur.

BIOS MEMORY SETTINGS

Some BIOS setup programs have settings for memory. Normally, most of these settings are to be left alone. In fact, manuals for Award BIOSs warn the technician never to alter the memory settings on the Chipset Features Setup page unless data is being lost. Data loss from memory is extraordinarily rare, so we also recommend leaving these settings alone unless directed to change them by support technicians *from the computer/motherboard manufacturer or the BIOS manufacturer.*

One memory setting you can change, as discussed earlier, is whether the memory should be ECC/parity or not. ECC/parity memory is not usually necessary except on file servers. An example of when you might change this setting is if you have some good non-parity memory from an otherwise irreparable computer and a computer that needs new memory of that type and speed, but that computer normally took ECC or parity memory. In the event that its BIOS has such a setting, change it to non-parity/ECC before removing all of the old parity/ECC memory and replacing it with the non-parity/ECC memory from the irreparable computer. Under normal circumstances, however, it is advisable to leave BIOS memory settings at their defaults.

For more information about BIOS settings, see your BIOS manufacturer's Web site, your motherboard/computer manufacturer's Web site, or access tech support at unicore.com.

6 | Magnetic Disk Drives

OVERVIEW OF HARD DRIVES (HARD DISK DRIVES, HDDs)

Hard disk drives are so named because they contain hard magnetic disks inside the housing. They are designed to store large quantities of information, and they don't need to be continuously powered in order to hold that data. The vast majority of PCs used today have at least one hard drive, and in almost all of these, the hard drive is used to store the OS, programs, and data. When a computer boots, depending on BIOS settings, the computer searches for boot files on different disk drives, most commonly the floppy drive first, then the hard drive, and then a CD drive. For regular use on any modern PC, the hard drive is the only one that is big

FIGURE 6.1   A standard PC EIDE hard drive.

enough to hold the required files. In fact, PCs that don't use hard drives are beyond the scope of this book. Figure 6.1 shows a typical PC hard drive. Note that laptop hard drives are physically much smaller.

Basic Hard Drive Characteristics

Externally, hard drives have a power connector, a data connector, and jumpers. We discuss jumpers later in this chapter. The power connector is connected to one of the drive connectors from the power supply, and the data connector is connected to the appropriate drive connector on the motherboard. Internally, hard drives have spinning magnetic platters and heads. *Heads* are small devices that store and pick up magnetic information from the platters; they have similarities to heads on cassette tape machines. Storage areas on the platters are divided into portions called *cylinders*, *sectors*, and *clusters*. Information about these parameters appears in the hard drive documentation and often on the paper label on the housing. When you go to the BIOS setup page that shows hard drive information, an example of which is shown in Figure 6.2, you might see some or all of this information and possibly more. Under the "type" category, there are usually three or more settings: User, None, and Auto (other settings might not apply to stationary hard drives). The None setting disables the drive. User allows the user to input the settings manually. If you choose User, the settings must match those of the drive exactly. Auto has the computer detect the drive information; on the vast majority of newer computers, Auto is the best setting.

This book is concerned only about what you need to know about hard drives in order to fix PCs. However, it will be very helpful to see the clear and simple explanation of how hard drives work at howstuffworks.com/hard-disk.htm, *or search* howstuffworks.com *for hard drives.*

NOTE

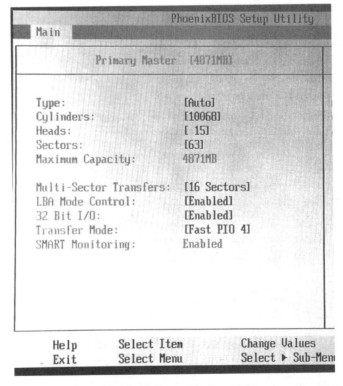

FIGURE 6.2 Hard drive information in a BIOS setup program.

SELECTING A HARD DRIVE

There are two main interfaces used today: Enhanced Integrated Drive Electronics (EIDE), and Small Computer System Interface (SCSI, pronounced "scuzzy"). SCSI drives perform better and have features that provide for higher reliability than EIDE drives. Not surprisingly, they are much more expensive than EIDE drives, and thus are used mostly in mission-critical business applications, and rarely in standard PCs. Because of this, SCSI devices are generally beyond the scope of this book, although some of the information in this chapter applies to SCSI also. There is a new interface, just becoming available as of this writing: Serial ATA (SATA). SATA drives are set to replace EIDE drives, and many new motherboards have connectors for both types.

We divide the factors to consider when selecting a hard drive into two categories: compatibility and quality.

Compatibility

The following factors must be considered to make sure a hard drive will work in a given system:

Form factor: Hard drive form factors aren't the same as other form factors. They have to do only with fitting the drive in the case, and thus are applicable only with internal hard drives. Desktop and tower computers are standardized for the 3.5-inch form factor, although it is possible to use smaller drives in one of these computers. (We discuss installing a small hard drive in a full-sized system later in this chapter). Laptops take 2.5-inch drives or smaller; check with the laptop documentation or Web site, or remove the drive and look at the label.

Ultra Direct Memory Access (UDMA) speed rating: This refers to the speed of data transfer between system memory and the hard drive buffer measured in megabytes per second and, at the time of this writing, has possible values of 33, 66, 100, and 133. Check the motherboard's maximum transfer speed and select the fastest hard drive the user can afford. Motherboards can accept any drives rated at their maximum speed or slower.

EIDE or SATA: As of this writing, some new motherboards have connectors for both, but older boards accept EIDE only. SATA expansion cards for PCI slots are available.

Quality

Any time you are purchasing a hard drive that is to be the main or only hard drive in a computer, you should take the following quality indicators into account. A cheap hard drive will provide poor performance in most cases, but might be well suited for file archiving when the files aren't accessed often.

Here are factors to consider when attempting to purchase the highest quality hard drive for the money:

Warranty: Previously, many hard drives came with a three-year manufacturer's warranty. More recently, one-year warranties have become most common. Try to get three years if possible.

Buffer (cache memory): This is high-speed memory that is used to store a small amount of data while it is waiting to be read from or written to the drive. As this significantly improves performance of the computer, the bigger the buffer, the better. 2MB is good; 8MB is much better, especially when the user works with graphics-intensive programs such as video editing or games, or other high-stress programs. Drives with less than 2MB of cache will likely provide poor performance.

Platter speed: The most common speeds are 5400 and 7200 revolutions per minute (RPM). The faster the platter spins, the faster data can be accessed and transferred.

EIDE or SATA: EIDE drives are the ones that PCs have been using for many years now. SATAs are just being introduced as this is written. SATA drives perform faster and more accurately than EIDE. An added advantage is that SATA cables are small, making for easier installation and better airflow than the standard ribbon cables used on EIDE devices. The smaller cables also allow for smaller computers.

HARD DRIVES AND OPERATING SYSTEMS

For it to store and retrieve data on a hard drive, and keep track of multiple partitions and multiple drives, significant portions of OSs have to be dedicated to managing hard drives. A *partition* is a portion of a hard drive recognized by the OS as a separate and complete entity; it is not the divider between these portions as the name suggests.

File Systems

The OS has to have a method of storing and organizing files on a drive. There are different *file systems* used by Windows and DOS to serve that purpose:

File Allocation Table (FAT): Better known today as FAT16 for its 16-bit file storage, this is the original DOS and Windows file system. Its storage efficiency is the lowest of all file systems in use and it is highly susceptible to fragmentation (portions of files spread out all over the drive resulting in slow performance and additional wear). Additionally, FAT16 limits file names to eight characters plus a three-character extension. The maximum partition size for FAT16 is 4GB. FAT16 is the only file system accessible in all versions of Windows and DOS, and is the only file system usable by the original version of Windows 95 and older. It is also the file system for floppy disks.

FAT32: FAT32 stores files more efficiently than FAT16 and has support for long filenames. FAT32 drives can be read by every version of Windows since the second version of Windows 95 (except for NT 4.0), and is the default file system for 98 and Me. The maximum partition size for FAT32 is very large, although there is a 32GB limit in Windows XP.

NTFS: The original version of NTFS was introduced with Windows NT. A newer version was introduced in Windows 2000, and it is the default file system for 2000 and XP. NTFS is somewhat resistant to fragmentation and allows for many of Windows 2000 and XP's security features not available in FAT16 or 32. The maximum size for an NTFS partition is two terabytes (TB), which is 2^{40} bytes, or 2048GB. Windows 9x and DOS cannot use NTFS.

To select a file system for a hard drive, you have to *format* the drive. When installing Windows 9x, you can use the DOS program FDISK, covered later in this chapter. When installing 2000 or XP, the OS setup program provides this service. You'll be shown a graphical display of all the hard drives installed on the system, and you'll be given your choice for installation of the OS. You'll also have the choice of file systems, and NTFS will be recommended.

Partitions and Drive Letters

Here are definitions of the terms used in this area:

Active partition: This is the partition that needs to contain the OS's boot files because the BIOS looks to this partition for them. You can, however, designate any partition as the active partition; if it is the wrong one, the computer won't be able to boot from the hard drive.

Basic disk: A physical disk that is accessible by any version of Windows.

Dynamic disk: A disk used in 2000 or XP that can use special features such as logical disk volumes that span more than one physical disk.

Extended partition: A partition that can exist only on a drive containing the *master boot record*. An extended partition does not get a drive letter. To use an extended partition, you must create one or more logical drives on it; logical drives are assigned drive letters. There can be only one extended partition on a physical disk and you cannot install an OS on an extended partition. The only reason to create an extended partition is if you want to have more than four partitions on a physical hard drive.

Logical drive: A partition created on an extended partition. A logical drive can be assigned a drive letter.

Master boot record (MBR): The area on a hard disk that contains boot files; this is the first sector on the disk.

Physical disk: A hard drive.

Primary partition: A partition that functions as a physically separate disk. You can create up to four primary partitions on a physical disk that contains the MBR, or three if you create an extended partition also. Primary partitions normally are assigned a drive letter by the OS.

Volume: Any area on a hard drive that has a drive letter assigned to it.

The most important thing to know here is that you must designate a partition as active in order to boot from it. However, the other items are likely to come up at some time or another.

Drive Letters

In a PC, physical disks are designated a number starting from 0. Primary partitions, logical drives, optical drives, and network drives are assigned drive letters between C and Z (a *network drive* is a folder or drive on another computer on a network that can be accessed as if it were a local partition on the hard drive). A and B are reserved for floppy drives. The order of automatic letter assignment is as follows:

1. The first primary partition on drive 0 gets C.
2. Subsequent primary partitions on any drive get D, and so on.
3. Logical drives get the next available letters.
4. Optical drives get the next available letters.
5. Network drives get any available letters.

This lettering system can cause the following complications: suppose drive 0 has one primary and one extended partition with one logical drive. Drive 1 has one primary partition. Because primary partitions come first, the primary partition on drive 0 is C, the primary partition on drive 1 is D, and the logical drive on drive 0 is E. Furthermore, if you add a second hard drive to a system with a logical drive on drive 0, the new primary partition takes the drive letter formerly held by the logical drive.

OS Hard Drive Control and Configuration

There are several Windows and DOS programs and commands to use to control and configure hard drives. When you are dealing with the only hard drive on a system, you are limited to what you can do in Windows. The reason for this is that Windows files are in use. In many cases, major changes won't be made until the computer is rebooted. The following sections are overviews of the programs.

FDISK

FDISK is a program that runs in DOS, and is useful mainly in 9x. Very old versions of FDISK aren't compatible with FAT32; if you run into this problem, it shouldn't be difficult to obtain a newer version from a Windows 98 or Me boot disk. No version of FDISK is compatible with NTFS. FDISK allows you to view partition information, create or delete a partition or logical drive, and set a partition to active status. FDISK is available on all 9x boot floppies, and in 95 and 98 by booting to DOS from the hard drive. When you get the command prompt, type FDISK. The first thing you'll see, unless you have a tiny hard drive, is a message asking if you want to enable support for large disks (larger than 504MB). Always answer yes (Y) to this prompt. The main menu then appears. You should usually start by viewing partition information by selecting number 4 from the menu. If you are installing a new hard drive, partition the drive as desired. Unless you have a compelling reason to have multiple partitions, such as setting up a *dual- or multiple-boot system*, create a single partition.

Partitioning with FDISK effectively deletes all data on the drive. If you are working with a used drive, make sure that the data is either backed up or unneeded before doing anything with FDISK other than viewing partition information or setting the partition as active.

FORMAT

Once you have completed partitioning with FDISK, your drive is not yet usable. The drive must be formatted with a file system. You do this with the FORMAT command. From the DOS command prompt, type FORMAT. For a list of switches, type FORMAT /?. Here is the syntax to use when formatting the C drive as FAT32:

```
FORMAT C: /FS:FAT32
```

After you press <Enter>, drive C, as shown in FDISK's partition information, will be formatted as a FAT32 partition. This will take some time, but when it is done, the partition will be usable. If you have set it active, you can install Windows on it. If you haven't set it to active, you can always run FDISK again and do so.

Any time you format a partition you necessarily delete all data on it. There are, however, programs such as Norton Unformat that can sometimes retrieve data from a formatted drive.

CONVERT (2000 and XP Only)

CONVERT is a command available in 2000 and XP that is used to convert a partition from FAT or FAT32 to NTFS. This is done in Windows at a command prompt. This cannot be undone in Windows without formatting the drive and deleting the data, although third-party software such as PartitionMagic® can be used to convert the file system back to FAT or FAT32 while preserving the data. The syntax to convert drive C to NTFS is as follows:

```
CONVERT C: /FS:NTFS
```

Press <Enter> and if the drive is in use, the conversion will occur at the next reboot; otherwise, it will start immediately.

My Computer

My Computer is available in all versions of Windows. If you select a partition and right-click it, you can perform a few tasks, which vary a bit from version to version. If you select Format from the menu that appears, you can format a partition. Naturally, you won't want to do this on a drive that you want to continue using, as this will delete all data on it. If you select Properties from the menu, the General tab shows you a pie chart showing used and free space on the drive. If you see a check box to enable DMA support, select it. *DMA* is a system that increases performance by reducing the amount of work done by the processor). If the drive doesn't support DMA, the box will be cleared at the next reboot. The Tools tab gives you access to error checking (ScanDisk), backup, and defrag programs.

Disk Management (2000 and XP Only)

All available disk-related tasks can be done in Disk Management. You can get there through Administrative Tools in Control Panel, and opening Disk Management from Computer Management, or by right-clicking My Computer, selecting Manage from the menu that appears, and opening Disk Management from Computer Management. This will show you a graphical depiction of all disks and partitions on your system. Note that by right-clicking a drive, you have access to certain commands, as shown in Figure 6.3.

If you make any changes in your disk configuration, make sure to edit the boot.ini file to match your changes. This can be a complicated procedure, but if you

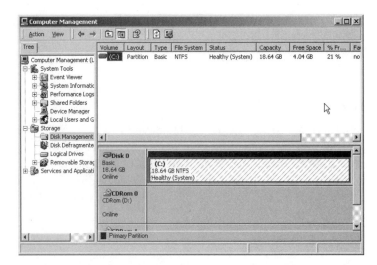

FIGURE 6.3 Disk Management on a simple Windows 2000 system.

don't, the computer probably won't boot afterwards. The only way to boot the computer after this happens is to use a Windows XP/2000/NT boot disk, with the boot.ini file on it edited to match the new disk configuration. Fortunately, Windows will remain intact. For information on making a boot disk for 2000 and XP, and on editing the boot.ini file, see Chapter 11, "Troubleshooting."

Disk Tools: ScanDisk, CHKDSK, and Defrag/Disk Defragmenter

We discussed these tools in Chapter 2, "System Configuration and Computer Hygiene."

HARD DRIVES AND MOTHERBOARDS

All standard PC motherboards today come with two EIDE channels, primary and secondary, as evidenced by connectors on the board. Each channel can handle two EIDE devices, one as the *master* and one as the *slave*. In this context, the terms *master* and *slave* really don't mean much, as everything a master drive can do, a slave drive can do also, although traditionally, the hard drive with the OS/boot files is installed as the primary master. This is not a rule, however. If the BIOS is set to detect any device as a boot device, then any one of the four can have the OS. The only restriction is that each channel cannot have more than one master and one slave drive. EIDE devices that can be connected to the EIDE connectors include hard drives, optical drives (CD and DVD), and Zip drives. Additional EIDE drives can be added to motherboards by using an EIDE expansion card (one manufacturer is Promise Technology, Inc. at *promise.com*). To use SCSI devices, a SCSI controller expansion card must be installed.

As we said before, many newer boards come with SATA connectors as well. With this interface, there is no such thing as master and slave, and only one device can be attached to each SATA connector.

HARD DRIVE REMOVAL AND INSTALLATION

It is *usually* not difficult to remove a hard drive from a desktop or tower computer for testing, virus scanning, data transfer, or disposal. The biggest problems you might run into are accessing the screws or having enough room to slide the drive out of the back of the cage. There are a number of steps to follow to install a new or replacement drive, but it usually isn't difficult either.

Hard Drive Removal

The first step in removing a hard drive is, with all the cables and power disconnected, to open the case and access the drive, as instructed in Chapter 4, "Cases and Power Supplies." You will probably have to remove four screws, two on each side of the drive, as shown in Figure 6.4. Then, remove the power connector and the data connector as shown in Figure 6.5.

FIGURE 6.4 Removing the screws that secure the drive to the cage.

FIGURE 6.5 Removing the power and data connectors from an EIDE hard drive.

Handle the hard drive with care. It shouldn't be subjected to physical shocks. See the video "Opening Different Types of Cases and Accessing Internal Parts" on the accompanying CD-ROM. The file is entitled Opening_the_Case.mpg.

Hard Drive Installation

There are several steps you need to take depending on whether the drive is new or you are reinstalling an existing drive.

Setting Jumpers

The first thing you'll want to do before installing a hard drive is to decide whether you want it to be a primary or secondary, master or slave, based on the other EIDE devices that are or will be installed in the machine. Then, make sure the jumpers are set correctly for master, slave, or cable select. Figure 6.6 shows a jumper panel that is set for the drive to be a master.

Cable Select is a setting that allows the slave or master condition to be determined by which connector on the ribbon cable the EIDE device is connected to. The cable and motherboard or IDE controller must support cable select in order to

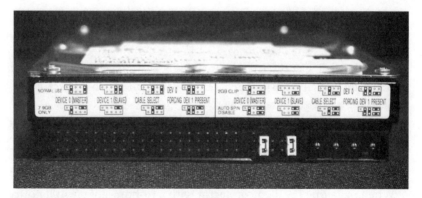

FIGURE 6.6 This jumper panel is set for master.

use it. Cables that do support cable select have three different colored connectors: black at one end for master, gray in the middle for slave, and blue at the other end for the motherboard (see Figure 6.7). Other cables with three connectors might support cable select. If you have two EIDE devices on one channel (primary or secondary), both or neither must be set to cable select. That is, you can't mix cable

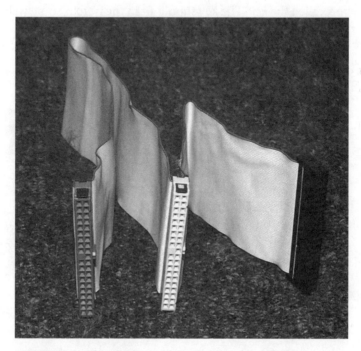

FIGURE 6.7 This ribbon cable supports cable select.

select and master or slave jumper settings on the same channel. Jumper settings are usually displayed on the drive label. If not, go to the drive manufacturer's Web site. For example, go to *seagate.com* and enter "cable select" in the search box. Then, open the article entitled *What is Cable Select and How Do I Configure my Seagate Drive to Use It?* This article gives an explanation of cable select, along with a jumper diagram for Seagate hard drives.

You can select whether a drive is primary or secondary by connecting the data cable to the appropriate connector on the motherboard or controller.

Ribbon Cables

When installing the data connector with a ribbon cable, you'll notice that one edge is colored differently from the others. That indicates pin 1. If you don't match up pin 1 on the connector with pin 1 on the drive, the hard drive will not work and might cause damage in some systems. In all full-sized hard drives, pin 1 is next to the power connector, as shown in Figure 6.8; notice that the stripe on the cable is next to the power connector.

Of course, it is just as important to connect the ribbon cable correctly to the motherboard, in the event you have removed it. The motherboard will also have a pin indication, as shown in Figure 6.9.

Also notice the notch in the connector. This is for the ridge in the cable connector, called the *key*. The key should fit in the notch. Some well-designed connectors are actually polarized—they will go in only the correct way. Thankfully, all SATA connectors are polarized.

FIGURE 6.8   Finding pin 1.

FIGURE 6.9 An EIDE ribbon cable connected to the connector on the motherboard. Notice the "40" on the opposite side of the cable's stripe, indicating pin 40.

There are two types of EIDE ribbon cables. Make sure that the ribbon cable is rated for the UDMA capacity of the hard drive and motherboard. Although all the connectors at the ends of the cables have 40 pins, cables for UDMA 66 through 133 have 80 conductors (wires). UDMA 33 cables have 40 conductors. The speed is printed on the cable. If the cable says 66, it is good for the higher speeds. If you use a 33 cable with a 66 hard drive or higher on a motherboard that supports the higher speed, the UDMA speed of the hard drive will still be held to 33.

You might see the term UltraATA *in place of UDMA. For the purposes of this discussion, there is no difference.*

Round Cables

Round cables are likely to all be designed to handle UDMA133. The rules for connecting them are basically the same as ribbon cables, but pin 1 is marked on the connector rather than on the wire. Round cables are much more expensive than ribbon cables, but are easier to work with and allow for better airflow. Search the Internet for round EIDE cables.

Make sure to tie off cables neatly. Use plastic wire ties, never rubber bands or twist-ties.

Hard Drive Bays

PC cases have a few different locations for hard drive bays. The most common is in a cage that holds drives horizontally at the front of the case. The second most common is the bay that holds drives vertically at the front of the case. The vertical bay is often used in smaller cases, or in larger cases for additional hard drives. If you are placing the drive horizontally, the label side should face up and the controller side should face down, unless it was previously installed and running in the opposite position. Then, connect the power connector.

Sometimes it might be necessary to install a hard drive in a 5.25-inch bay, the type usually used for optical drives (CD and DVD). There are adapters that allow you to do this. See Chapter 7, "CD and DVD Drives," for more information on optical drives and 5.25-inch bays. There may come a time when you want to install a 2.5-inch laptop drive into a regular computer. This requires an adapter for the data connector for a temporary situation, and a full kit for a permanent installation. To find an adapter, search the Internet for "2.5 hard drive to 3.5 adapter." If you can't determine which pin on the notebook hard drive is pin 1, consult the manufacturer's Web site. Unlike others, 2.5-inch laptop style hard drives do not have a separate power connector; the power connector is part of the data connector. There are two rows of pins with a space between it and the 4-pin jumper block. The first pin after the jumper block is pin 1, and the last pin at the opposite end on the bottom row is the positive power. If you connect this wrong, you might be connecting a power lead to a data pin, which, once the computer is powered on, will damage the drive and possibly the motherboard. Figure 6.10 shows the connector on a 2.5-inch hard drive.

We recommend to always remount a hard drive in the same position (right-side up, upside down, vertical) it was in originally, or it might fail sooner than it would otherwise. This is based solely on our personal experience.

Notebook/Laptop Hard Drive Installation

Unfortunately, there is no standard location where notebook manufacturers put their hard drives. On some machines, you might find that simply removing a single screw on the bottom of the machine and removing the plastic plate gives you full access to the hard drive. Other machines require you to remove the keyboard (see Chapter 9, "Input Devices," for more information). Still others have the hard drive in a slot on a side panel. Unless you have the first type, you will probably have to go to the manufacturer's Web site for service information. Once you find the hard drive, however, replacing it should be easy; the connector is usually polarized (goes in the correct way only). For more information, search the Web for notebook hard drive installation.

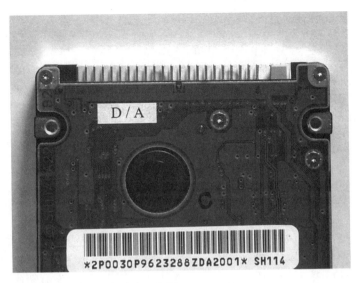

FIGURE 6.10 2.5-inch hard drive connector.

Hard Drive Setup

Once the drive is in place, there is a series of steps to perform to set up the drive and prepare it for use. The first is to make sure the BIOS recognizes the drive.

Hard Drive BIOS Settings

As long as it has such a setting, it is best to set the BIOS to Auto, so that it detects the hard drive settings itself. Manually entering these settings might slightly reduce the time it takes for a computer to boot, but it won't be significant enough to make it worthwhile. Some motherboards auto-detect the drive the first time and set the parameters so that they don't have to detect the drives each time. The other option is often called User, meaning that the user sets the parameters. If you feel you need to set the information manually, the information is usually printed on the drive label, or is available from the drive manufacturer's Web site and includes such items as cylinders, heads, write precomp, landing zone, sectors, and size mode.

Also, look in the BIOS setup program for a S.M.A.R.T. drive setting. This feature reports potential problems with the hard drive. Sometimes it will report that a hard drive is ready to fail. This will hopefully give you time to back up the data to another drive before you lose it all. Certainly, no harm can come from enabling S.M.A.R.T., so as long as the setting is available, it should always be enabled.

Disk Partitioning and Formatting

The next step is to partition and format the drive as described earlier in this chapter. In addition to FDISK, there are other setup programs you can use. In fact, just about all hard drive manufacturers offer installation, diagnostic, and other utilities free for download from their Web sites. Ontrack Data Recovery Services (*ontrack.com*) has enhanced versions of some of these utilities for sale. These utilities have many advantages over FDISK and FORMAT, including the capability of formatting partitions as NTFS.

ON THE CD The Industry Contacts document on the CD-ROM lists hard drive manufacturers. Visit their Web sites and look for downloads for installation, diagnostic, BIOS size limitation, and other utilities.

TIP *Early in the Windows 2000/XP installation process, you are prompted to press the F6 key in case you want to install drivers for a special drive controller. You must do this if you want to install the OS on a SCSI or SATA hard drive. This option is available for only a few seconds.*

When you set up Windows 2000 or XP from scratch or perform a *clean install* (installing an OS on a formatted drive, as opposed to running an upgrade), you can boot from an installation floppy or CD and follow the prompts. At a certain point you'll be shown a graph of available partitions and you'll be asked how you want to proceed. You might be able to use existing partitions or delete them and let Setup create new ones for you. You simply answer the prompts concerning the installation partition and file system you want. Then, Setup formats the partition as set. There is no need to pre-format a drive before installing 2000 or XP.

NOTE *You might come across a function in a BIOS setup program or elsewhere called "low-level formatting." Never do this; it would likely ruin the drive and invalidate the warranty. The point of low-level formatting is to do a complete format and erase everything to eliminate a virus or prepare the drive for a new user. This includes data that the manufacturer wrote onto an otherwise inaccessible portion of the drive. If you need to perform this operation, use the drive manufacturer's utility. In Seagate's case, for example, the procedure is called "Zero Fill" because it replaces all data with zeroes, and is done with Seagate's Disk Wizard software.*

Third-party disk management programs such as Power Quest's PartitionMagic (*powerquest.com*) have many features that aren't available in Windows or from any of the utilities that come with new hard drives. You can use PartitionMagic to create, delete, undelete, re-size, hide, merge, or move partitions, as well as change the file system or drive letters, all without losing data. These and many other features make it an especially useful tool for a technician to have, especially if you discover that you have finished installing an OS only to discover that you made an error in partitioning or formatting. You can use Partition Magic to correct the error without having to start all over.

Once you have installed, formatted, and partitioned the drive, you should be ready to install the OS.

TROUBLESHOOTING HARD DRIVES

Hard drives are a common culprit in PC problems. These problems can range from easily correctable to disastrous. As mentioned earlier in this chapter, making sure S.M.A.R.T. drives are enabled in the BIOS will be helpful to catch some of these problems sooner than they otherwise would be caught. This section covers some common hard drive problems and solutions.

Operating System Is Missing

One of the most obvious signs of a hard drive problem is an error message early in the boot process saying that the system can't find an OS. However, before jumping to conclusions, make sure there is no floppy in the floppy drive. It is most common for a BIOS to be set to boot first from a floppy, so if there is a non-bootable floppy in the drive, you'll probably get a message such as "Non-system disk or disk error," or "ntldr is missing." Remove the floppy and restart before taking any other measures.

If a computer is in early stages of booting or is running in DOS, pressing <Ctrl> + <Alt> + <Delete> will restart the system.

If there is no floppy in the drive and you continue to get a missing OS message, it is time to check the hard drive for problems. You can try the following:

A. Listen for hard drive activity and look at the indicator light on the case. The light should flicker and you should hear some sounds. Buzzing or clicking, however, is a possible sign of drive failure.

B. Check the BIOS to make sure that it recognizes the hard drive. Set the BIOS to autodetect the hard drive and to enable S.M.A.R.T. drives.

C. Check the power and data cables. Make sure they are plugged in correctly and securely. If the data cable looks damaged, try a replacement cable. Try disconnecting the power cable and using another one from the power supply.

D. Check the hard drive jumpers. Make sure there aren't two slaves, two masters, or a mixture of slave or master and cable select.

E. Run a diagnostic program such as Micro-Scope or PC Certify, or a utility offered by the hard drive manufacturer or Ontrack (*ontrack.com*). Also helpful are the Partition Magic Rescue floppies. You can boot the machine with these and run the program even if Partition Magic isn't installed on the system. You can access drive information and check for errors, as well as perform other operations. Just make sure to use a version of Partition Magic as recent as the OS installed on the system. For example, running a version of Partition Magic older than 7.0 on Windows XP or 2000 with Service Pack 2 or later will likely produce false error messages.

If you use a hard drive software utility, make sure to read the directions carefully, and, if so instructed, back up the data before running tests. In addition, make sure to follow the terms of the software license for any program you run.

F. Use a hardware-based EIDE hard drive tester such as the Western Digital Quick Tester (*wdc.com*).

G. Run FDISK and select number 4 from the menu to view partition information. Note that if the partition is formatted as NTFS, FDISK will label the partition only as a non-DOS partition. Sometimes the use of drive overlay software such as EZ-BIOS will actually interfere with the system's recognition of the drive.

H. Remove the hard drive and check it on another computer. Look for the Windows folder to make sure it is intact, and scan the drive for viruses.

I. Try a different EIDE device in the same channel to make sure the problem isn't in the motherboard or EIDE controller.

J. If there is another EIDE device on the same channel, disconnect it and boot the computer. One malfunctioning drive can cause the other device to stop working.

The System Doesn't Recognize the Full Capacity of the Hard Drive

There are a few different reasons why a computer might not make full use of a hard drive.

Many BIOSs are limited as to the maximum size of a supported partition. In the past, the only way to get around these limitations was to partition the drive so that each partition fit into the size limitation. However, today, unless the computer is very old, there are more satisfactory ways to get around this problem. The following list will be a helpful guide.

Enable large drive support in the BIOS, if available. This includes a setting called LBA support.

Check for a BIOS update. The source of the update should show a list of changes from the previous BIOS version. If there have been any BIOS versions released after the one installed on the computer but before the newest update, you might have to view them to see if any of them have a fix to this problem.

Install drive overlay software. This is available for download from the hard drive manufacturers, although it's not always called "drive overlay" software. If the computer locks up on boot and the hard drive is larger than 33GB, check to see if the BIOS is Award 4.5x. If so, drive overlay software should solve the problem.

Remove drive overlay software. Oddly enough, this software can sometimes cause the problem it was designed to solve, especially if it is installed on a newer computer. You will probably have to boot the computer with the drive overlay floppy and elect to uninstall the software once you get to the main program page.

Other Hard Drive Problems

Disk too full: Whenever a system runs poorly or if you get Windows Protection errors, check to make sure that at least 10 percent of the drive is unused. The paging file and other temporary files need this space. If less than 10 percent of the disk capacity remains, you will have to delete or transfer some data to another location. You might have to install the hard drive on another computer to do this. Another choice is to copy all or some of the data onto a larger drive and install the new drive in the computer. We discuss data backup later in this chapter.

The system suddenly can't read data on the drive: This is a sign of possible hard drive failure. If Windows is still running, run ScanDisk (9x), or Error-Checking/CHKDSK (2000, XP) (see Chapter 2 for more information). Make sure to select the "Thorough" and "Automatically fix errors" check boxes on ScanDisk, or the "Automatically fix file system errors" and "Scan for and attempt recovery of bad sectors" check boxes on Error-Checking/CHKDSK before running. You can also try the methods described in the previous list under "Operating system is missing."

If you have removed a hard drive from a Gateway computer with 98 or Me, and installed it in another machine and find that the second machine can't read any data from the drive, Gateway's Go Back utility might have been installed on the drive. Reinstall the drive in the Gateway machine, boot to Windows if possible, and uninstall Go Back. To do this, go to Control Panel, Add/Remove Programs.

If Windows stops running, you can boot a system with a Windows 98 or Me startup disk and scan a FAT or FAT32 partition by typing SCANDISK at the command prompt and pressing <Enter>. With NTFS partitions, you'll have to use a third-party program such as Norton Utilities or Partition Magic. Diagnostic programs such as Micro-Scope and PC Certify can also be very helpful.

Hard Drive Trouble Indicators

Some hard drive problems are indicated by blue screens or a message in 2000 or XP's Disk Management. This will usually require you to write down the entire error message and search Microsoft's Knowledge Base. In Disk Management, there is a status indicator on each partition's graph. Underneath the drive letter, size, and file system you'll see a word; hopefully the word is "Healthy," although you could see words like "Failed" or "Unreadable." For more information, access the Help files in Computer Management and search for "healthy." Then, select "Disk status descriptions" or "Volume status descriptions" and click the Display button.

If you get these indicators or other serious error messages, but the drive appears to work, there is no time to waste to back up important data, covered next.

For more help with hard drive problems, go to *http://howto.lycos.com/lycos/ series/1,,5+26+35994+34536+24365,00.html*, or go to *lycos.com*, click Computers, and navigate to the hard drive section.

SAVING DATA

Anyone who has important data is advised to back it up regularly. Few of us, however, do so. However, if you have an indication that a drive is about to fail, you might be able to save the data before it does. There are various ways to do this. First, you could copy the data directly. You can install the replacement hard drive into a separate computer on its own channel and transfer the data over a network, or barring that, you could install the replacement hard drive into the same computer on the other channel. Disconnect an optical drive if you have to. The XCOPY command is particularly good for this.

XCOPY

While you could manually transfer data in Windows, the XCOPY command gives you the advantage of certain options that streamline the process. Using the following switches when copying from the C drive to the E drive causes the system to copy hidden and system files, and continue copying even if some files are bad, among other benefits:

```
XCOPY C: E: /E /V /C /I /F /H
```

For more information, see the description of XCOPY in Appendix C, "Command-Line Tutorial." You can also open the command prompt and type XCOPY /?. This will provide the command's syntax and list the switches.

Another way to copy blocks of data is by using software such as Drive Copy™ or Drive Image® from PowerQuest®(*powerquest.com*). These programs have to be installed, but they work much faster than XCOPY.

Backup Programs

There are also backup programs that take all the data to be backed up and create a single highly compressed file. These programs provide a way to back up and restore data, including OSs and programs, exactly the way they were. Early Windows Backup programs could store the backup only on the local drive, floppies, or on a network drive, although the backup file can always be moved to another drive once the backup is complete. The most common backup program is Backup Utility for Windows, better known as Windows Backup, available in Start > Programs (All Programs in XP) > Accessories > System Tools. The interface for Windows Backup is simple (see Figure 6.11). Just follow the wizard.

There are many third-party backup programs on the market, most of which offer more features than Windows Backup does.

Hard Drive Crash

If you have a hard drive that has absolutely ceased to work no matter what steps you have taken to restore it, it has probably *crashed*. To recover the data, your only option might be to send the drive to a recovery company such as Ontrack (*ontrack.com*). This is an expensive operation, so it is done mainly when the data is critically important.

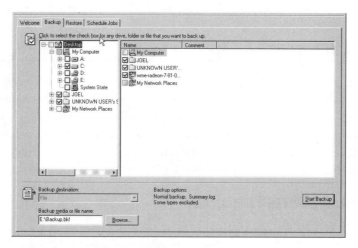

FIGURE 6.11 Windows Backup.

File and Settings Transfer Wizard

Introduced with Windows XP, the File and Settings Transfer Wizard allows you to set up a new computer running Windows XP as close as possible to the old one running Windows versions 95 through 2000, including NT 4.0. Available in Start > Programs (All Programs in XP) > Accessories > System Tools, this wizard is easy to follow. Early versions have been troublesome, however. To correct any problems, make sure to install Service Pack 1 or later on Windows XP before proceeding.

RAID

RAID stands for "Redundant Array of Independent (formerly "Inexpensive") Disks." RAID is a collection of hard drives in a computer that is used for performance enhancement and/or fault tolerance. Windows server versions (Windows NT and 2000 Server, and Windows Server 2003) have built-in support for some levels of RAID, but hardware-based RAID systems provide better performance. The most basic level of RAID uses two hard drives to increase performance, while higher levels store data on two or more drives so that if one fails, the data won't be lost. SCSI drives are usually used in RAID systems. In hardware-based RAID systems, it is common for the drives to be removable; they are kept in a caddy that is accessible through an opening in the case. When one fails, it can easily be replaced. More advanced systems employ *hot-swappable* drives. These are drives that can be removed and replaced without shutting down the system. Naturally, all this technology is much more expensive than standard PCs, so it is used mainly in business and government situations in which downtime and/or data loss would be catastrophic to the operation of the organization. For more information on RAID, see *raid-web.com*, and search the Web for more articles; there are many.

REMOVABLE STORAGE DEVICES

There are several different types of removable storage devices. We discussed removable full-sized hard drives in the section on RAID. There are additional uses for these. One is for drives containing data only (no OS or programs) that can be easily switched from machine to machine, although networks usually do that job. Another use is as an easy way to switch OSs on a single computer, a job usually done by setting up the different OSs on different partitions.

USB and FireWire (IEEE 1394) Drives

USB and FireWire are external drives that connect easily into the appropriate port. They are especially good for backup and transferring large amounts of data from one machine to another without using a network connection, and they are hot-swappable (consult the manual to be sure). These take drive letters, just as internal hard drives. They cost a bit more than internal drives because of the housing and external power supply. When installing one of these drives, make sure you follow the directions exactly, especially order of installation. You can expect problems if you don't. If you are asked to get one of these drives working after someone installed it incorrectly, you'll have to uninstall the drive and start over again.

PC-Card (PCMCIA) Hard Drives

PC-Card hard drives are credit card sized drives that fit into the appropriate Type II or III PC-Card slots on notebook computers and the occasional full-sized computer. Recent models by Kingston (*kingston.com*) and other companies hold several gigabytes of data. However, because of their extraordinarily small size, they don't have much buffer, so they are good mainly for data archiving on notebooks. These drives are usually easy to set up and they do get a drive letter from the system. They are also hot-swappable, but if Windows is running, make sure to stop the device by clicking the Eject or Unplug Device icon in Windows' system tray, or in the Add/Remove Hardware wizard (or equivalent depending on Windows version) in Control Panel. Failure to stop a PC-Card device before ejecting it can damage the device.

Microdrives

Microdrives are even smaller drives used in certain computers and digital cameras. A Hitachi (*hgst.com*) 4GB drive using a single 1-inch platter should be coming on the market as this book is released. There are adapters available to plug microdrives into PC-Card slots.

When formatting an external hard drive, take into account the different computers in which it might be used. You wouldn't want to format a drive as NTFS if it will be shared with a notebook running Windows 9x.

Flash Memory Cards

Flash memory is memory that doesn't need continuous power to maintain its data. Therefore, it can be used in place of a disk drive. Flash memory has the advantage over disk drives of having no moving parts, so it is much more resistant to damage than the spinning platters and fast-moving heads of a hard drive. If flash memory eventually gets to the point where it exceeds the speed of hard drives for a comparable cost, it will possibly replace hard drives and possibly all disk drives. Flash memory is also adaptable to PC-Card slots.

Diagnosing Removable Storage Device Problems

These devices can fail just as regular hard drives can. Follow all drive troubleshooting instructions that apply to these devices. Moreover, with the USB and FireWire drives, drivers could be a problem—either the driver could be corrupted or the installer didn't follow the instructions. Uninstall the device and reinstall the drivers, making sure to follow the directions to the letter. See Chapter 2 for more information on device drivers.

FLOPPY DISK DRIVES (DISKETTE) OVERVIEW

Floppy drives were the original storage drive type in PCs. The IBM PC, circa 1981, had two 5.25-inch floppy drives, each with a capacity of 360KB. There were no other storage devices. 1.2MB versions of these came out years later, and the 3.5-inch version that we use today came out after that. There was an attempt to circulate 2.88MB floppies, but they really didn't catch on.

These days, floppy drives are on their way out, although the vast majority of new computers still come with them, with the exception being notebooks. While

FIGURE 6.12 Standard opening, standard drive.

many of the most common uses for floppies have been taken over by CD-RWs, removable hard drives, Zip drives, and network connections, at the moment, floppies are still essential for tasks such as starting computers that won't boot otherwise, or running programs such as disk utilities that can't run in Windows. This is because the drivers to run floppy disks are included on all BIOS chips, meaning that floppy disks can run as soon as the BIOS gets to them. More recently, however, this has become true for optical drives as well.

Selecting a Floppy Drive

New floppy drives available today are nearly all good quality. If the case has an opening that shows the entire floppy faceplate, as shown in Figure 6.12, the only consideration is that the color of the faceplate matches the computer case, if that is important to the user. Many cases, however, have openings for proprietary floppy drives, an example of which is shown in Figure 6.13. In this case, if you have a selection of used drives, you can try to match up a faceless drive, such the one shown in Figure 6.13, or try to order a new drive from the case or computer manufacturer.

FIGURE 6.13 Proprietary opening, proprietary drive.

Floppy Drive Installation

Motherboards have one floppy connector, and many newer motherboards support only one floppy drive. A computer can have no more than two floppy drives. About the only need these days for two floppy drives is if the user has 5.25-inch disks to access. In this case, the 3.5-inch drive should be A and the 5.25-inch should be B. A small power connector (see Figure 6.14) is used for 3.5-inch floppy drives. A standard floppy drive ribbon cable has three connectors: one for A, one for B, and one for the motherboard connector (see Figure 6.15). You'll see that a floppy cable has a twist. The twist should be nearest the A drive. If there is some compelling reason to switch drive letters, such as having to use the B drive as a boot drive (only A can be a boot drive), this should be possible in the BIOS. The other option is to change jumpers, but they differ from drive to drive and tend to be confusing.

The data connectors for 5.25-inch floppy drives are not the same as those for 3.5-inch drives. If you need to install a 5.25-inch floppy drive, you'll need a floppy cable with a choice of two connectors to use for the B drive. That type of cable allows connection of either a 3.5-inch or a 5.25-inch device as the B drive. Remember, the A drive is always the one nearest the twist in the cable.

Just about every case has a space dedicated to a floppy drive. Look for a 3.5-inch bay that corresponds to an opening in the front of the case (shown in Figure 6.16).

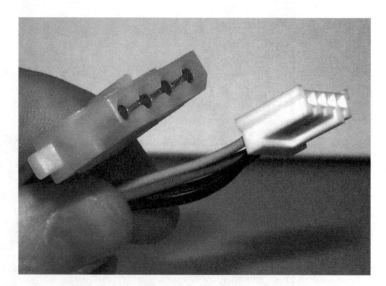

FIGURE 6.14 The large connector is for hard drives, optical drives, and 5.25-inch floppy drives. The small connector is only for 3.5-inch floppy drives.

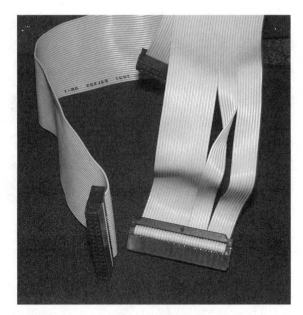

FIGURE 6.15   One floppy cable with a twist.

FIGURE 6.16   A bay usable for floppy drive.

FIGURE 6.17 Pin 1 markings can be vague.

Just as in hard drives, you'll have to match up pins 1. Pin 1 on the cable has a stripe, and there will be some type of marking on the drive as shown in Figure 6.17, and on the motherboard, as shown in Figure 6.18. The drive markings can be cryptic, but know that if pins 0 and 34 are marked, pin 1 will be next to pin 0, and on the opposite side from pin 34. Other drives have only a red mark. Once you ascertain which side pin 1 is on, it is a good idea to mark it on the drive with a fine-tipped permanent marker. However, damage won't occur if you make a mistake with the data cable; if the floppy drive light stays on continuously, it means that one end of the data cable is in backward.

Finally, make sure that the BIOS is set correctly for the floppy drive(s) in the system.

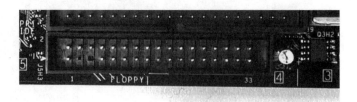

FIGURE 6.18 Pin 1 marking on the motherboard.

Diagnosing Floppy Problems

There aren't many different types of problems with floppy drives. The one mentioned previously is that of the light staying on continuously, indicating that one of the data connectors is in backward. If the drive doesn't seem to work at all, either the data or power cable might not be in all the way. The only other problem is trouble reading from or writing to the disk. First, try a new disk—floppy disks are prone to damage. If that doesn't work, try using a cleaning kit. Search the Web for "floppy drive cleaning kit." These should be very inexpensive.

Don't use an important floppy to test a drive; a bad drive can damage a floppy disk and/or its data.

Formatting Floppies

Floppy discs come from the factory already formatted for PCs or Macs. The easiest way to erase all the data on a floppy is to format it again. In Windows, right-click the drive in My Computer and click the Format command. If the disk has been working and you are in a hurry, select the Quick Format check box. Quick Format skips the step of checking the disk for bad sectors. If the data has been corrupted, or you have the time, leave this box clear. You can also do this at a command prompt, which is important if you are in DOS. The command is as follows:

```
FORMAT A: /Q
```

The Q switch instructs the system to do a quick format.

All floppies will be formatted as FAT16.

Making a Windows 9x Startup Disk

To make a Windows 9x startup disk, insert a floppy in the drive of a Windows 9x computer. Then, go to Add/Remove Programs in Control Panel, and click the Startup Disk tab.

For more information on floppy drives, go to *pcmech.com/floppy.htm*.

ZIP AND *JAZ* REMOVABLE DISK DRIVES

Zip and Jaz drives use proprietary removable disks in sizes running from 100MB to 2GB. These drives get a drive letter and are fast and easy to use. Windows Me and later versions don't need to have software installed in order to use them. Mac-formatted disks and PC-formatted disks are available. A Mac can usually use a PC disk, but a PC needs third-party software to be able to use a Mac disk. The disks are rather reliable, but of course are subject to bad sectors and magnetic or physical damage. The disadvantage to these drives is that the removable disks are much more expensive than CD-RWs and recordable DVDs, which can be had for under $1 apiece, and can be formatted to act as a regular magnetic disk.

7 CD and DVD Drives

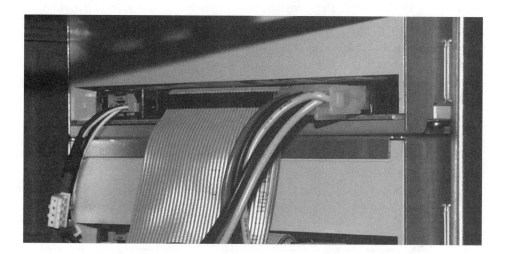

CD/DVD DRIVE OVERVIEW

Compact Disc (CD) and Digital Versatile Disc (DVD, formerly Digital Video Disc) drives are called *optical* drives because microscopic pits embedded into the discs are read by measuring reflected laser light. Read-Only Memory (CD-ROM) drives became popular around 1994 and represented a major improvement over floppies for program installation. They can also be used to read from CD data discs. Eventually came CD-R drives, which allowed discs to be *burned* (recorded) once only. There weren't too many of these made as they were quickly replaced by CD-RWs, which can be used with both single-use and rewritable discs. DVD-ROM drives were next. These are used to play DVD videos and read from data DVDs. More and more programs are becoming available on DVDs as well.

The term ATAPI *refers to IDE optical drives.*

NOTE

Unfortunately, there are several different incompatible types of DVD writable drives available, and the industry has not settled on a standard. The different types include the following:

DVD-R: Can write to a blank disc once. The discs are compatible with most recent DVD video players.

DVD-RW: Can be written and rewritten to. The discs are compatible with most recent DVD video players.

DVD+RW: Can be written and rewritten to. They can read and write to DVD-Rs. The discs are compatible with some DVD video players.

DVD-RAM: Can be written and rewritten to. The discs are *not* compatible with most DVD video players as of this writing.

Blu-ray Disc: A format not yet available as of this writing that allows for up to 27GB of data to be stored on a single DVD disc.

Some multi-standard drives are available. There are also discs with multiple layers and discs that can be flipped over to record on the other side, increasing the data capacity. Stay tuned; the industry will probably eventually come to an agreement on a single standard.

SELECTING OPTICAL DRIVES

There are only a few considerations in selecting an optical drive.

Interface

So far, internal drives come only in two interfaces: IDE and SCSI. IDE is the same interface as EIDE as it applies to hard drives, and thus the optical drives are connected to the same cables as the hard drives. See Chapter 6, "Magnetic Disk Drives," for more information on the IDE interfaces. SCSI drives are simply additional devices in the SCSI chain. SCSI controllers and consequently, SCSI drives, are found almost exclusively in heavy-duty business computers. Serial ATA optical drives will be available eventually.

External drives once came with parallel interfaces (they connect to a parallel port on the computer) and SCSI, but now are available in USB and FireWire. You should select the fastest interface the user can afford. Also note that USB 2.0 is faster than the USB 1.1, so if you are using a USB 2.0 drive with a computer that has only a USB 1.1 interface, the drive will operate at the slower speed.

Speed

Speed of optical drives is based on the data transfer rate of the original CD-ROM drives, 150 kilobits per second (Kbps). For example, the data transfer rate of a 52x CD-ROM drive is 52 × 150, or 7.8 megabits per second (Mbps). Even the fastest optical drives, however, are slower than hard drives.

CD-RW Speed

A CD-RW, also known as a *CD burner*, has three speeds listed in its specifications. The first number represents the speed of writing to a CD-R, the second is the speed of writing to a CD-RW, and the third is the speed it reads a disc. In the case of a combo drive that offers a DVD-ROM along with a CD burner, a fourth number is the speed the drive reads a DVD, but see the next item for an explanation of DVD speeds.

DVD Speed

There are combo drives available that offer DVD and CD burning capabilities. In these cases, there are so many numbers in the specifications that each is spelled out (or should be) wherever it is displayed. The single DVD-burning speed, however, is much faster than the CD's 150 Kbps, and can vary from standard to standard. The actual speed in Mbps should be spelled out in the documentation.

The maximum speed of the blank media (writable discs) in any format must match or exceed that of the burner in order for the burner to operate at its maximum rated speed.

REMOVAL AND INSTALLATION

IDE optical drives are connected the same way as EIDE hard drives, so see Chapter 6 for information. Set the jumpers for primary/secondary, master/slave, or cable select, just as you do with EIDE hard drives. The BIOS should be set for autodetect for each optical drive. Also, pin 1 is almost always next to the power connector, which is the same type of power connector used for hard drives. Screws are used on each side of the cage to secure the drive. The only differences are that optical drives have to be installed in a 5.25-inch bay with an opening in the front of the case, and that an audio cable usually has to be connected. Figure 7.1 shows a typical example of an installed optical drive.

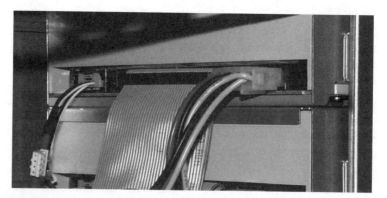

FIGURE 7.1   A typical CD-ROM drive installation.

To remove a drive, shut off the power, remove all cables from the computer, and open the case. If there could be any question about reconnecting the drive, make a diagram of which connectors are connected where. Make a note of the drive select jumper position. This is especially important if you will be removing other drives as well. Next, remove the data, power, and audio cables. Then, remove the screws fastening the drive to the cage and pull out the unit. To replace a drive, follow the instructions in Chapter 6 for installing a hard drive, except for the differences described here.

Mixing Drives with Different UDMA Ratings

As is true with hard drives, you normally wouldn't want to have drives of different UDMA ratings—for example, an Ultra ATA UDMA 100 drive on the same IDE channel as an Ultra ATA UDMA 66—unless the motherboard or IDE controller came with a program such as Intel's Application Accelerator. See Chapter 6 for more information.

Audio Cables

For most optical drives to play analog audio from audio CDs or video discs with audio, there is an audio connector on these drives. These get connected to the audio header connectors on the motherboard or sound card. Some motherboards have two or more of these, as shown in Figure 7.2.

If you have one drive and two connectors, use the header connector for CD-ROM in. If you have two drives and two connectors, connect the drive that will be most likely used for audio playback to the CD-ROM in and the other to the AUX in. If you have two drives and only one connector, the user will be limited to one of

FIGURE 7.2   Audio header connectors on a motherboard.

the drives for analog audio playback (digital audio playback can be heard without an audio cable being connected at all; it is transmitted via the data cable). If one of the drives is a DVD drive, you'll want to connect the audio connector to it. In this case, instruct the user to play audio CDs in the DVD drive. Figure 7.3 shows an audio connector on an optical drive.

FIGURE 7.3   Optical drive audio connector.

Proprietary Faceplates

Often, a computer manufacturer will design their cases for aesthetics and will include an odd-shaped front opening for optical drives. It is often hard to acquire a replacement for these drives by the time they fail. If you have a large supply of used drives or can match the original manufacturer's drive closely enough, you might be able to get a good match by removing the faceplate carefully from the original and fitting it on the replacement. Usually, you will need to modify the case slightly or place the drive in a different drive bay if available. There have been times that we have opted to get a brand new high-quality case with a power supply, and transfer the motherboard and all internal parts to the new case as well as install a new standard optical drive. This might actually be a better and more aesthetic long-term solution as long as all the components will fit properly in the new case.

Driver, Firmware, and Software

Windows, in almost all cases, will automatically install all necessary drivers for optical drives. Once the drive is installed, the programs supplied by the manufacturer that allow for use of the drive's features can be installed. These are usually "lite" versions of programs. The user can purchase full versions of these programs for added functionality. In addition, newer versions of Windows Media Player and other media players such as RealPlayer™ (*real.com*) have the *multimedia* functions built in. Windows Media Player is standard with Windows, and updates are frequently available either through Windows Update (see Chapter 2, "System Configuration and Computer Hygiene"), *microsoft.com/downloads*, or *microsoft.com/windows/windowsmedia*. In addition, data-burning capabilities are built into My Computer in Windows XP, as shown in Figure 7.4.

In most cases, a drive's firmware should be left alone. If you are researching a problem and find that a firmware update is necessary, go to the manufacturer's Web site and follow the directions exactly.

Remember, you run the same risks when updating component firmware as when you update a motherboard BIOS. If you make a mistake, you might render the drive useless!

Installing and Configuring External Optical Drives

USB and FireWire drives can be very simple to install. Follow the manufacturer's instructions carefully and *read them first* before you connect anything. In most cases, USB drives will require that the software be installed before the drive is ever connected to the computer. Some USB drives might be able to be plugged in to a

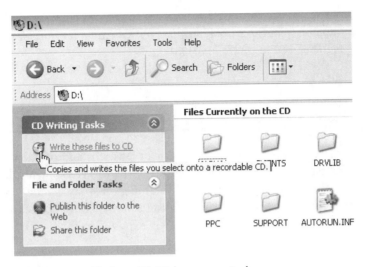

FIGURE 7.4   Windows XP CD burner controls.

PC with Windows Me, 2000, and XP directly without any driver installation at all because the drivers are built right into the firmware of the drive.

With FireWire, the drive is usually plugged into the computer after it is running and the OS will recognize the drive and install Windows native drivers. If the drivers were not installed originally with Windows, you will probably be asked to insert your Windows installation CD. After your drive is properly detected, you can install any applications needed to use the drive, such as software for CD burning, movie editing, music production, and so forth.

BACKUPS ONTO OPTICAL DISCS

Microsoft Backup, which comes with Windows except for XP Home Edition (Start > Programs/All Programs > Accessories > System Tools > Backup), can use optical drives. Many third-party backup programs have this capability as well. Elect to back up to a file and then store the file, if it will fit, on a CD-RW or writable DVD. You can use software to burn a disc, or better yet, format a rewritable disc so that it can be used just as a magnetic drive. Most or all CD-burning software has a function for formatting the disc. To format a disc could take between 25 and 45 minutes. When it is completed, files and folders can be dragged and dropped, or cut/copied and pasted into and out of the rewritable disc. This makes these discs very convenient to use for backups. Keep in mind that formatting a rewritable optical disc will preclude its use in a DVD or CD video/music player.

Windows Backup can be installed on XP Home Edition. See Chapter 11, "Troubleshooting," for more information.

MAINTENANCE OF OPTICAL DISC DRIVES AND DISCS

The same cleaning kits you use to clean lenses in audio/video optical disc players can be used to clean lenses in computer drives. It is also helpful to spray the inside of the disc drawer with Blow Off or a similar air spray. Do not use any chemicals or solvents anywhere near a drive unless it is designed for it. Cleaning doesn't need to be done often unless the computer is exposed to dust, tobacco smoke, or other pollutants.

DIAGNOSING OPTICAL DISC PROBLEMS

The list of problems that can occur with optical drives isn't huge.

Disc Read Problems

The most common problems are related to reading from discs.

Repairing Disc Scratches

If you find that a drive cannot read a disc, the first thing to do is to examine the disc for damage. If the disc has a crack, there is little hope of saving it. If there is no serious visible damage, try the disc in another drive you know to be working. If the disc still can't be read, the problem is most likely to be in the disc. Scratches can often be repaired using a scratch repair kit. Follow the directions on the kit. This might be a good time to copy the files to a hard drive folder and then burn a new disc, as long as this doesn't violate copyright laws. Most computer supply stores can stock or can order you a hand-operated or motorized CD cleaner. Be aware that you might have to get a different type of tool for data CDs and DVDs.

Drive-Related Disc Read Problems

If the disc is good in other drives, the problem *should* be in the drive. Try another known good disc in the drive. If the drive still will not consistently read the disc, you should start by using a compressed air spray and a vacuum hose to blow out the dust. If all else fails and you feel comfortable with it, you can sometimes carefully disassemble the drive and find hairs and dust in the works of the drive and remove it. If you then carefully reassemble the drive, it might work again. This step should be used only as a last resort.

Read Failures of CD-R or RW Discs in ROM Drive

You might run into a situation in which you try to read a CD-R or CD-RW in a CD-ROM drive, but the disc isn't recognized. There are a few reasons why this could occur. One is that the disc was not finalized after being burned. The disc should be taken back to the machine it was burned on, and then finalized. Another possibility is that the CD-ROM drive is so old that it was not designed to read these discs. While there is an outside chance that the drive manufacturer might have a firmware update that will allow the drive to recognize these, your best bet is usually to replace the drive with a new one, especially considering how inexpensive they have become.

Problems Writing to a Disc

It is common, when writing to a disc, to get *buffer underrun* errors. These errors indicate that the data is being read at a different rate than it is being written. The result of these errors is that the destination discs become beverage coasters. Newer drives are designed to avoid these errors, but if you have this problem, there are a few ways to reduce the chance of this from occurring. One way is to copy all the files to a single folder on the hard drive first. The other is to lower the writing speed in the burner program. Another is to free up resources by closing all unneeded programs that are running. For ways to free up resources, see Chapter 2. These steps can be taken individually, or together to gain the best results. For troubleshooting a particular problem, it is recommended to try them one at a time to see what gives the best results. If you consistently have problems writing to CD-R and CD-RW discs, it might be more cost effective, due to lower prices, to purchase a newer, faster CD-RW drive with more buffer memory. Today's drives often come with 4 or 8MB of buffer, and other technology designed to minimize failures.

Occasionally, a particular drive might have a problem with a certain brand of disc. Once you find a disc brand that works, try to stick with it and you will be likely to have fewer failures.

Other Drive Problems

Does a drive simply fail to work or even open? Try going into Device Manager, removing the drive, and then rebooting the system. The drive might very well work normally again. In Windows 9x, the IDE controller might not have the appropriate drivers. If the optical drive is connected to the secondary IDE controller in some versions of 9x, Windows might not be able to recognize the drive if the IDE drivers for the chipset are corrupt or not installed. You can usually test this by attaching the optical drive as a slave to the hard drive on the primary IDE controller and restarting Windows. If the drive is now recognized and working properly, this is most likely the problem. The solution is to reinstall the IDE bus mastering controller software drivers, or if you only have two IDE devices in the system, you can leave the optical drive connected as a slave on the primary.

Certain CD-burning programs can cause problems opening the drive. For example, Roxio Easy CD Creator™ 5.0 on XP might cause the drive not to open after a CD is burned. Roxio offers a software *patch*, at *roxio.com*, that solves this problem, but you can open the drive before downloading the patch by opening the Direct CD application and clicking Eject.

In case a disc gets stuck in the drive, if you need to remove a disc while the computer's power is off, or if there is a disc in a drive that's not installed in a computer, you need a highly specialized tool to open the drawer. The tool is a straightened paper clip. If you look closely at the front of the drive, you'll find a tiny hole. Insert the clip in this hole and push until the drawer opens, as shown in Figure 7.5.

In case an Me, 2000, or XP user wants to listen to audio CDs through the front panel headphone jack, and it doesn't work, it's probably because the CD-ROM drive is configured for digital playback. Either instruct the user to use the speaker or headphone jack on the soundcard or speakers, or disable digital playback by accessing the drive's properties in Device Manager and clearing the "Enable digital CD audio for this CD-ROM device" check box.

Another problem that can occur is excessive noise when the disc is spinning. Although some noise is normal, if you hear a loud buzzing or grinding noise, there are two main possibilities: either the disc has a loose label that is flapping against the top of the drive, or the drive is broken or worn out.

FIGURE 7.5 Freeing a captive disc.

BOOTING FROM A CD-ROM

In older DOS-based systems, including Windows 9x, you often couldn't boot from a CD. This is because DOS CD drivers couldn't be loaded before DOS boots. The *El Torito* specification allows that problem to be overcome. Most CD drives for many years meet that specification. Furthermore, in newer machines, the BIOS is designed to load drivers needed to allow the CD drive to work. This makes it possible to install Windows 98SE/Me/2000/XP without using installation boot floppies. Simply set the BIOS to boot first from a CD drive, insert the installation CD, and boot the machine. This also makes floppy drives obsolete; you can make boot CDs for Windows 9x or for 2000 and XP. In 9x, you will need to either copy the boot files from a boot floppy or from the hard drive, because the Windows Setup boot disc creation function won't work directly with a disc other than a floppy.

CD-ROM Doesn't Work in DOS

If you have a boot floppy for Windows 9x and you need to access files on a CD, simply select "Start computer with CD support" when you are so prompted. If you still do not have access to the CD-ROM, your drive might be too old to support the generic drivers on the Windows 9x boot floppy. If this option does not appear with your boot floppy, which would occur if the boot floppy were from an old version of 95, then you might have to manually install the device drivers that come from the manufacturer of the CD-ROM drive. Visit their Web page for DOS CD-ROM drivers and follow their instructions. Other options include borrowing a boot disk from a newer version of Windows, or downloading a boot disk from a Web site such as *bootdisk.com*. For more information on boot disks, see Chapter 11.

8 Video, Sound, Modems, and Network Adapters

VIDEO OVERVIEW

Video is the single most important feature of a PC. Even in the two situations that don't require video, servers and blind people's computers, video is still essential. In the case of servers that aren't regularly accessed by users, you still need video on occasion for configuration, repair, and other operations. Blind people use screen readers and keyboards to use their computers, but screen readers don't work until the OS boots. Consequently, repairs and other operations often require a sighted technician to see the monitor. It is because of video's high level of importance that the BIOS allows the video adapter to provide base VGA video as soon as the computer is powered on. *Base video* is enough for clear text: 640 x 480 *pixels* (the smallest picture elements) and 16 colors. *Video Graphics Adapter* (*VGA*) is a video standard used by PCs for many years. *Super VGA* (SVGA) is a major improvement, but it is based on VGA and the monitor connectors are the same. (See the end of Chapter 3, "Motherboards and Their Components," for more information on ports.) Figure 8.1 shows a monitor plug and a corresponding VGA connector.

Video Adapter (Graphics Adapter, Video Card) Overview

Many computers come with video built into the motherboard. However, many motherboards don't have built-in video, and some that do also have AGP slots for additional or replacement video adapters. There are also PCI video adapters available, although PCI isn't considered the best interface for video. There are several reasons to use separate video adapters:

■ Users may want better video performance than their motherboard provides.

■ If built-in video fails or is troublesome, it can be disabled in the BIOS and an expansion card used.

Sometimes, inserting an expansion video card automatically disables built-in video in the BIOS.

■ Users might need to use two or more monitors simultaneously, and multiple adapters or a specially designed video adapter is necessary for two or more

FIGURE 8.1   VGA connectors.

monitors. Recent Windows versions support multiple monitors for different purposes, including having all monitors show the same screen, having one screen spread across more than one monitor, or even having a different screen on each monitor. For more information on multiple monitors in Windows XP, search Windows XP's Help and Support for "multiple monitors."

Dualview in XP is similar to multiple monitors, but works with laptop/notebook computers. With Dualview, the laptop's built-in screen is the primary monitor, and a monitor that the user attaches to the external VGA port is the secondary monitor. For more information on Dualview, search for it in XP's Help and Support.

As covered in Chapter 3, there are also DVO header connectors for DVI digital video adapters in some motherboards, and built-in DVI ports in others. As of the time of this writing, most PC motherboards have either built-in VGA ports or AGP slots for VGA video cards. Digital video capability might or might not be present.

Selecting a Video Adapter

High-quality video is necessary for any graphics-intensive activities such as Web surfing, high-graphics games, video and photographic editing, and others. High-quality video has two main components: general quality of the video adapter and monitor including the chipset, and amount and type of video memory. To understand the importance of sufficient video memory, it is necessary to understand how the amount of video memory affects the screen resolution and *color depth* (the total number of different colors a video adapter can output to the monitor). The easiest way to show this is through Tutorial 8.1.

TUTORIAL 8.1   SETTING DISPLAY PROPERTIES IN WINDOWS (ALL VERSIONS)

1. Access Display Properties in one of two ways:
   A. Double-click Display in Control Panel (see Chapter 2, "System Configuration and Computer Hygiene," for information on Control Panel).
   B. Right-click any spot on the desktop with no icons and select either Properties or Active Desktop > Customize my desktop from the menu that appears.
2. On the Display Properties page, click the Settings tab. A page such as the one shown in Figure 8.2 appears.

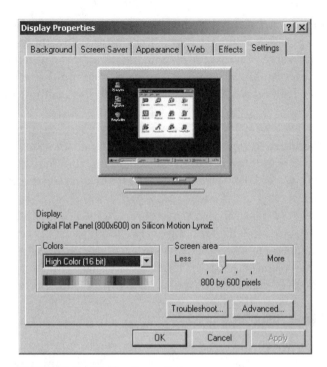

FIGURE 8.2 Display Properties.

3. Click the down arrow next to the Colors box. You should see a choice of color depth. Table 8.1 lists the possible choices.

TABLE 8.1 Display Colors

Color Depth	Number of Colors	Useful for
16 Colors	16	Text and very simple graphics
256 Colors	256	Text and simple graphics
Medium (16 bit)	65,535	Text and most general graphics use, plus video editing and most photography editing
True Color (24 bit) or High Color (24 bit)	16,777,216	Text and any but the most demanding graphics use
Highest (32 bit) or True Color (32 bit)	4,294,967,295	Text and the most demanding graphics use

It is most doubtful that you will see all of these choices. Old video adapters don't support the higher color levels, and newer ones might not show the lower or even support some of the intermediate levels.

4. Move the slider in the area labeled "Screen area," "Screen resolution," or equivalent. You'll see that as the numbers change, the image in the sample screen on the page changes in size correspondingly.
5. Click OK or Apply. Regardless of whether you have changed color depth or resolution, in most or all cases, you'll be shown the new screen and will be prompted to accept or reject the change. In some cases, the results will be unsatisfactory and you'll have to change back. Other things that could happen include lowering of one parameter as you raise the other, or having few or no choices at all. These conditions could be caused by several factors, as listed in Table 8.2.

Video Memory

So, you can see that the capacity to display high-quality video depends on video memory. Fortunately, you can get the highest color depth and excellent resolution with amounts of memory that are modest by today's standards. People successfully use computers with 2 to 8MB of video memory, although they might see slower

TABLE 8.2   Display Setting Anomalies

Anomaly	Possible Causes
No choices in either resolution or color depth, or both.	Certain LCD screens can display video at only one preset resolution.
	Design limitation of the video adapter or monitor.
	The computer is in Safe Mode.
	There is a problem with the adapter or its driver.
One parameter decreases as the other one is increased. simultaneously.	Lack of sufficient video memory to support high resolutions and large color palettes
The image is odd-shaped.	The aspect ratio of the selected screen resolution does not match that of the screen (4x3 for computer monitors).
The page displays unusable or poor quality video.	The settings exceed the capability of the video adapter or monitor.

loading of graphics on the screen and slower Web surfing. Video adapters with enormous amounts of memory—in the 1GB range—are available. For consumer use, 256MB is the most available at this time, although this number will probably be higher by the time you read this. These high-powered adapters can provide good resolution for large-screen high definition television (HDTV). They are great for three-dimensional and other special effects, and those who are into the latest computer games will want the most video memory they can get. However, a mere 8MB allows for 1024 x 768 resolution and 32-bit color simultaneously with memory to spare, settings that are good for the vast majority of computer users with typical monitors.

Just as in main computer memory, video memory comes in different types. Single Data Rate (SDR) and Double Data Rate (DDR) are the most common types. DDR is faster, so its performance will be better. Video cards with more and faster memory have the potential to provide better performance than others, but there is a point of diminishing returns. It is probably not worthwhile to have a great video card installed in a computer with a slow processor and limited amount of main memory.

In some computers with video built into the motherboard, video memory is part of the main memory. There is a BIOS setting to determine how much of the main memory to dedicate to video. Unless there is a large amount of main memory, the decision becomes a trade-off between video performance and overall computer performance.

Other Elements of Quality Video Adapters

When your motherboard comes with built-in video, you basically choose graphics by the quality, features, and reputation of the manufacturer in much the same way you would choose a video adapter card to install on the motherboard. With a separate video card, however, you have more choices, and that can be confusing.

One big manufacturer of video chipsets, ATI, makes their own video cards and sells chipsets to other video card manufacturers. Even though the chipsets might be identical, video cards from different manufacturers might be different. The same is true for video chipset makers such as nVidia who do not manufacture their own video cards. Be careful to choose a company that has great support and supplies driver updates readily.

Video Adapter Interfaces

Video adapters are available in AGP, PCI, and other older interfaces.

Accelerated Graphics Port (AGP)

AGP represents an advancement over previous video interfaces. It allows for more efficient transfer of data between the chipset and the graphics controller.

There have been three different connectors used for AGP. These are designed so that only the correct card can be inserted into a given slot. Each connector represents a different standard that includes a different signal voltage and other parameters.

PCI Video Cards

PCI video cards are rarely used for primary video adapters anymore; they are almost always used when built-in video fails or to feed video to second monitors. In the late 1990s, however, there were systems in which the video did come in PCI.

DVI Video

DVI video is becoming more popular, especially as digital flat-panel monitors become more commonplace. DVI video is available mainly in AGP video cards and as built-in video. DVI video can be better and faster than analog video. A computer's VGA port outputs analog video that the video adapter has converted from digital using a *Random Access Memory Digital-to-Analog Converter (RAMDAC)* chip. All flat-panel monitors are digital, but those with VGA connectors have to convert the analog signal back to digital. Video that has been converted from digital to analog and back to digital again loses some quality. Therefore, it is best to use a digital flat panel monitor with a DVI output. Early digital flat panel monitors used oddball video connectors: the MDR-20 and the Plug & Display connector. The DVI connectors shown in Chapter 3 aren't compatible with these, but a few adapters are available. Search the Internet to find them.

For more information on DVI, see Chapter 3, or go to *matrox.com/mga/ products/tech_info/dvi_backgrounder.cfm*.

Older Video Interfaces

The only other interfaces you could run into on PCs built since the mid-1990s are ISA, which fit into ISA slots, and VESA Local (VL) Bus. VL Bus adapters fit only into VL Bus motherboard slots. These rather long slots are found only on PCs from the mid-1990s.

Speed

Video speed comes from the type of AGP port, the chipset, the RAMDAC chip, and the type and amount of video memory. With applications that are used to manipulate images, greater speed and memory amount allows for much faster loading and manipulation of images. Moreover, the faster the RAMDAC chip, the faster the refresh rate. We discuss *refresh rates* later in this chapter.

Removal and Installation of Video Adapters

Video adapters are removed and installed similarly to other expansion cards. AGP slots might have optional retention clips to hold them in place (retention clips are covered later in this chapter).

To upgrade a video driver, go to Add/Remove Programs in Control Panel and uninstall the drivers, if present. If prompted to restart the computer, say No, and shut down instead. Remove the existing video card and install the new one, following the manufacturer's directions exactly. For onboard video, follow the same instructions, obviously omitting the step of removing the video card. Install the new card, start the computer, and go into the BIOS and look for a setting to disable onboard video. If there is such a setting, disable it. Then, finish booting the computer to test the new video.

Video chipset maker nVidia® (*nvidia.com*) provides a single set of drivers, called Detonator™, which will work with any card with an nVidia chipset, regardless of the card's manufacturer. ATI (*atitech.com*) has a similar driver set called Catalyst™, although it doesn't cover all ATI chip cards.

Diagnosing Video Problems

The best thing about video problems is that you know immediately if your computer has them. An additional plus is that it is usually easy to troubleshoot video problems; compared to many other categories of computer problems, there aren't that many things that can go wrong. Table 8.3 lists many common video problems and possible solutions.

Viruses can sometimes affect video. One virus causes a pinwheel image to almost completely cover the screen. Use the usual antivirus procedures as covered in Chapter 2.

Bent Pins

If, in a VGA connector, one pin is not making contact with the corresponding terminal in the socket, the video will be degraded. It is common to be missing one color in the event this happens. Use a small probe such as a thick sewing needle, needle-nosed pliers, tweezers, or hemostats to try to gently straighten the pin. Know, however, that such a pin has been weakened and runs the risk of breaking off. In the event that the cable is permanently attached to the monitor, it is recommended to attach a VGA extension cable and never remove it. This protects the pin from breaking off, which would require an expensive monitor repair or replacement, and also protects the video port from getting a pin fragment stuck in it, which would also require replacement.

TABLE 8.3 Common Video Problems and Solutions

Problem	Troubleshooting and Possible Solution
No video	Make sure the monitor is powered on, connected to the computer, and that the brightness control is not turned all the way down. If the power indicator is blinking or glows orange, that means there is no video signal coming from the computer. Try another monitor or connect the dark monitor to a different computer. If there is no video at boot, listen for the POST beep code and/or use a POST card (see Chapter 11, "Troubleshooting," for more information on POST beep codes and POST cards). Try removing the hard drive and scanning for viruses. Try installing a known good video adapter.
Video at low resolution with splotchy colors	Try to adjust the settings from 640 x 480 resolution and 16 colors. The video driver might be corrupted. Update or reinstall the driver. Try installing a known good video adapter.
Artifacts (parts or shapes of windows continue to appear on screen after the window is closed); other unwanted spots appear on screen	Reinstall or upgrade the video driver. Scan for viruses.
Line appears on screen	Swap the monitor with a known good monitor. Reinstall or update the video driver.
One or more colors missing	Check the VGA connector pins. If the monitor cable is replaceable, swap it with a known good cable. If not, swap the monitor with a known good monitor.

Troubleshooting Specialty Video Devices

For *video capture devices* (video cards that include *composite video* inputs for connection to VCRs and older video cameras, or cards with FireWire ports that connect to digital video cameras), and video cards with TV outputs, a common problem is that Windows installs the wrong driver. Uninstall the existing driver and follow the manufacturer's instructions to install the correct driver.

Monitor Settings

Today's CRT monitors (those with television-like picture tubes) can handle the highest settings computer users are likely to want to use. If you run into a situation, however, in which an old monitor is displaying unusable video, it is possible that the Windows video settings exceed the capabilities of the monitor. You will have to diagnose the source of the problem. If you are able to read the text that appears on screen as the system is starting but the video becomes distorted and unreadable once Windows starts up, then the settings are most likely too high for the monitor. If the image is distorted from the moment you start up the computer, then it is possibly a video adapter issue. If it is the former, you will have to start Windows in Safe Mode, which will give you basic settings that almost all monitors will work with. While in Safe Mode, set the Display Properties to a lower setting and restart Windows. At this point, you might very well decide to get a new monitor that can display higher settings rather than live with a low resolution. You can try to find the monitor's specifications on the Web and set the Display Properties accordingly. If you can't find this information, which is possible, you'll have to try lower settings until you find a combination that works.

The monitor itself will have settings for shape and size of the picture, brightness and contrast, and others. In addition, virtually all monitors manufactured for the last several years have an energy saving system. When the video signal from the computer stops, the monitor goes into a low-power state, and the power indicator light begins to blink or turns from green to orange. Some monitors, however, show a test pattern or no-video message in certain circumstances such as when the power comes back on after a failure and the computer is still off.

Refresh Rate

A monitor (or television, for that matter) produces a picture by having an electron beam scan a grid of microscopic light-emitting elements. The *refresh rate* is the rate at which the beam scans all the elements—the entire screen—once. The rate is expressed in Hertz (Hz), which means cycles per second, so that a rate of 60 Hz means that the electron beam scans the screen 60 times every second. Rates that are too low have noticeable flicker. If the rate is set too high for a given monitor, the video can be unusable and the monitor can be damaged. The higher the refresh rate, the less apparent the flicker will be. Rates of 70 Hz or higher should provide flicker-free video for most people. The refresh rate should be set only as high as necessary to minimize flicker—higher rates, even if all the components support it, can cause other problems such as reduced contrast. To adjust the refresh rate, follow Tutorial 8.2.

TUTORIAL 8.2   SETTING THE REFRESH RATE

Note that some systems don't have a refresh rate setting.

1. Follow Steps 1 and 2 of Tutorial 8.1 to access the Settings page of Display Properties.
2. Click the Advanced button.
3. Click the Monitor tab (if there is one).
4. Click the down arrow next to the frequency and select a new frequency.

AGP Retention Clip

Loose adapters in AGP slots are often the culprits for video problems. Retention clips that retrofit to most AGP slots were introduced to hold them in place. Figure 8.3 shows an AGP retention clip in place. If a PC with this type of AGP slot loses its video for no apparent reason, try a retention clip. The video adapter you use must have a notched tab to work with the retention clip.

Dot Pitch

Dot pitch is a measurement of how close the picture elements are to one another. The closer they are, the higher the resolution can be, so the lower the number, the better. Cheap monitors have larger dot pitches and are harder on users' eyes. Select .028 mm or lower.

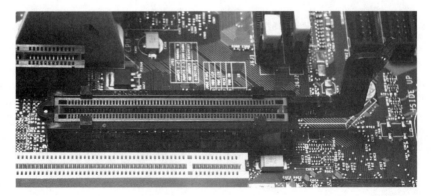

FIGURE 8.3 AGP retention clip.

Testing Displays

There are a few ways to test monitors. DisplayMate® (*displaymate.com*) offers testing utilities and hardware for any type of video display. They have products for end users, technical users, and advanced users. If you plan to test monitors, their products are definitely appropriate.

General computer testing utilities, such as products from PC Certify and Micro-2000, and even some products that are released by computer makers also include video tests. See Chapter 11 for more on general diagnostic products.

Monitor Installation

In the vast majority of cases, monitors need only to be plugged into the video adapter outputs, be they SVGA or DVI. Some monitors are recognized and installed automatically by Windows. In some situations, Windows will need a driver in order for the monitor to display more than *base video*. This is most likely to happen with an older version of Windows, or a monitor that uses new technology.

SOUND OVERVIEW

Sound cards range from simple built-in features to elaborate two-piece devices with physical control panels that mount into a 5 1/4-inch drive bay. The basic purpose of sound cards is to allow the user to hear sounds played by the OS and programs, along with music from audio CDs and other audio files, plus sound from DVD and other types of videos. In addition, these allow for voice communication using software such as Yahoo Messenger, AOL Instant Messenger, and Windows Messenger, along with Internet telephone calls, voice-recognition software, and other uses.

Sound Card Removal and Installation

Sound cards are physically installed and removed in the same way as any other card using the same interface (PCI or ISA), except that there are likely to be analog audio cables connected to it inside the computer. On a motherboard with onboard sound, there will also be audio connectors. These connectors are for connecting analog audio to optical drives, modems, and other devices. Some of these connectors are polarized, but even if they aren't, the worst that can happen is that the right and left audio channels could be reversed. Figure 8.4 shows the audio connectors on a sound card.

FIGURE 1.1 A typical PC system.

FIGURE 2.13 Jumpers and microswitches.

FIGURE 2.23 A computer dedicated to virus scanning and data backup.

FIGURE 3.8 If the motherboard has this 12-volt connector, it must be connected. The connector from the power supply is in the inset.

FIGURE 3.9   AT power connector.

FIGURE 3.19   Installing a processor.

FIGURE 3.20   3-pin processor fan connectors.

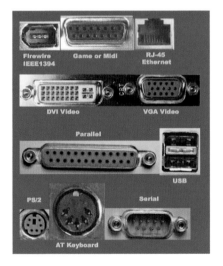

FIGURE 3.23   Common Ports.

FIGURE 5.6 Inserting a SODIMM in a notebook computer.

FIGURE 7.5 Freeing a captive disk.

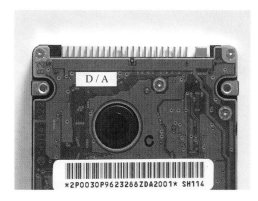

FIGURE 6.10 2.5-inch hard drive connector.

FIGURE 8.3 AGP retention clip.

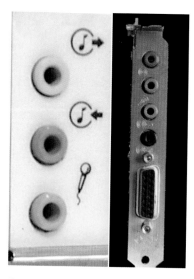

FIGURE 8.5 A sound card jack panel.

FIGURE 9.8 The removable panel type of laptop keyboard removal.

FIGURE 9.9 Treat the ribbon cable with care.

FIGURE 11.2 The Micro 2000 POST card.

FIGURE 8.4 A sound card's audio connectors.

External Sound Connections

Sound cards can vary as to the number and type of external inputs and outputs. The most basic, usually found on motherboards with built-in sound, have three:

- **Microphone input:** This is for a computer microphone, although battery-powered condenser mics usually work in these jacks.
- **Line input:** This is for an external line source such as a cassette deck or CD player's line outputs.
- **Speaker/headphone output:** This is a headphone-level output that can sometimes drive small, non-amplified speakers. They are usually connected to amplified speakers.

A sound card with a built-in amplifier would have full-power speaker outputs, able to drive most non-amplified speakers. More advanced cards have a whole assortment of inputs and outputs. On many cards, the icons that identify each jack are very difficult to see and interpret, especially when you are struggling just to see any part of the back of the computer. Consult the manufacturer's documentation. Figure 8.5 shows sound card jack panels.

Now look carefully at Figure 8.5. The concentric arcs represent sound waves. An arrow pointing toward the center indicates a line input, while an arrow pointing away from the center represents a line output. The microphone and speaker icons are more illustrative than are the others.

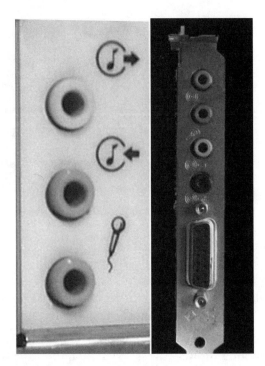

FIGURE 8.5   Sound card jack panels.

Diagnosing and Repairing Sound Problems

There are a number of steps you can take to correct sound problems. First, make sure the speakers are powered, turned on, and turned up. Make sure all external connections are correct, and that the cables aren't damaged. Run System File Checker (see Chapter 11). Reinstall the sound drivers. Sometimes, you'll have to re-move the device in Device Manager, shut down the computer, remove the card, restart the computer and uninstall any programs that came with the sound card, and then shut down the computer again. Then, follow the manufacturer's direc-tions for installing the card, or just reboot and see if Windows will install it cor-rectly. If you have any trouble with resource conflicts, which would be evidenced by instant lockups, go into the BIOS and make sure Plug and Play is enabled.

Selecting a Sound Card

A basic sound card is good for most people. High-end models are good for gamers and musicians. Some people like to have surround sound with their computers, so surround sound models are common.

MODEM OVERVIEW

Oddly, modems are often confused with the computer itself. A *modem*, as discussed in this chapter, is a device that connects a computer to a standard analog telephone line, the kind to which your telephone is connected. Modems are used for dial-up Internet service, telephone use such as faxing, wide area network (WAN) connections, and the antiquated, but still-used terminal connections, which are beyond the scope of this book. You might have noticed that modem speed has been stuck at a maximum of 56 Kbps for several years. That is because the amount of data that can be transmitted across an analog telephone line might have reached a physical limit. Consequently, although there have been improvements in accuracy of data transfer and the capability of connecting and holding onto a telephone line, modems haven't gotten any faster than 56K. Because of this limit, Internet service has moved away from dial-up and toward different broadband technologies. As a result, modems are now not usually built into newer motherboards (except in laptops, which are often used where the only network access is through telephone lines). There are a few motherboards out there with modem risers. These are slots that take proprietary modem cards. If one of these modems fails, it is cheapest and easiest to remove it and install a standard modem in a PCI or ISA slot, if possible.

Internal vs. External Modems

Internal modems are PCI or ISA expansion cards. They tend to be simple to install; just follow the manufacturer's directions if available. They receive their power from the slot. External modems are less common today, but are still around because internal modems are often optional these days. External modems traditionally plug into a serial port on the computer, although there are USB modems available today as well. The advantages to external modems are that you don't have to be a technician to install one and they can easily be moved from computer to computer. The disadvantages to serial-port external modems are that they require external power and are more expensive. Most or all USB modems are powered by the USB ports and aren't as expensive as serial port modems. Figure 8.6 shows a PCI modem, a USB modem, and an external serial port modem.

PC-Card modems are designed for laptops without built-in modems, or those whose built-in modems are broken. They tend to be expensive. Many of these come with *dongles*, which are small cable assemblies that connect the card to the telephone jack assembly. Dongles are usually delicate and replacements have to be ordered from the manufacturer. Better designs are available that have the phone jacks built into the card. Figure 8.7 shows two PC-Card modems.

For an alternative to PC-Card modems, try an external USB modem.

FIGURE 8.6 Three different types of modems.

Use of Serial Ports

Older PCs often came with up to four serial ports, while newer machines usually come with one. These ports are referred to as COM 1 through COM 4. Traditionally, COM ports 1 and 4 use IRQ 3, and COM ports 2 and 3 use IRQ 4. If you have ever installed an internal modem, you have probably noticed COM ports with numbers up to 12. These COM ports that are numbered higher than the highest numbered physical COM port are called *logical* COM ports.

FIGURE 8.7 PC-Card modems.

Selecting a Modem

Even though modem speed hasn't changed since 1998, modems have gotten better. You might recall that picking up a telephone while an early 56K modem was connected to the Internet on the same line caused the modem to instantly disconnect the connection. Fortunately, that problem was abated in subsequent modems.

WinModems vs. Controller-Based Modems

If you look at modems, you might notice that some have very few components soldered onto the circuit board. If these have PCI or ISA connectors, then they are probably WinModems (if they don't have PCI or ISA connectors, they are probably riser modems). If they have a lot of components, they are probably controller-based modems. As you might have guessed, controller-based modems are more expensive than WinModems. WinModems let Windows do much of the work that controllers do in the more expensive modems. Consequently, that means that the processor has extra work to do. For that reason, WinModems don't work well in any systems with slow processors, and should never be used in a computer with a Cyrix processor. Therefore, if an old computer needs a new modem, don't install a WinModem.

Faxing and Voice

Virtually all modems sold in the last several years have faxing capability. Using supplied "lite" software, retail software, or fax programs built into newer versions of Windows, users can send and receive faxes. Fax software installs itself as a printer; to send a fax, open a document or image file and use the Print command. There are three ways to access the Print command in almost all programs:

■ Click File > Print
■ Click the printer icon
■ Type <Ctrl> + <P>

You will see a dialog box similar to the one shown in Figure 8.8. Select the fax software as a printer and click Print. The fax program should open. Many users with scanners print documents, scan them, and then fax them. This is necessary only if you have to write something, such as a signature, on the document. There are sketch programs available that allow you to store a signature image that you can paste on a document. For example, if you have a Synaptics touchpad (pointing device), a program is available free from *synaptics.com.*

Modem Removal and Installation

External modems are simple to install; just plug in and install the software, with the order depending on the instructions to the particular model. Internal modems are installed physically just as any other expansion card. Many will be installed automatically by Windows.

Software that uses modems, such as faxing programs or dial-up Internet software like AOL, have provisions to search for the modem. Therefore, it is a good idea to look in Device Manager to see how many COM ports are installed in the machine. Look for the Ports (COM & LPT) listing and click the plus sign. Hopefully, you won't see any more than the number of physical COM ports installed on the system. Then, when you install the modem or modem-using software, look for the COM port the system uses. If the port number is the same as one of the physical COM ports, it is usually wise to change it. To do this, open up Modem Properties in Device Manager or in Control Panel > Phone and Modem (or equivalent). Click the Advanced tab to get a page similar to the one shown in Figure 8.8.

If you change it, make sure to change it in modem-using software too. Then, check all programs that use the modem: dial-up Internet, telephone networking, telephone dialing and answering systems, and fax programs. Either change the COM port manually in these or have the programs redetect the modem.

Diagnosing Modem Problems

Modems can be troublesome. If you have a telephone communications problem, there are a number of things you can do to check to see if the modem is working.

It bears repeating that the message often seen in the properties of any hardware device, "This device is working properly," is often wrong. However, if you see "This device is not present, not working properly, or does not have all the drivers installed. See your hardware documentation (Code 10.)," you can bet that it is right.

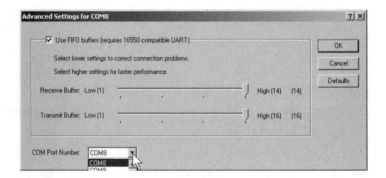

FIGURE 8.8 Advanced modem properties.

Here is a list of places in Windows where you can check to see whether a modem is working:

A. Modem Properties in Device Manager, General page: If you see a message that indicates a problem, the modem might need to be reinstalled or replaced. Follow the directions in Chapter 2 or from the modem manufacturer to reinstall the driver.

B. Query Modem: Go to Modem Properties from either Control Panel or Device Manager and click the Diagnostics tab if one is present. Then, click the Query Modem button and wait for the report. If the last couple entries in the report indicate OK, the query hasn't detected a problem. You will often see the line "COMMAND NOT SUPPORTED" at one point in the report. You can ignore this.

C. HyperTerminal: Go to Start > Programs (or All Programs) > Accessories > Communications > HyperTerminal, if it is installed. You will be prompted to set up a connection. Give it a simple name; you won't be saving it. Figure 8.9 shows this page.

FIGURE 8.9 Naming a HyperTerminal connection.

Then, enter a single-digit telephone number. Make sure your modem is listed in the Connect using box. Click OK and you will be prompted to dial the number you entered. Click Cancel. You will see a blank HyperTerminal window. Type "AT" and then press <Enter>. A working modem should respond with "OK," as shown in Figure 8.10. Then, you can close HyperTerminal and elect not to save the connection.

Some malfunctioning modems can nonetheless pass every one of these diagnostic tests.

It is also a good idea to test a suspect modem with every function in which it can be used on the computer. This is to rule out the possibility that a program, rather than the modem, is malfunctioning. For example, if a modem works with faxing and Phone Dialer (Start > Programs (or All Programs) > Accessories > Communications > Phone Dialer), but not on the Internet, it is likely that the problem is in the Internet software or service rather than with the hardware.

You might find that Phone Dialer doesn't work properly in Windows 2000 on certain machines no matter what you do. However, Windows 9x's Phone Dialer (dialer.exe) might work in the newer Windows versions. If the modem will dial a number in Phone Dialer but do nothing else, the problem might very well be the hardware; we had a batch of new PCI modems that did this. The modems weren't recognized by the Plug & Play system and had to be installed manually because they were defective.

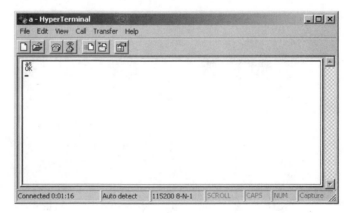

FIGURE 8.10 Autodetecting the modem in HyperTerminal.

It is unfortunately common to get certain numbered error messages such as 619 or 693 when trying to connect using a modem. You might try several times in a row and get several different error messages. Often, these error messages bear no relationship to the truth. When you get one of these, first attempt to rule out the problem that the message indicates, assuming you can understand the message. The problem could be as simple as a bad telephone cord, the Caps Lock being on and altering the password, or that the telephone line is in use. Other possibilities include problems with the remote computer or service, or incorrect password or username. If the computer locks up every time you try to connect, you probably have a resource conflict. See Chapter 2 for information on resolving it.

Make sure that the user doesn't plug a modem into a PBX telephone line. Even though PBX systems can use RJ-11/14 telephone connectors, the voltage and signal are different. This can damage the modem, but it might merely cause the computer to lock up.

Once you have ruled these out, the next step is to reboot the computer, especially if you have a laptop. With some laptops, a design flaw causes certain functions not to work after the computer comes out of standby or hibernation. Rebooting might solve other problems as well. If none of these steps works, delete the connection and recreate it. If you still have the problem, it is time to try new hardware. Swap the modem for a known good unit and retry the connection. This is the perfect time to try an external modem if you have one. If you still can't connect, and the modem is removable, try it in another system.

If a built-in modem on a laptop fails and you have reinstalled the driver to no avail, unless the laptop is under warranty, your only recourses are to install a PC-Card modem or use an external serial or USB modem. You might want to disable the built-in modem in the BIOS, if such a setting exists. Note, however, that sometimes seemingly permanent modem failures can occasionally resolve themselves over time.

Modem Cables

Different external serial modems use an assortment of different types of cables. Make sure the cable is actually a modem cable; other cables might fit, but that doesn't mean they'll work. Also try testing the cable in a cable tester. With USB cables, it is often easy to swap with a known good cable.

For information on troubleshooting network connections, see Chapter 10, "Troubleshooting Internet Connections."

Cable and DSL Modems

Cable and DSL modems are external devices used to connect computers to a broadband (high-speed) Internet connection. DSL models connect to the telephone line *without a DSL filter*. A *DSL filter* is a device that blocks the DSL signal from interfering with regular telephone conversations; these are usually provided by the DSL provider. DSL modems are connected to the computer either through a USB cable or an Ethernet network cable. Cable modems are similar to DSL modems, but they connect to a television cable instead of a telephone line.

Modem/Sound Card Combinations

No longer manufactured, modem/sound card combinations are very difficult to get drivers for. The best way to deal with failed modem/sound card combos is to replace it with individual components. If you have only one free slot, you can probably replace the modem with an external modem.

NETWORK ADAPTERS (NETWORK CARDS, NETWORK BOARDS, NETWORK INTERFACE CARDS, NICs, ETHERNET ADAPTERS)

Considering how complicated networking can be, network adapters are rather simple. They are among the easiest devices to install; simply follow the manufacturer's directions. Cards made by 3Com and Intel are often installed automatically by Windows. Others, including external USB models, require driver disks, but are still easy to get up and running.

Selecting a Network Adapter

Older network adapters came in myriad types, but today's cards are mostly Ethernet cards. *Ethernet* is a network standard that almost exclusively uses *Cat 5/Cat 5e* UTP (unshielded twisted pair) cables with RJ-45 connectors. *RJ-45* connectors are very similar to standard RJ14 modular telephone plugs, but are twice as wide and have eight wires. Many of today's motherboards come with built-in Ethernet adapters. Ethernet transmission speeds have increased from 10 to 100 to 1000 Mbps. Older cards worked at a fixed speed, preventing their connection with any network device running at a different speed. Newer cards, however, can automatically switch to a lower-than-maximum speed to match the device they are directly connected to, be it a router, switch, hub, or other Ethernet adapter. The vast majority of Ethernet network adapters on the market will work fine for most users with home or small business networks, or high-speed Internet service that requires network adapters.

Wireless Network Adapters

Wireless models come in various types to work in desktops or laptops. They require wireless routers to work. They work similarly to cordless telephones; they have to stay within a certain distance of the base (router) to maintain a connection.

Diagnosing Network Adapter Problems

Many things can go wrong with networks, but not many problems can occur with the adapters; usually, they either work or they don't. Check in Device Manager to see if there is a problem. If reinstalling the driver doesn't fix the problem, it is probably time to replace the card.

If Device Manager indicates a working adapter, it is a good idea to check the cable. Use a tester, or swap it with a known good cable.

NOTE

Make sure to use the right cable for the job. RJ45 telephone cable, if it is not Cat5 or Cat5e, will not be reliable for network transmission. There is also such a thing as a crossover cable, which is used only for a direct connection between two computers with Ethernet adapters, or between two central devices such as hubs, switches, or routers. A crossover cable won't work for a connection between a central device and a computer, and a straight-through cable won't work with a two-computer network or between two central devices. Crossover cables should be marked on the cables' insulation. If there is any doubt, you can check it with a cable tester. Please note that general networking is beyond the scope of this book.

9 Input Devices

*I*nput devices are devices that allow the user to input data into a computer. The most obvious input devices are pointing devices (mice and their equivalents) and keyboards. Other input devices include such things as microphones used in the case of voice recognition systems. This chapter is limited to discussion of keyboards and common pointing devices.

POINTING DEVICES

The most common pointing device is the mouse. Others include the trackball, touchpad, and track stick ("pencil eraser") controls found on some laptops. All but the last one come in different forms.

Pointing Device Types

Pointing devices can be divided into interface type, features, and detection system.

Mouse Interfaces

Mice can be connected to PCs in at least one of four ways: serial (DB-9 female connector), PS/2 (the small, round, 5-pin connector), USB, and infrared or radio frequency wireless. Many mice come with adapters so that an individual mouse can be used in both PS/2 and serial ports, or both PS/2 and USB ports. More information about these follows:

> **Serial:** This is the original interface used in personal computers. Serial devices are hot-pluggable. Although new computers no longer come with serial mice, the vast majority of computers have serial ports, so a serial mouse is the perfect choice when the built-in PS/2 port fails. In fact, serial mice used to come with drivers on floppy disks, although Windows 95 and later have the drivers.

> **PS/2:** This is the standard mouse interface for the vast majority of computers with ATX and similar motherboards. These computers have dedicated PS/2 mouse ports that can be used only for PS/2 pointing devices and those adapted to PS/2. These devices *are not hot-pluggable*; plug in and remove only with the computer's power off. There is no guarantee that ignoring this warning will fry the motherboard, but it is not worth the risk. Windows installs PS/2 mice transparently to the user unless the device has unusual features, in which case, a software disk might be needed.

Many laptops have one PS/2 port. A keyboard or a pointing device can be plugged into this port. Y-connectors are available that allow both a pointing device and a keyboard to be plugged in simultaneously. However, not all Y-connectors work with all brands of laptops; there are at least two types of Y-connectors for this purpose. Make sure to match up one that will work with the brand you're using.

> **USB:** This is the standard mouse port for many new computers. However, because most computers still have PS/2 mouse ports, unless the mouse you want is available only in USB, it is a good idea to use a PS/2 mouse. This is because

there are many devices that use USB ports, but only one that can use a PS/2 mouse port, so you might as well save the USB port for some other device. Most of the feature-laden mice use USB. USB devices are recognized and installed by Windows, and many come with software disks. Windows, however, has drivers for almost all commercially available mice. USB mice are also good choices for replacements when PS/2 ports fail.

Wireless: Wireless mice use one of the other interfaces in this list. They come in two varieties, infrared and *radio frequency* (*RF*). The RF types are usually preferred because the receiver and mouse do not have to be directly in line of site of each other. The mouse runs on battery power, so plan to have spare batteries on hand or at least hold on to a basic wired mouse in case of an emergency.

Detection Types

Mice come in two detection types: mechanical (ball) and optical. Ball mice have rubber-coated metal balls that roll over a surface. This is the cheapest and most common type. It is also the most troublesome because the mechanical parts get clogged with dust, lint, and hair, and they also break. They usually need mouse pads, or at least table or desktops of a certain texture to work well.

Optical mice use a reflected red LED light to detect movement. Early optical mice sometimes required certain types of surfaces, but since then, optical mice have become easy to use and much more reliable than ball mice.

Mouse Features

The most common feature is a scroll wheel. This allows the up-and-down scrolling of a window by turning the wheel with your thumb, rather than clicking on the scroll arrows or moving the scroll bars on the screen. The next most common feature is an ergonomic shape.

Non-Mouse Pointing Devices

Trackpads, touchpads, and track sticks are the most common. The track sticks are found in the center of laptop keyboards. Touchpads are commonly found on laptops, although they are also available built into separate keyboards, or as freestanding devices. Trackballs can also be found in any of those locations. These devices, shown with others in Figure 9.1, are often very helpful for people who experience wrist pain from excessive use of mice.

Touchpads have no moving parts, so they tend to be very reliable. The most common manufacturers of touchpads are Synaptics (*synaptics.com*) and Alps (*alps.com*). Free software available from the manufacturers or the computer maker

FIGURE 9.1   Pointing device assortment.

provide touchpad users with many features such as scrolling, tapping for left-clicks, and click-and-drag operations with one finger (not requiring the use of the mechanical mouse button).

Pointing Device Configuration

Although there is considerable configuration possible in the Control Panel Mouse applet, most settings are typically left at their defaults. Microsoft has done a good job of setting these defaults. It is helpful to be familiar with these settings so that you aren't bewildered when you encounter unusual pointing device behavior. This applet looks like the one in Figure 9.2 unless extra pointing device software is installed.

The most useful settings in this applet include double-click speed, which is useful for older people and others who have trouble double-clicking. There is also a setting for right- and left-handers that reverses the functions of the left and right mouse buttons. There is a whole host of settings of pointer appearance and speed. Windows Me and XP come with a check box that causes a circle to appear around the pointer when the Ctrl key is pressed, although it doesn't always work in Windows Me. There is also a Click Lock setting that allows clicking and dragging without holding down the button. Another setting is in more than one place in some versions of Windows: single- or double-click to open an item is both in the Mouse applet and in the Tools > Folder Options command in any Windows Window.

FIGURE 9.2   A typical Mouse applet from Windows Me.

Removal and Installation of Pointing Devices

As covered earlier in this chapter, removal and installation of these devices isn't complicated unless you are trying to replace a pointing device that is built into a laptop, a repair that is beyond the scope of this book. The main point to remember is never to plug in or unplug a PS/2 device with the computer powered on. Other points to remember are:

■ Don't reverse pointing device and keyboard PS/2 connections. This will cause neither device to work, and you'll have to shut off the power without a proper shutdown to switch the connectors. You might see badly labeled connections, such as the one shown in Figure 9.3. In this case, the keyboard port is on the bottom and the mouse port is on the top.
■ USB devices are hot-pluggable and are recognized as new hardware.
■ Serial mice can be safely plugged in or removed while the computer is running.

Diagnosing Pointing Device Problems

Pointing devices are not the culprit in most computer problems, but because they are almost indispensable, the problems they do have are important to repair quickly.

Error Messages

There is only one common error message related to pointing devices, a message indicating that Windows didn't detect a mouse. The message is accompanied by a note that a serial mouse can be attached right away, but that to install a PS/2 mouse,

FIGURE 9.3   Badly labeled PS/2 ports.

you'll have to shut down the machine. If there actually is no mouse connected, the solution is obvious. If a PS/2 mouse is connected, the first thing to check is that the mouse and keyboard connectors aren't reversed. Again, switch them only once the computer has been shut down. If the pointing device is installed correctly, however, there is a problem. The pointing device could be dead, so swapping a known good device should confirm that. For this reason, it is a good idea to keep various types of mice around any computer shop. If a known good mouse doesn't work either, then the problem could be in the port. First, check the BIOS setup program to make sure that the port in question hasn't been disabled. Then, unless the port is PS/2, check in Device Manager for the same thing. If the port is disabled or not installed in Device Manager, attempt to enable it or reinstall it. If you still can't get it to work, the port might be disconnected or broken. In an older computer, the serial port might not be part of the motherboard. The cable from the port to the header connector on the motherboard might be detached, damaged, or connected to the wrong header connector. Of course, these possibilities are unlikely unless someone opened the case and made changes. If the port cannot be fixed, the simplest solution is to use a pointing device with a different interface. In an AT computer that accepts only serial pointing devices, you can try a different serial port, if there is one available. If not, you might be able to replace the port or add a new one. Search the Web for these replacement parts if you don't have old ones available. But remember, AT computers are probably not worth the time involved to fix.

Jerky Pointer

There are two possibilities for jerky pointers. One is a dirty or damaged mechanical ball mouse or trackball, and the other is that a computer's CPU and memory are being used heavily. The latter should be ruled out first. Often, use of memory- or processor-intensive hardware such as printers, scanners, or optical disc burners cause the pointer to be jerky. There are several ways to determine if this is the case. First, a damaged or dirty mouse will not spontaneously start working normally; if it does, the problem is probably not in the device. Another way to tell is if the computer reacts slowly or erratically to everything you try. For example, if you press the Windows key (shown in Figure 9.5, appearing in the section on keyboards) or click Start, but the Start menu takes a noticeable amount of time to appear, the problem is probably not related to the mouse. In 2000 and XP, you can check Windows performance in Task Manager; look for a high percentage of CPU time being used. In 9x, look at the Performance tab of the System applet for the percentage or resources remaining. If the number is low, something might be draining resources. Sometimes, Windows will run poorly for no apparent reason.

If everything appears to be working normally, except for a jerky pointer, and the pointing device is a ball mouse or trackball, try cleaning the device. It is probably a good idea to save your open files and close all programs to avoid clicking anything that can cause problems. You could also clean the device while the computer is shut down.

To clean a ball mouse, twist and remove the bottom plate in the direction of the arrow as shown in Figure 9.4. Remove the ball. You will probably find grit and stringy substances around the rollers. Pull out this debris. Air spray such as Blow Off can be helpful. Replace the ball and plate and try the mouse again. If this doesn't help, try a new or known good mouse. If the new mouse solves the problem after a cleaned old mouse is still jerky, discard the old mouse. If the new mouse doesn't solve the problem, you'll have to go back to the drawing board. It will be helpful to try both mice in a different computer. Make sure to note which mouse is which; if necessary, mark the bottom of the old mouse with a permanent marker.

FIGURE 9.4 Opening the bottom of a ball mouse.

Similar problems will occur in mechanical trackball-style pointing devices. The balls can be removed by pulling them out, or by pushing from a hole in the bottom. Use an air spray and blow out the dust.

Of course, to avoid the problem of contaminated mice, recommend an optical mouse or touchpad to the user.

Lockups

Lockups are when the computer stops responding to any input. The mouse pointer freezes, keyboard commands are ignored, and the screen doesn't change. The tell-tale sign of a lockup is when the Num Lock light on the keyboard (if there is one) doesn't change when the <Num Lock> key is pressed. However, because the most obvious sign of a lockup is the frozen pointer, many users are convinced that the problem is in the mouse. Many mice are sold to consumers who want to repair a lockup. In fact, a bad mouse can lose the capability to move the pointer, but the screen will still change and keyboard commands will still be accepted. However, lockups are much more common culprits of frozen pointers. We discuss lockups in more detail in Chapter 11, "Troubleshooting."

The Center Mouse Button

You have most probably noticed that some mice have three buttons. Software that comes with the mouse can be used to configure the center button for a number of different functions such as the Enter key. Most people didn't program these, so this type of mouse never really caught on.

KEYBOARD OVERVIEW

Keyboards are also crucial devices in the vast majority of computers. Keyboards can be had for under five dollars, and for several hundred dollars. Keyboards come in versions for different languages. There are *Dvorak* keyboards, which have the alphabet laid out in a pattern conducive to faster typing than the QWERTY type, which was designed for old typewriters to keep the typebars from jamming. Some keyboards come with features such as ergonomic shapes or built-in touchpads. Some have extra buttons used for turning the computer on and off, connecting to the Internet, controlling audio CDs, or opening any program designated by the user.

Not everyone is familiar with all the keys on a keyboard, so an explanation of some of the lesser-known keys follows.

- **Windows key:** Opens the Windows Start menu. See Figure 9.5.
- **<Print Screen|Sys Rq>:** There are various abbreviations of this key label. This key doesn't actually cause the screen to print, at least in Windows. If it is enabled, pressing this key copies the screen to the clipboard so that if you open any document or image program and use the Paste command (<Ctrl> + <V> or Edit > Paste), the screen image appears in the document or image program. Holding the <Alt> key when you press Print Screen stores just the active window in the clipboard.
- **<Pause>:** If Quiet Boot or its equivalent isn't enabled in the BIOS, lots of valuable information about hardware can appear on the screen early in the boot process. Some of this information moves down the screen at about the same pace as the credits after a television show. Use the Pause key to stop this movement so you can actually read it.
- **<Num Lock>:** This key toggles the numeric keypad on and off. It also, as stated earlier in this chapter, can be used to test for a lockup as long as there is a working Num Lock light. If pressing the key has no effect, you can be almost certain that the machine is locked up. If the Num Lock light responds to the key, the computer isn't locked up, although it could be in a virtual lockup condition in which the pointer moves, but nothing really responds in a reasonable amount of time. The <Caps Lock> key can be used for the same purpose.

FIGURE 9.5   The Windows key.

- **<Home>, <End>:** These keys move the cursor to the beginning and the end of a line in a document, respectively. Holding down the <Ctrl> key when pressing these causes the cursor to move to the beginning and end of the entire document, respectively.

Keyboard Interfaces

There are four main interfaces for keyboards:

- **PS/2:** All varieties of ATX motherboards, except "legacy-free" models, come with PS/2 keyboard connectors. The same rules that apply to PS/2 mice apply to PS/2 keyboards. Plug in and unplug these only when the power is off, and don't attempt to plug any other device into a PS/2 keyboard port. Windows installs these keyboards transparently. Models with extra features need software disks from the manufacturer. Adapters exist to plug a PS/2 keyboard into an AT port, or vice versa.

- **5-Pin DIN (AT):** All varieties of AT motherboards come with these keyboard connectors. These are the only type of keyboard that can be used in a computer with one of these motherboards. Although there should be no problem hot plugging an AT keyboard, it is better to be safe and turn off the computer first.
- **USB:** These are hot-pluggable devices. Some have their own auxiliary USB connectors, which are handy for USB mice.
- **Wireless:** These come in the USB and PS2 varieties and can be either infrared or RF controlled.

Keyboard Maintenance

There is one overriding rule that must be followed when cleaning a keyboard: *don't let it get wet!* Keys and the body of the keyboard can be cleaned with a slightly damp cloth, but don't let water get underneath the keys. The most common damage that

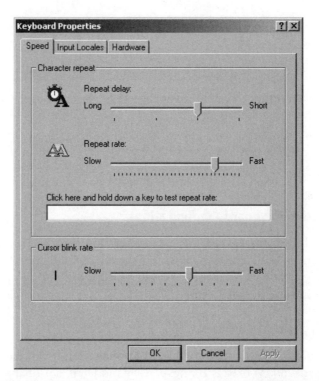

FIGURE 9.6 Speed page of the Keyboard applet in Windows 2000.

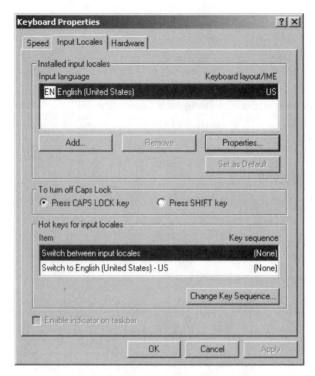

FIGURE 9.7   Input Locales page of the Keyboard applet in Windows 2000.

occurs to keyboards is when someone spills liquid into them. Air sprays such as Blow Off are great for removing dust. Sprays are available to clean the surfaces of keyboards; make sure they are designed specifically for computer keyboards.

Troubleshooting Keyboard Configurations

What little configuration that can be done for the main functions of a keyboard can be done in the Keyboard applet in Control Panel. Figures 9.6 and 9.7 shows a typical Keyboard applet from Windows 2000. As with pointing devices, it is helpful to be familiar with these settings.

Repairing Keyboard Problems

Keyboards are generally trouble-free unless subjected to liquids or physical shock. If a broken keyboard is an inexpensive model, it is probably best to replace it. The cost to replace the unit is usually lower than the value of the time it takes to attempt to fix one. That being said, some keyboards are more expensive, some are no longer available, and some users are "attached" to their keyboards. If you have a situation like this, disassemble the keyboard, if possible, and carefully clean the internal components inside. Then, reassemble the keyboard and try it out. If you are careful, you are unlikely to cause any further damage, and hopefully you can fix the problem. If a liquid has spilled into the keyboard, you should spray the non-residual contact cleaner on the surfaces under the keys. Use cotton swabs to clean the surfaces. This cleaning spray is expensive; expect to use up to $10 worth cleaning one keyboard.

Keyboard Error Codes

The only error message you're likely to encounter is the six-beep (usually) POST code indicating a keyboard or keyboard controller problem. If this happens, and replacing the keyboard doesn't help, unless the motherboard is under warranty, your only solution will be to use a USB keyboard if the computer has a USB port. If not, it is probably time to retire the motherboard.

Laptop Keyboards

Laptop keyboards are essential to the portability of a laptop. Imagine trying to tote a laptop or use one on a plane if you have to use a separate keyboard. The most

FIGURE 9.8 The removable panel type of laptop keyboard removal.

common reason to have to replace a laptop keyboard is if liquid spills on it, but the rest of the machine still works. Laptops vary widely in how to remove the keyboard, and laptop manufacturers vary widely in providing such information. For example, IBM® makes detailed service instructions for its ThinkPad® laptops available on its Web page (*ibm.com*), while many other companies do not make this information available on the Web. There are two common ways to remove a laptop keyboard. One is, with the power off and battery removed, to look for a removable panel around the keyboard. There might be a screw or two holding it in place (see Figure 9.8).

Remove the screw(s) and then the panel. You might then see a screw holding in the keyboard. Remove the screw and lift the keyboard slightly. Look underneath to see where the ribbon cable is, as shown in Figure 9.9. Make certain not to stress the ribbon cable as you lift the keyboard out of the way. The other method some manufacturers use is to look at the bottom of the laptop and remove any screws marked with "K" (see Figure 9.10). Then, gently lift the keyboard out following the previous instructions to prevent damage to the ribbon cable.

FIGURE 9.9 Treat the ribbon cable with care.

FIGURE 9.10   The "K" screw.

 If liquid has spilled on a laptop, do not attempt to power it on until you or a technician experienced in portable computers has determined that there is no liquid present anywhere in the system. See Chapter 11 for more information on attempting to rescue a laptop that has been exposed to liquid.

10 Troubleshooting Internet Connections

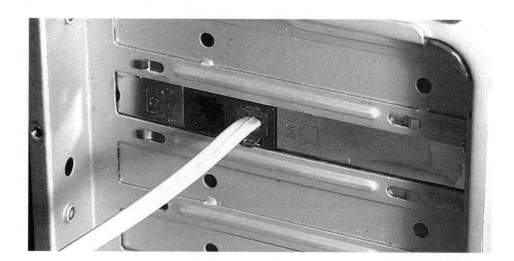

INTERNET CONNECTION PROBLEM OVERVIEW

Failure to connect to the Internet is a very common reason why people request service for their computers. We'll cover two main types of Internet connections here: dial-up and high speed. Each type has its own problems, with some overlap. The problems can be put into main categories:

- You cannot connect to the *Internet Service Provider* (*ISP*).
- You can connect to the ISP, but you can't open Web pages and/or use e-mail.
- You can connect to the ISP and open Web pages and use e-mail, but your connection is very slow, and/or you get disconnected frequently.

There are many causes of each of these problems, too many to cover them all here. We will attempt to cover common problems here. However, as is the case with other problems, there are times that everything is set correctly, and the hardware is OK, but Internet connections still don't work. When this happens, it might be because of OS corruption serious enough to require a clean install, or it might be one of those Windows things that happens for no real reason, and sometimes resolves itself with no real reason either.

We don't cover wireless Internet specifically in this book, although some of the information in this chapter does apply to it.

When setting up or troubleshooting a connection, there are some simple rules to follow, as we discuss in the following sections.

Basic Connection Problems

- **Call the ISP first:** There could be an outage in your area. There is no point in troubleshooting before you rule out an outage.
- **ISP settings:** Every ISP has its own requirements and specifications for connection configuration. Make sure you follow them.
- **Username and password:** Many connection problems could be avoided if users always used the correct username and password. This means that typos must be avoided and that the Caps Lock shouldn't be toggled on. In addition, some ISPs require you to enter your entire e-mail address (such as name@ domain.com) as a username, and some require only the username (the part before the "@.")

DIAL-UP CONNECTIONS

Although high-speed Internet service is becoming much more common and affordable, dial-up is still the most common as of this writing. In many rural areas, dial-up is the only option. Additionally, if you have high-speed Internet service at home, but you take your laptop to a distant location such as a motel or a relative's house, your only Internet access might be through dial-up.

Problems Dialing Up to an ISP

The first thing you need to do to troubleshoot a dial-up connection is to make sure that the hardware is connected correctly. If you are using a built-in modem in a desktop computer, make sure the telephone line is connected to the jack on the modem labeled *line*, or with a picture of a telephone jack, as shown in Figure 10.1.

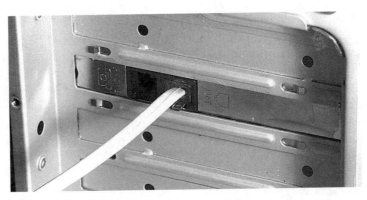

FIGURE 10.1 Connect the phone line to the phone jack.

In addition, make sure that the other end of the cable is connected to the wall jack. If the installation has a surge suppressor with telephone line protection, the telephone line needs to be connected to the line jack on the surge suppressor, with another telephone cord connecting the surge suppressor's output jack to the modem's line jack. If there is a telephone, hook it up to the telephone jack on the modem; it's the one labeled *Tel*, *Phone*, or with a picture of a telephone. Sometimes, there is a problem with the surge suppressor. To test it, plug a telephone into the output jack on the surge suppressor and listen for a dial tone. If you get no dial tone, and the line jack is connected to the telephone line, there might be a problem with the surge suppressor. Bypass the problem by connecting the telephone line directly to the computer.

Try connecting a telephone to the telephone line and dial the access number and listen to be sure you hear a modem on the other end. If you do not connect to a modem on the other end, you might have to modify the telephone number you are calling to reach the access number. If the call connects but you do not hear a modem, you will have to find an alternative access number to dial.

Never connect a computer modem to a PBX business telephone line. The voltage is different from a regular telephone line, and it could damage the modem, or at the very least, lock up the computer.

If you still get no connection, plug a telephone directly into the wall jack to make sure the telephone line works.

Other items to check include the telephone cords themselves: make sure they're good. If you are using a PC-Card modem with a dongle in a laptop, make sure it's working. A *dongle* is a cable that plugs into the end of the PC-Card and has a telephone connector on the other end (other PC-Card devices, such as network adapters, sometimes use dongles as well). Dongles tend to be delicate, especially where they plug into the PC-Card.

If the modem or the COM port the modem uses was changed at any time after setting up the connection, the connection might not recognize the new modem. Attempt to select the new modem in the connection's properties, have the ISP software detect the new modem, or delete and set up the connection from scratch. We discuss connection properties and setting up and deleting connections later in this chapter.

Does the Modem Work?

Obviously, if the modem doesn't work properly, you're not going to be able to connect. Follow the instructions in Chapter 8, "Video, Sound, Modems, and Network Adapters," for troubleshooting modems.

The Hardware Is OK, but I Still Can't Get Online

There are a myriad of different problems you can have connecting to the Internet related to configuration. The first thing to consider is whether you use a program provided by the ISP, such as AOL, or if you are using Windows dial-up networking. The programs vary greatly, so if you do have a problem, you'll have to consult the program vendor. Windows configuration can, however, play a big part in connecting, even if you're using third-party software.

ON THE CD

The Industry Contacts file on the accompanying CD-ROM has a section on ISPs.

NOTE

If you're using a free ad-based Internet service, you'll probably have a difficult time getting anything beyond automated technical support.

The main configuration problems are related to the following:

- Selecting the modem.
- Dialing the correct numbers, including the area code if necessary, the code to disable call waiting, codes required to get an outside line, even calling card numbers.
- Username and password.
- Any other settings required by the ISP.

Windows Dial-Up Networking (9x), Network Connections (2000/XP)

Access Internet connection wizards in these places:

9x: Dial-up Networking is accessible in Control Panel, and often in My Computer. Create new connections and access existing ones in Dial-up Networking.

2000: Create new connections using the Internet Connection Wizard. Although this can be started in several places, it is always available through Start > Programs > Accessories > Communications > Internet Connection Wizard. View existing connections in Network & Dial-up Connections, also accessible through the Communications folder.

XP: Create new Internet connections by using the New Connections Wizard, accessible through Start > All Programs (or Programs) > Accessories > Communications > New Connection Wizard. Access existing connections in Network Connections, also accessible in the Communications folder. XP also has a Network Setup Wizard, which allows some Internet configuration such as sharing an Internet connection with other computers and enabling or disabling the built-in *Internet Connection Firewall* (*ICF*). We discuss the ICF later in this chapter.

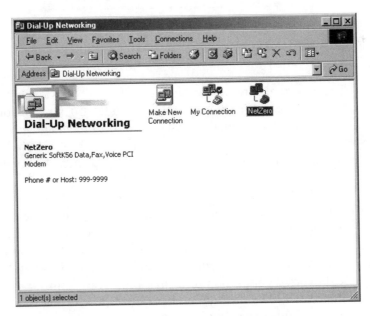

FIGURE 10.2   Dial-up Networking in Windows Me.

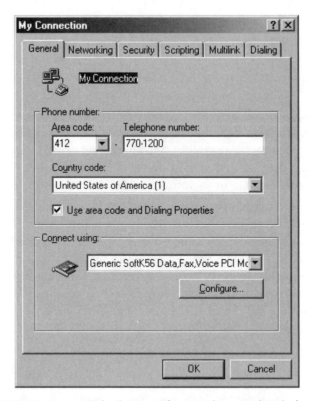

FIGURE 10.3 A connection's General properties page in Windows Me.

The 9x wizard is rather simple. The 2000 and XP wizards are also simple, although they offer more choices. Early in each wizard, you'll be prompted to select a modem. If there is no modem installed, or the modem is dead, Windows will attempt to detect and install the modem. Install or troubleshoot the modem before starting the wizard. If there is more than one modem, make sure to choose the correct one.

The main issues with dial-up connections are dialing the correct numbers, using the right username and password, and setting up any requirements from the ISP and local telephone company. To see a connection, open Dial-up Networking or Network Connections. You should see all the dial-up connections on the computer along with an icon to add a new connection, as shown in Figure 10.2.

Right-click a connection and click Properties from the menu that appears. You'll see a page like the one in Figure 10.3. (The dialog boxes that appear vary among the Windows version, but they are similar.)

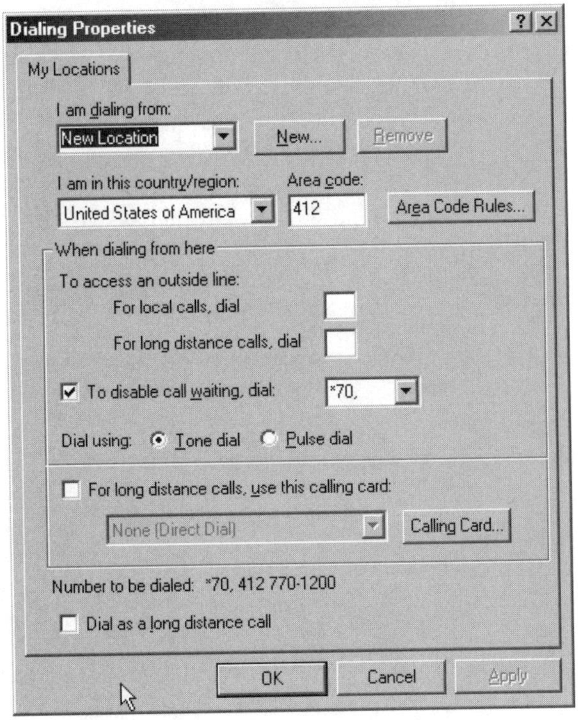

FIGURE 10.4 My Locations.

Some of the other tabs in this dialog box have settings that might prevent connection if set improperly. Look at Figure 10.4. This page is very useful if you use the computer in different areas where other numbers need to be dialed. Click the Area Code Rules button, shown in Figure 10.5.

Area Code Rules can be a very important page now that more and more areas require 10-digit dialing for local calls. The settings are self-explanatory. Another important page is the Dialing page, shown in Figure 10.6. The three option buttons at the top of this page don't affect the capability of connecting, but setting them correctly can make the difference between an unhappy and a happy computer user:

- **Never dial a connection:** Selecting this button means that Windows will never dial a connection unless the user chooses to connect.
- **Dial whenever a network connection is not present:** This is the setting to choose if you want to always be connected whenever Windows is running. This is great for high-speed Internet, and occasionally useful with dial-up, but it can

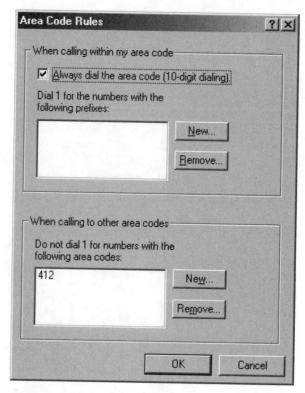

FIGURE 10.5 Area Code Rules.

also be extremely annoying to the user, especially when using a laptop that is not connected to a telephone line, high-speed line, or wireless network source.

■ **Always dial my default connection:** This setting will cause the computer to dial the default connection whenever the user opens a Web browser (such as Internet Explorer) or clicks an Internet link in a document, whenever the computer is not already connected to the Internet. Many people like this setting, although some don't.

These three settings also appear in Control Panel > Internet Options on the Connection page. Internet Options is also accessible from the Tools menu in any Internet Explorer page.

There are times when you'll be setting up new connections. Here are a few tips that can help streamline your experience with 2000's and XP's wizards:

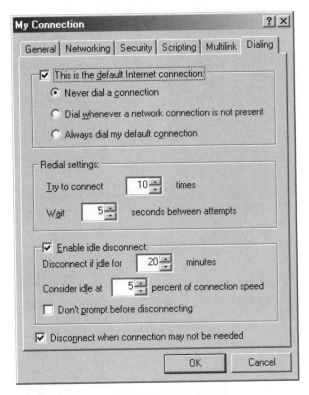

FIGURE 10.6   Windows Me Dialing page.

- 2000's and XP's wizards give you the option of setting up a new Internet account, and 2000's gives you the option of transferring your existing Internet account to your computer (2000's is shown in Figure 10.7, XP's in Figure 10.8). These make use of Microsoft's Internet Referral Service, which can't list every ISP available in every area. Forgo these options and use the choice to set up your account manually unless you want to use MSN®.
- Figure 10.8 also shows an option to use the CD provided by the ISP. If you want to use the ISP's CD, there is no reason to use the wizard. Simply insert the CD and run the program.
- When running XP's wizard you'll be prompted to enable the ICF. It is a good idea to enable this for any *direct* connection to the Internet, as long as no other firewall is running on the system. If you dial up to an ISP or have one computer that connects to a DSL or cable modem, this is considered a direct connection. We discuss firewalls later in this chapter.

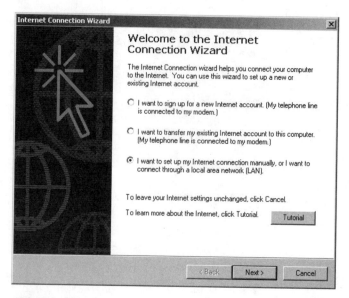

FIGURE 10.7   Choose the third option with Windows 2000.

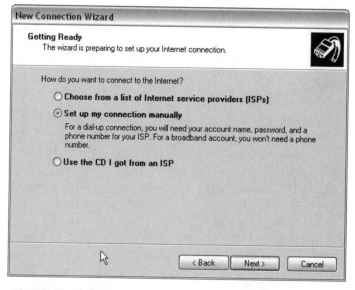

FIGURE 10.8   Choose the second option with Windows XP.

Dialing Rules

Dialing rule settings are accessible from the Phone and Modem applet (or equivalent) in Control Panel, and from buttons in the wizards and the connection pages. These rules purport to give the user control of exactly how the computer dials numbers, including the appropriate area code, calling card numbers, and other codes. These settings are supposed to be in effect for any connection on the computer with the "Use area code and dialing rules" (or equivalent) check box selected, as shown in Figure 10.9.

In 2000, it sometimes doesn't seem to matter how you have Dialing Rules configured and if you have the connection configured to use them; the rules will often be ignored.

TIP

> *If you run into the problem of dialing rules being ignored in 2000, and you're sure that everything has been correctly configured, try rebooting—it sometimes helps.*

Dialing Rules also allows you to set up separate rules for different locations as shown in Figure 10.10; select the one you want for your location.

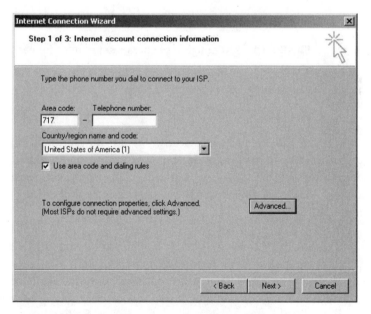

FIGURE 10.9   2000's wizard page with the "Use area code and dialing rules" check box selected.

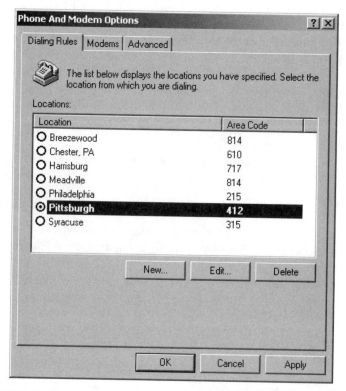

FIGURE 10.10   Configure a separate set of rules for each location.

You can edit the rules by selecting the location and clicking Edit. This applet gets rather deep in levels of dialog boxes you can edit. On the Calling Card page, in addition to being able to use some preset calling cards as shown in Figure 10.11, you can add additional calling cards by clicking New and editing the page shown in Figure 10.12.

TIP

Make sure that Dialing Rules are being used by listening to hear if enough digits are being dialed. If you have configured your laptop to use a calling card from a hotel room and the system ignores the settings, you could fail to connect, call someone else's room, or dial long distance without a calling card and most likely be charged an astronomical amount of money by the hotel.

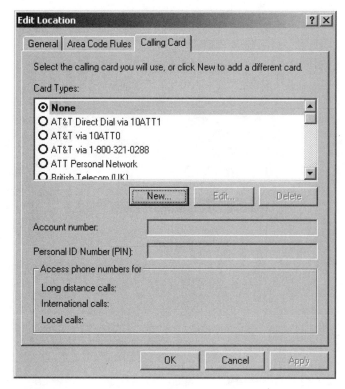

FIGURE 10.11   Calling card use in 2000.

Troubleshooting Broadband (High-Speed) Connections

Because general networking is beyond the scope of this book, this section covers only direct broadband connections to the Internet, and not connections through a local area network (LAN).

Generally, broadband Internet connections are made with ISP software. This software can vary widely; therefore, most troubleshooting should be done with the assistance of the ISP's technical support department. However, Windows XP allows broadband connections without the use of ISP software, as shown in Figure 10.13.

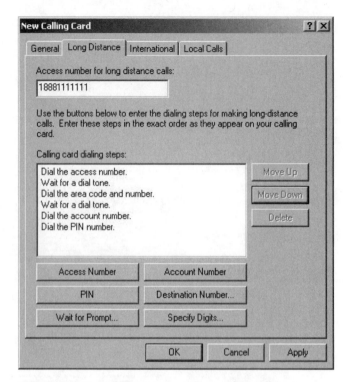

FIGURE 10.12 Adding a new calling card in 2000.

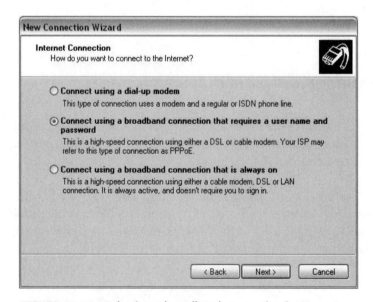

FIGURE 10.13 Selecting a broadband connection in XP.

Using XP's broadband feature is desirable any time the ISP's software becomes troublesome. Regardless of whether you're using the ISP's software or XP's feature, you'll get a connection dialog that could be similar to a dial-up connection dialog. Sometimes a "phone number" is displayed, usually 111-1111. As mentioned earlier, the most common configuration problems in this type of connection are incorrect use of username and password, and the Caps Lock function being toggled on in the event of case sensitivity of either.

Broadband Hardware Issues

The two most popular types of consumer and small business broadband connections are *Digital Subscriber Line (DSL)* and *Cable Internet*.

DSL: DSL transfers data across regular analog voice telephone lines at a different frequency than voice conversations, allowing voice and data to flow simultaneously. To keep the Internet signals from interfering with voice, fax, and even dial-up signals, *DSL filters* must be attached to every telephone jack on that telephone line (or one heavy-duty filter used for all the other jacks). Don't forget to install filters on *every device connected to the telephone line except the DSL modem.* This includes fax machines, computer modems, alarm systems that dial the telephone, and utility (water, gas, electricity, etc.) meters. The individual DSL filters should be connected between the telephone jack and the device. Figure 10.14 shows an assortment of DSL filters.

FIGURE 10.14 An assortment of DSL filters.

To connect DSL to your computer, use a standard telephone cable to connect the wall telephone jack to a DSL modem (or DSL router). *Do not* use a DSL filter on this connection. The modem connects to the computer either with an Ethernet cable to an Ethernet adapter (see Chapter 8) or to a USB port (unless the DSL modem is an internal expansion card). Any of these cables or devices represents a potential point of failure. If you rule out everything else, it is likely that the modem (or router) is the problem. Make sure the modem is powered and connected, and that all cables are intact. You can also check the telephone line by unplugging the telephone cable from the DSL modem and plugging it into a telephone. You should hear a dial tone with no interference. (The interference comes from the modem, not the telephone line.)

If DSL is being used where there are multiline telephone jacks, make sure the DSL modem is connected to the correct telephone line.

Cable Internet: This makes use of cable television cables, which already have a great deal of *bandwidth*. A television cable gets connected to a cable modem that connects to the computer either through an Ethernet cable to an Ethernet adapter (see Chapter 8), or through a USB port. Because televisions and VCRs have tuners, there is no problem with interference. Cable modems simply tune to a frequency not used by television channels.

Here are some items to check when troubleshooting suspected cable Internet hardware problems:

- Check for a damaged television cable.
- Did anyone install or remove a cable splitter? Cable modems can be finicky. If the signal is too strong or weak, the Internet connection might fail. Splitters reduce the signal strength by a factor equal to the number of extra outlets in use.
- Make sure the Ethernet or USB cable is good. The Ethernet cable in most cases must not be a crossover cable (see Chapter 8).
- Check the cable modem for power (or if the modem is an internal expansion card, check its status in Device Manager.

After connecting or reconnecting a broadband modem, you'll have to wait for the ready light or equivalent to indicate that the connection was made, often by the light glowing steadily and not flashing. This usually takes a minute or two. If it doesn't indicate a connection, the problem could be the modem or the telephone/cable line. Call the ISP.

There are a great many Web pages with useful information for troubleshooting broadband connections. Search for *DSL troubleshooting* or *cable modem troubleshooting*.

YOU CAN CONNECT, BUT YOU CAN'T OPEN WEB PAGES

The first thing to do in this situation is to call the ISP. There might be a glitch on their end. Barring that, three types of situations can cause this type of problem:

- Configuration
- Malware
- Virus infection

Solve the latter two by using procedures described in Chapter 2, "System Configuration and Computer Hygiene," and Chapter 11, "Troubleshooting." We discuss configuration here.

Internet Options

The information here applies to Internet Explorer 6.0, but most will apply to other versions.

Internet Options is a group of settings accessible from Control Panel or from the Tools menu of any Internet Explorer page. Its settings can affect the performance of the Internet. Figure 10.15 shows the General page of Internet Options.

The General Page

This page has the following pertinent settings:

- **Home page:** Use this to select the Web page that appears when Internet Explorer is opened. If a rogue program changes it, you can change it back here.
- **Temporary Internet files:** These files can take up a surprising amount of disk space, and large amounts of files can even slow Internet performance. *Cookies* are small files that remember data the user entered for the next time the user visits the same Web site where the cookie came from. For example, when a user regularly visits a Web page that makes use of a logon, such as Yahoo.com, cookies are the files that allow Yahoo! to recognize the user every time he visits (if the page is so configured). Some cookies are used for nefarious purposes, but we'll discuss that later in this chapter.

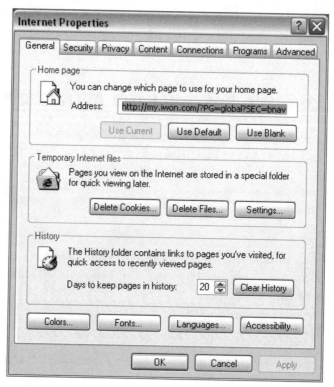

FIGURE 10.15 Internet Options General page from XP.

- **History:** History allows a user to click on the arrow next to the address bar and select a previously viewed Web page. Clearing the history will clear this list.

Security and Privacy Pages

These pages are used to set various options related to security. Keep the sliders too low, and malware and viruses can become easier to contract. Keep the bars too high, and you won't connect to too many pages or be able to download files. If you are prompted to "enable cookies," these pages are where it's done. It's possible that you'll have to use a custom level by clicking the button and selecting or clearing the check boxes within. Sometimes, you are prompted to enable cookies by a Web page or program and you discover that cookies are already enabled. On the Privacy page (shown in Figure 10.16) is an Advanced button. If you click it and select the check box to "Override automatic cookie handling," and then elect to accept first- and third-party cookies and to automatically allow session cookies, you should have no more trouble. You might want to set the settings back to the way they were after the

FIGURE 10.16   Privacy page.

page or program has finished. If it still doesn't work, it usually indicates malware or virus infection.

Content Page

The crucial settings on this page are the Content Advisor and the Certificates section. The Content Advisor is a system to block Web pages that contain profanity, nudity, violence, and/or sex. These systems are notorious for blocking legitimate sites and allowing offensive sites to slip through. The main problem here is if the user wants to disable or configure the advisor but can't remember the password. Search the Internet for *lost Content Advisor password*, or see Microsoft Knowledge Base article 155609 (See Chapter 11 for information on viewing Knowledge Base articles).

Certificates are documents that certify that an entity communicating via the Web is who it purports to be. Too high of a setting on the Security page and you'll

FIGURE 10.17 The Content page.

have Web pages blocked or you'll receive prompts to block them based on problems with certificates. Sometimes, even Microsoft pages can be blocked by too high a setting. Figure 10.17 shows the Content page.

We have all seen the prompt when attempting to download files to accept or reject the download. Each of these dialog boxes contains a check box to "Always trust content from…" Selecting these check boxes is desirable when the content provider is a known trustworthy entity such as Microsoft or your antivirus program provider—doing so will eliminate these prompts. The content providers (called *publishers*) are stored on the page that appears when you click the Publishers button.

Connections Page

The pertinent settings on this page are the Setup button, which opens up the Internet Connection Wizard; the option buttons in the middle, which are the same as the ones discussed earlier in this chapter except that they apply to any Internet connection; and the LAN settings, which are used only if the computer is connected to the Internet via a LAN. By clicking the LAN settings button and selecting the "Automatically detect settings" check box within, the computer should be able to connect to the Internet simply by having a network cable carrying an Internet signal connected to the network adapter. Figure 10.18 shows the Connections page.

Programs and Advanced Pages

The Programs page is used to set the default programs for certain activities. The most important one is the e-mail program. If you click an e-mail address link anywhere in Windows, a document, or a Web page, the program displayed here should appear automatically. However, this is one of those settings that, in 2000 and XP, has to be made in one other place as well. If you click the Start menu and look at the top portion, you will usually see a command called *Set Program Access and Defaults*. This option seems to have priority over the one in Internet Options.

FIGURE 10.18   The Connections page.

The Advanced page has highly technical settings that should be left at their defaults unless you are instructed by Microsoft support personnel or documents to change them.

DATA TRANSFER SPEED ISSUES

Speed of data transfer is affected by viruses and malware, just as the inability to get Web pages at all. There are, however, some other steps you can take to try to resolve these issues.

Telephone Line Problems

Windows Dial-up Networking and most Internet software have an indicator of connection speed. Usually, you can view the speed by moving the pointer over the appropriate icon in the System Tray, as shown in Figure 10.19.

If you have slow speeds, such as under 38 Kbps with a 56K modem, and/or the Internet connection is frequently dropped for no apparent reason, the problem might be in the telephone line. Hotel room telephone lines often have extraordinarily slow speeds; it is unusual to connect at *faster* than 19 Kbps from a hotel room, regardless of whether the property is a cheap motel or a four-star property (although some hotels are installing new telephone systems allowing faster connections). There is nothing that the user can do about it unless the hotel has a high-speed network connection, as a small, but increasing number, do. The user should test the connection speed from different residential telephone lines. Chances are that most will be faster than hotel lines are. If, however, the connection speed is very slow or the connection gets dropped frequently in a residence, there might be a problem with either a noisy telephone line or with the ISP. To attempt to rule out

383 bytes received 1748 bytes sent @ 48000 bps

FIGURE 10.19 Viewing the Internet connection speed.

the ISP, the user should sign up for a free ISP such as NetZero (*netzero.net*) or Juno (*juno.com*) just to test the connection speed and reliability (assuming that the free service isn't using the same telephone number to connect as the primary ISP is). If they are significantly faster or more reliable, the problem is most likely with the ISP. If they are no faster or better, the problem is probably in the telephone line. This could be a problem with internal house wiring or with external telephone company wiring, or both. Have the user check with the telephone company, noting the possibility that there could be a substantial charge in some cases for the telephone company to repair house telephone wiring.

Call Waiting and Voice Mail

When setting up a dial-up Internet connection, the user must know if the line has Call Waiting from the telephone company. *Call Waiting* is the feature that signals someone during a telephone call that another call is coming in and allows switching between one call and another. Normally, those users with Call Waiting wouldn't want to be disconnected from the Internet every time another call comes in, so most or all connection programs have a provision to dial the deactivation code before the telephone number. In most or all cases, this code is *70 (1170 with a pulse-only line). However, having the software programmed to dial this on a laptop will likely cause the connection attempt to fail when dialing from a telephone line without Call Waiting, such as a hotel room. Therefore, the user should not use *70 when setting up a connection to use on a line without Call Waiting.

Telephone company voice mail is very helpful for those who have dial-up Internet service. With voice mail, the telephone will never be busy. If the user has both Call Waiting and voice mail, the call waiting should be disabled in an Internet connection. A problem that can occur with voice mail is if the telephone company uses a pulsing dial tone to indicate a new message. In some cases, the modem will not detect a dial tone. To solve this problem, either listen to all your messages before trying to connect, or add three commas to the beginning of the telephone number to dial. Commas are seen as pause indicators by the system.

There are also Internet answering machines and software. We haven't tested any of the hardware devices, but their advertisements say that they allow incoming calls to come in when the telephone line is connected to the Internet. The most notable software-based system is the CallWave® Internet Answering Machine® (*callwave.com*). This software requires Call Forwarding from the local telephone company. You simply forward the calls from the telephone line to a toll-free number provided by CallWave, and callers will hear an announcement prompting them to leave a message. Their message will then be played on your computer while you are online. AOL has a feature to accomplish this as well for an extra charge.

FIREWALLS

A firewall is a program or hardware device that keeps hostile attackers from accessing a computer's data. Firewalls can help prevent virus transmission, and overall, they are good to have. Unfortunately, configuration of some firewalls can be painstaking. Without proper configuration, certain firewalls can block all Internet access.

Certain products come with firewalls. For example, Linksys routers act as firewalls, but the router firmware also makes available a trial version of a software-based firewall. Trend Micro's PC-Cillin antivirus program comes with a firewall that, at least in recent versions, won't deactivate even when the program settings indicate that it is disabled. (To disable it in 2000 or XP, go into Services and disable the Trend Micro personal firewall service there.) As mentioned earlier, Windows XP comes with the ICF.

Here are some basic recommendations about use of firewalls:

- Use of more than one firewall on a system will probably stop most or all Internet traffic. Stick with one.
- If you are using Internet Connection Sharing in 2000/XP, enable the ICF or use another firewall product.
- If you use a *proxy server* to connect to the Internet, don't use a firewall, except on the proxy server. (It is not necessary to know what a proxy server is for our purposes.)

See XP's Help and Support for more information about the ICF.

TROUBLESHOOTING E-MAIL

Although there are several e-mail programs (called *clients*) that people use, in addition to Web-based e-mail such as Hotmail® and Yahoo®, Outlook® Express is the most common (besides AOL). The reason is that Windows and Internet Explorer come with Outlook Express. A few problems are common with Outlook Express, as we discuss here.

Outlook Express and General E-Mail Information

We will be covering Outlook Express version 6 here, the latest as of this writing. Much of this information applies to other e-mail programs as well.

The problem most people have with Outlook Express has to do with a change in their account. If there are any errors, you might not be able to send or receive mail. You must set up new accounts using the wizard. The wizard is very simple to use, as long as you have all the correct information from the ISP. To access the wizard, open Outlook Express. There might be icons for it all over the Desktop, but you should be able to find it in the Start menu program list. The first time you start it, the wizard will open. Just follow the prompts. If Outlook Express has already been configured, you can access the wizard by going to Tools > Accounts > Mail and clicking the Add button (see Figure 10.20). This adds another e-mail account to Outlook Express. If the ISP has any unusual configuration requirements, you might have to configure the account manually anyway. To do this, select the name of the account in the Mail page and click Properties. You'll get a page like the one shown in Figure 10.21.

The key to successful configuration of most of these pages is not to make any typos. If there are connection problems, compare what is entered in these text boxes to the information provided by the ISP, letter by letter if you have to.

Some ISPs require the full e-mail address to be entered in the username box, and some require just the username portion (the part before the @). Sometimes, such as when the ISP is separate from the e-mail domain, you might be required to use a % in place of the @.

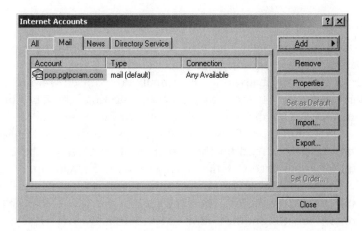

FIGURE 10.20 Add an e-mail account.

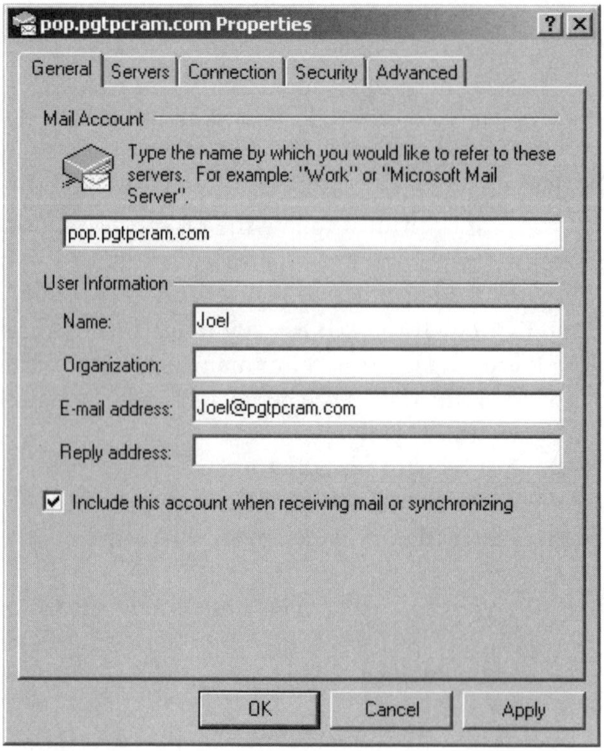

FIGURE 10.21 General properties.

The Servers page (Figure 10.22) contains some of the most important information. The server names must be right. Don't use @ in place of periods in the server name; normally, only the e-mail address itself will use the @. In addition, don't select the "My server requires authentication" check box unless the username and password are different from the one for incoming mail, a rare occurrence.

The Connection (Figure 10.23) page gives the option of selecting the Internet connection to be used for the particular account. If you have multiple ISPs and multiple e-mail accounts, this is where you match them up.

The Security page has various options that you would configure based only on instructions from the ISP. The same goes for the Advanced page (Figure 10.24), except for the setting at the bottom. Most ISPs allow you to get e-mail on your local computer and on the Web. Many business e-mail accounts are monitored by more than one person. Selecting the "Leave messages on server" check box allows other users to download the same messages on their computers, and keeps the messages available on the ISP's Web page. Users who have this box selected will have to

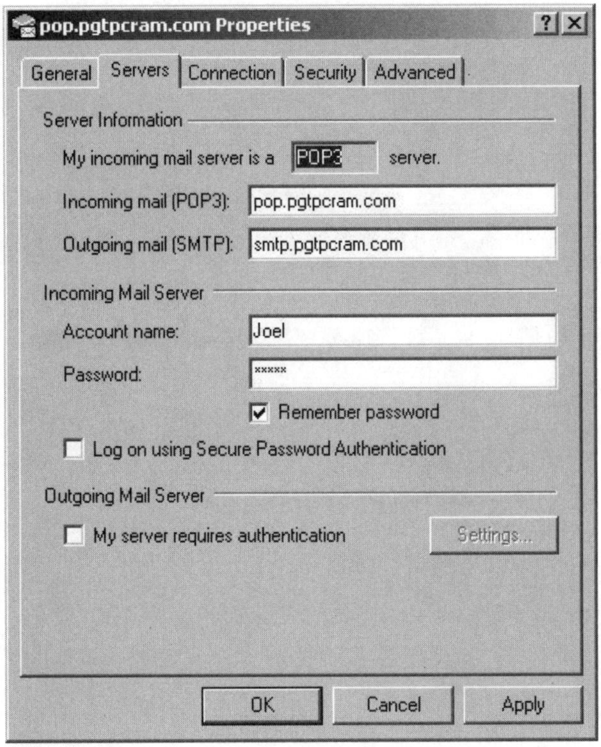

FIGURE 10.22 The Servers page.

regularly delete the messages from the server to keep from using up their quotas and/or disk space.

Common Outlook Express Problems

Incoming attachments won't download: Especially after updating Outlook Express in Windows Update, you might find that attachments won't download. This is because the update selects the "Do not allow attachments to be saved or opened that could potentially be a virus" check box. Go to Tools > Options and click the Security tab to find this check box. See Microsoft Knowledge Base article 329570 for more information (Chapter 11 has instructions for searching the Knowledge Base).

Attachment pages are blank: Sometimes, attachments download but aren't visible. This usually indicates a problem in the attachment as sent. If you can't get it to appear, download it to a folder, right-click it, click Open With, and

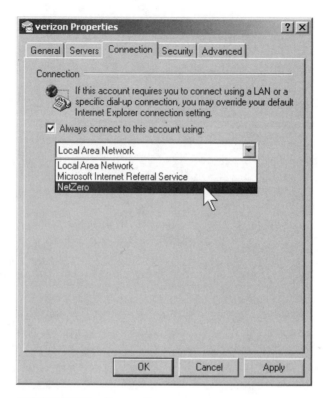

FIGURE 10.23 Connection page.

select Notepad from the list. Among all of the useless characters you should find the message, as long as there are no images.

Attachments come up with many pages full of numbers or nonsense characters: The computer doesn't have a program capable of opening the attachment. Contact the sender and ask what program the attachment was created in.

Dial-up settings are wrong: Different users have different needs as far as how they read their e-mail. Many dial-up users prefer to open Outlook Express and have the system automatically dial their ISP, download their messages, and then disconnect. This way, they can read their mail and write replies without tying up their telephone lines. After they finish their replies, they click to send and the system again dials up to the Internet just long enough for the messages to be sent. The problem occurs when these settings are reset. Users can become rather unhappy when that happens, because it's not always easy to find the location to change these settings. Go to Tools > Options and click the

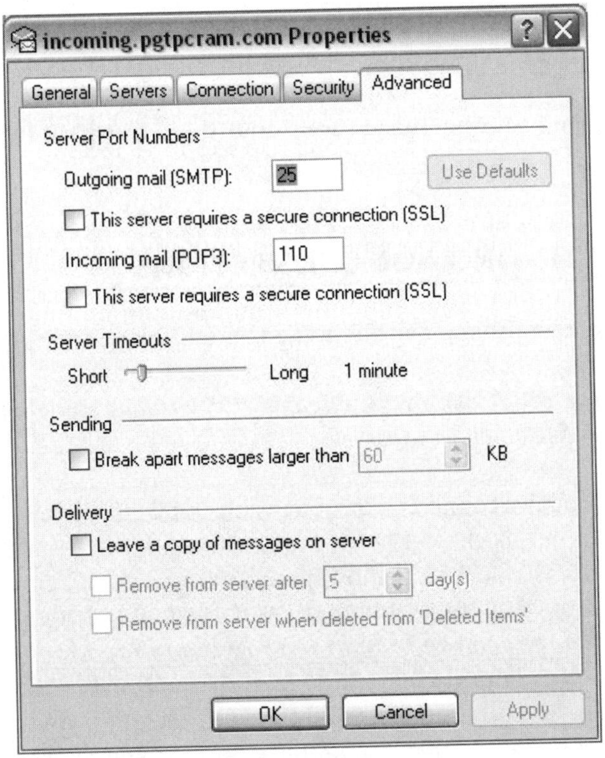

FIGURE 10.24   Advanced page.

Connection tab. If you want the connection to disconnect after downloading or uploading, select the "Hang up after sending and receiving" check box. The Change button on this page directs you to Internet Options as discussed earlier in this chapter. Make changes to suit the user, but remember that these changes will affect Internet Explorer as well.

Backing Up Outlook Express

Full system backups will include Outlook Express data files. Outlook Express folders aren't real Windows folders. Messages and Outlook Express folders are actually stored in a single or a few files. The same goes with address book information. If you are doing a manual backup of Outlook Express data, in 2000 and XP, copy the Documents and Settings\[username]\Application Data\Microsoft\Outlook Express folders. It's a little harder to find in 9x; you can look in Windows\Application\ Data\Identities\ and Windows\Profiles\[username]\Application Data\Identities.

The easier way is to click Find or Search from the Start menu and enter *.dbx in the text box. This will search for all files with the .dbx extension, which is where Outlook Express' data is stored. Copy the contents of all folders with these files.

When restoring, make sure to put these files back in the same or equivalent folders.

TROUBLESHOOTING AOL CONNECTIONS

AOL is the most popular ISP in the United States and in many other countries.

Because AOL took over CompuServe™, virtually everything we say about AOL applies to CompuServe as well.

If you have connection problems in AOL and you have tried some of the hints provided in this chapter to no avail, you can try uninstalling and reinstalling the program. Use the Add/Remove programs applet in Control Panel and let it completely remove all copies it finds. In AOL versions 6, 7, and 8 (possibly in earlier versions too), you can go to Start > Programs > America Online (or equivalent) > AOL System Information and then clear the browser cache and check the error messages. You can even uninstall the AOL adapter from the Utilities tab as shown in Figure 10.25, and then reboot the computer and reinstall the AOL software.

If you are able to sign on to AOL but get an error message when you try to load a Web page, there might be a problem with *TCP/IP*. AOL uses a software device called an *AOL adapter* that actually shows up in Device Manager as a network adapter. There are two AOL adapters in all versions since AOL 5. Removing these and restarting the computer might solve the problem. The best place to do this is AOL System Information, shown in Figure 10.25.

If you have been using AOL 6 or later, after uninstalling AOL, your address book and most of your settings will be saved. If you are using an earlier version, copy the contents of your address book before uninstalling. You will then need to redo all your settings after installation.

Since Windows 95B and C allow a maximum of four TCP/IP connections by default and AOL will try to use two of them, you might run into a problem if your computer has too many other TCP/IP connections. Check to see if there are any unused TCP/IP connections in the network settings and remove them. To do this, double-click Network in Control Panel. The applet will open to the Configuration page. Look for any TCP/IP listings in the network components box, highlight it, and click Remove. Click OK. You'll have to reboot the computer for the new settings to take effect.

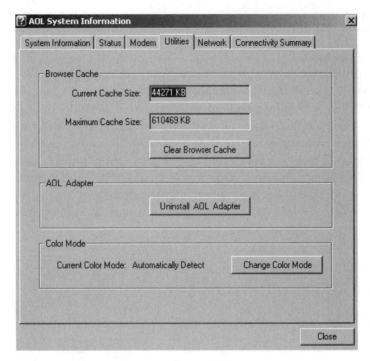

FIGURE 10.25 AOL System Information.

If AOL is unable to find your modem, you might need to reinstall or replace the modem. If you have tested the modem and determined it to be okay, then you might need to go into Setup, remove the modem, and let AOL find your modem again. Depending on what version of AOL you are using, the dialog boxes vary slightly, but the option to get into Setup is at the bottom of the Sign On screen window in all versions.

If AOL has been installed for awhile and suddenly you keep getting disconnected, and you have ruled out faulty cables and modem, you might need to select the access numbers button on the Sign On screen and get updated telephone numbers to dial.

If you get a message that the modem would not initialize, you can turn the power to the modem off and on again if it is an external. If it is an internal modem, restart the computer.

If you click the Help button from the Sign On screen, you can get lots of help there. Go to Setting up your computer to connect to AOL > Resolving Connection Problems > Disconnections to the AOL service > I get disconnected from the AOL service. Doing so attempts to repair your AOL connection automatically.

MISCELLANEOUS ITEMS

As discussed in Chapter 2, certain hardware devices, including modems and network adapters, have problems working with certain programs and Windows versions. If you search for support articles (see Chapter 11), be sure to specify the modem brand and model number, or the chipset's identifying information.

Some ISPs require a *terminal window* to be called up to log on to the Internet. Hyperterminal, discussed in the modem troubleshooting section of Chapter 8, is a terminal program. When setting up a connection to this type of ISP, you'll notice a check box on one of the wizard pages that will call up a terminal window. Select it. The ISP should be able to provide instructions.

11 Troubleshooting

TROUBLESHOOTING OVERVIEW

So, you have a computer with a problem. Where do you start? Sometimes, that answer is obvious. If you have a machine that won't power on, the first thing to check is if the power is connected. Then, check the power supply. Is the voltage switch set correctly? Is the power supply on-off switch in the *on* position? If the answer to these is yes, the next thing to do is try a known good power supply. If that works, you have found the problem. Occasionally, that won't work either, but then you have reason to suspect a bad motherboard; there aren't too many other possibilities.

More often, however, the source of the problem won't be so obvious, or it will seem obvious, but nothing you try works. While experience helps more than anything else, there are certain principles and concepts that ease the job of diagnosing a computer.

All Might Not Be What It Seems

All might not be what it seems. The best example is when the computer locks up, as discussed in Chapter 9, "Input Devices." Many people see that the pointer freezes and assume that their mouse just broke. They buy a new mouse, and unless the computer locks up immediately, they think the the problem is solved. Here's what happened to me on two laptops. The machines wouldn't go into standby or hibernation, and attached printers stopped printing. In every case, the error messages blamed the problem on the driver of an item that was working normally: in one case, it was the keyboard driver; in another, a COM port driver; in the third, a network adapter driver. The problem, however, had nothing to do with these drivers. In fact, keyboard and COM port drivers rarely, if ever, exhibit any problems. The problem in each case turned out to be the recent installation of a USB device; a scanner, a Web cam, and a hard drive. Even with the device disconnected, the mere presence of one of these drivers in the system caused these problems. Uninstalling the drivers, and in the case of the Web cam, removing every vestige of the software, solved the problem. The oddest thing is that all three of the USB devices worked perfectly.

So, to repeat the question, how do you know where to start? For those who work in technical support for certain notorious hardware and software companies, the answer is anywhere but with their product. However, if you're trying to find the real reason, the first thing you'll have to accept is that a given problem could be caused by almost any component in a system. Therefore, the troubleshooting procedure should start with the most likely culprit and then proceed to the next most likely once the most likely has been ruled out. If nothing is obvious, there are other ways to find the problem, which we discuss throughout this chapter.

There comes a point at which it is not worthwhile to diagnose a problem, such as when you'll be spending more time and/or money than the computer is worth, or when it would be easier to simply back up the data, if desired, format the hard drive, reinstall the OS and programs, and restore the data.

Basic Troubleshooting Rules

There are basic rules to follow when troubleshooting:

- **Make only one change at a time:** If you make more than one change at a time, you won't know which change solved the problem. If a change you made didn't help, undo the change before trying the next one.
- **Record all changes:** It can be very difficult to remember all the changes you've made, especially if you've tried several. There's no sense in repeating changes; and if you haven't solved the problem and need to turn the machine over to another technician, the machine should be the same as when you got it.
- **Keep a record of all error messages:** We discuss error messages later in this chapter.
- **Seek assistance:** Others might have experience with the problem you are having. Ask colleagues. Look on the manufacturer's or developer's Web site for their knowledge base or *frequently asked questions (FAQs)*, or call the company. In many cases, there is a simple fix or software patch to solve your problem. You can also search the Internet for the problem; in many cases, there are forums where people post problems and others give recommended solutions. You can find tips on obtaining tech support later in this chapter.

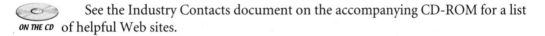 See the Industry Contacts document on the accompanying CD-ROM for a list
ON THE CD of helpful Web sites.

Questions to Ask

There are a series of questions to ask when you begin to troubleshoot a problem:

- **Is there an error message or beep code?** We discuss error messages and beep codes later in this chapter.
- **Had the computer been physically moved just before the problem started?** When a computer is moved, cables often become disconnected, including the power cord. If the computer has been moved from one place to another and the case sustains enough shock, internal components can become partially or fully dislodged.
- **Were any changes made to the computer just before the problem surfaced?** These changes include configuration changes, or installation or uninstallation of hardware or software.

Diagnostic Tools

Thankfully, trial and error isn't the only way to diagnose a problem. Many hardware- and software-based tools exist to let you know what is wrong. Many of these were discussed in previous chapters. A few others are described here:

- **CheckIt (*smithmicro.com/checkit*):** There is a series of programs designed to help you diagnose and fix PC problems. The most relevant title is *CheckIt Professional*, which has a battery of tests for just about every aspect of the computer. Additionally, it has professional features such as the capability of running from a bootable floppy. This is similar to Micro 2000's Micro-Scope. CheckIt offers a POST card as well.

- **AMI Diag (*ami.com*):** This is very similar to CheckIt Professional.

- **Diagnostic Utilities from Hardware Manufacturers:** Many computers come with their own diagnostic utilities. For example, HPDiag comes with Hewlett-Packard computers and some other HP products.

- **Norton SystemWorks (*norton.com* or *symantec.com*):** This is a set of programs including Norton Anti-Virus and Norton Utilities. Norton Utilities has a set of tools that can be used to solve hard drive and other problems. It is a useful program, but one of its main features, the capability of running in the background to prevent problems, can be troublesome. There was a case in which a user found that he had only 3GB of space left just one day after having 24GB left, but Windows showed no evidence of additional files. It turned out that a program he ran was creating and deleting 1GB temporary files, and a feature of Norton Utilities, Delete Protect, was rescuing these temporary files from deletion. The user finally found the files in the Norton Recycle Bin. In fact, if you encounter a computer with an inexplicably small amount of remaining hard drive space, and the computer is running Norton Utilities, check the Norton Recycle Bin. Of course, the anti-virus program is particularly important (see Chapter 2, "System Configuration and Computer Hygiene," for more information on viruses). Norton and others even have a program that can "unformat," possibly saving data from a drive that has been formatted.

- **McAfee Clinic (*mcafee.com*):** In addition to the highly recommended *Virus-Scan Online* (that works on all versions of Windows), McAfee Clinic has several programs, all online only, that can solve computer problems. Unfortunately, most of these programs run only on Windows 9x and not on 2000 or XP. The most helpful programs in the set are FirstAidOnline, which includes a registry cleaner and some other assorted utilities, and UninstallerOnline, which includes a very helpful utility called QuickClean, which deletes unnecessary files.

While these are very helpful for Windows 9x, many other programs available perform similar functions and do work on all versions.

McAfee has many programs available to download or purchase that can be installed on a system to diagnose and repair many problems with Windows.

- **Registry cleaners:** There are many other registry-cleaning utilities available, most of which work with all versions of Windows. A notable one is RegCleaner, available free from *jv16.org*.

Information-Gathering Utilities

There are also utilities designed simply to obtain information from your computer. This information includes installed hardware and software and even some software registration codes. Again, some of these were discussed in previous chapters:

- **System Information:** Available from Start > Programs (or All Programs) > Accessories > System Tools, this applet provides a comprehensive report of many aspects of the computer. Figure 11.1 shows a System Information report.

FIGURE 11.1   A sample System Information report on Windows XP. Note the open Tools menu.

■ **Belarc Advisor:** Belarc is a great program that can be used to get a wealth of very useful information from a computer. Download free from *belarc.com*, but note that Belarc's license allows personal use of Belarc Advisor only; it is not licensed for any commercial purpose. Therefore, use it only on your own personal computers.

■ **McAfee and Norton:** McAfee FirstAidOnline and Norton SystemWorks have information-gathering programs.

Two Excellent Diagnostic Programs

PC Certify (*pccertify.com*) and the Micro-Scope diagnostic program by Micro 2000 (*micro2000.com*) are useful in many ways. They operate by using their own proprietary OSs that bypass DOS and Windows problems. Their OSs read the system hardware and report a complete list of information that can help to diagnose the PC. They can also run hundreds of tests on components such as memory, video, hard drives, floppy drives, and CD drives. They will also help to determine if you have hardware conflicts, and will allow you to see which IRQs are being used and which are available so you can get things straightened out. They also can be used to perform a low-level format and a secure wipe (complete erasure) of a hard drive. They are useful in running burn-in tests and creating a report of the results. A *burn-in test* is a series of individual tests run over a course of several hours for the purpose of certifying a newly built computer.

POST cards are available from each company (Micro 2000's is shown in Figure 11.2). They are used when a system will no longer boot up or run the diagnostic software. They will help in determining the cause of a dead system and can tell you whether the problem lies in memory, processor, a PCI or ISA slot, video system, and so forth. They come with guidebooks filled with POST codes for most BIOSs. The guidebooks list the meaning of each code and provide recommended solutions. They are big time savers and can eliminate many hours that would be spent swapping components.

Many other companies make products designed to perform the same functions. They range in price and vary from slight to great in their abilities to diagnose different problems.

The biggest advantage to this type of software and a POST card is that you can rule out or correct hardware issues before you try to deal with software issues. For example, if you are installing a new component and are having trouble with it, you can first see if the component is defective. You can then see if it needs to have jumpers changed, if applicable. Afterward, you can go ahead and troubleshoot the software and driver issues. You can see that this process will save you lots of time rather than installing and uninstalling drivers and software over and over again when the problem was hardware all along.

FIGURE 11.2 The Micro 2000 POST card.

It is a good idea if you do this type of work on a regular basis to have tools like this available so you can get the problems diagnosed quickly and cost-effectively. If you are just an occasional hobbyist, then you might find that swapping components and trial and error are just fine for you.

TIP

OBTAINING ASSISTANCE

As covered elsewhere in this book, obtaining assistance is crucial to effective and timely repair. There are two categories of assistance sources: manufacturers and information sharing groups.

Manufacturers

This includes hardware manufacturers, software developers, ISPs, and any organization that provides a product or service that you are troubleshooting. Help can be available in any form, including telephone support, live chat, e-mail, Usenet newsgroups, Web page form submission that leads to various types of responses, and others. Manufacturers prefer that their customers use self-service help such as FAQ pages and knowledge base searches, and often, this provides the information you need. A *knowledge base* is a collection of articles providing all information made available by a manufacturer. Many businesses force you to try self-service support before they supply contact information. This is usually reasonable, because some people will ask questions the answers to which are easily found in the product's documentation. With some other companies, however, important information is nowhere to be found; self-service support pages contain nothing but a rehash of the product's inadequate help files; and even if you can locate contact information, getting personalized support is about as easy as having your teeth pulled. Some other companies are easy to contact but often provide useless or incorrect information, and still others give you the runaround either because of incompetence or because they apparently hope you'll just go away. Fortunately, there are enough businesses that make good quality products and provide good or excellent support, that there is usually no need to buy from the bad ones.

TIP

When visiting a Web page, you'll almost always find assistance under the "Support" heading.

Some support is free of charge, especially under warranty, but some requires payment. Charges can be prohibitive. For example, one company charges $25 to troubleshoot an out-of-warranty inkjet printer, and there is no guarantee that the printer will work when you're done. With the cost of these printers so low today, you're usually better off buying a new printer, even if that means you've just wasted $60 on new ink cartridges. We discuss printer troubleshooting later in this chapter.

Knowledge Base Searches

The best way to search a knowledge base, and for that matter, the Internet, is to use few keywords to start with. Do not use "and," "or," "the," and so forth. If you get too many responses, you can narrow the search with exact phrases. (Here you can use the aforementioned small words.) If you get too few responses, or none at all, broaden the search with fewer keywords. Also realize that many sites' search engines don't work well. Sometimes you won't get anything no matter how you search.

To reach Microsoft's Knowledge Base, go to *support.microsoft.com* Advanced searches can be very helpful. Click Advanced Search in the upper left-hand corner. You'll have options such as specifying the Microsoft product, searching for any of the words, all of the words, or the exact phrase, among others. Despite the fact that Microsoft's Knowledge Base has literally hundreds of thousands of articles, there will still be situations in which you can't find what you're looking for.

Microsoft numbers its Knowledge Base articles with six-digit numbers. To search for a specific article, go to http://support.microsoft.com, *click the Knowledge Base Article ID Number Search link under the Search the Knowledge Base link, and enter the article number in the box. In case this page changes, you should be able to find instructions on the support page.*

Microsoft's Knowledge Base as well as other companies' knowledge bases are full of articles about hardware devices identified by brand and model number, or by chipsets, that have problems when used with certain versions of Windows or programs. If the problem could be related to hardware, it is a good idea to identify the device in the search dialog.

Searching for Error Messages

Perhaps the most important category of items to search for is the error message. Often, error messages are identified by numbers, but provide either cryptic descriptions or no descriptions at all. Therefore, the only way to find out what they mean is by searching the Internet or a particular site's knowledge base. Try searching on the manufacturer's Web site first, and try in different ways until you get a useful response. For example, if you get the message "Internal error 46," you could try searching for the full message text or just the number. You could also try searching for "error" or "error messages," and hopefully you'll get a list of error messages or a place to search for the specific message. Sometimes you won't find any information, but often you will. If you find nothing, search for the full text of the message on a search engine such as Google. It is usually helpful to use the search engine's advanced search function and select to search for the exact phrase. If you do, however, it is crucial not to make any typos; if you make even one typo, you might not get any hits.

To make it easier to copy the exact text of error messages, as long as the computer is booted to Windows and is still running, you can use the <Print Screen> key. This key does not print directly; see Chapter 9 for instructions on its use.

To search for Microsoft error messages, go to *support.microsoft.com*, click *Advanced Search and Help*, select the product, or select *All Microsoft products* if you're not sure, enter the message verbatim (unfortunately, you probably won't be able to copy and paste the message), select the exact phrase search type, and then click the arrow. Also follow these guidelines if you get a "blue screen of death," officially known as a stop error. For more information on stop errors, see Chapter 2.

Tips for Obtaining Personalized Assistance

It will be extremely helpful to follow these simple guidelines to get effective assistance.

- Before you seek assistance, write down everything you want to ask.
- Call the support desk if you can. Although fewer and fewer companies offer free telephone support, especially out of warranty, some companies still do. However, it is rarely a good idea to pay for telephone support because the rates are often between $35 and $200 per problem.
- Have access to the system when you call.
- Be polite. Whether or not you think support personnel know what they're talking about, let them think you think they do. They will be more willing to help and escalate problem to supervisors if necessary.
- Always provide as much information as possible, especially when e-mailing. For example, writing "My sound doesn't work" isn't particularly helpful. Identify your exact OS version, your hardware (such as computer or motherboard model number, processor speed, amount of memory, and model of hardware that pertains to your question), and any other piece of information you think might be pertinent. Also include information about what happened when the problem first occurred, what changes you made, if any, before the problem occurred, the steps you have taken to resolve the problem, and so forth. Many times, you'll have to fill out a Web form with this information. Even if the form asks for information that you're sure couldn't possibly pertain to your problem, answer these anyway, because leaving out the information will only delay the answer.
- Expect to answer questions you've already answered. Support personnel always seem to ask you for information that you provided earlier. Just tell them again. Don't make an issue about it; doing so will only delay assistance.

Information-Sharing Groups

These often take the form of *Usenet newsgroups*, or other similar forums on Web pages. Some, such as Microsoft's public newsgroups, are monitored by experts, and some aren't. There is no guarantee that anyone will respond to a particular post, and there is also no guarantee that information provided will be accurate or useful. Despite these limitations, however, you can often get the help you need from these groups.

There are many Web pages with articles and forums that are searchable from Web search pages such as Google (*google.com*). Frame your topic as succinctly as possible and click the Search button. Very often, you'll find some useful information.

 See the Industry Contacts document on the accompanying CD-ROM.

ON THE CD

BOOT FLOPPIES

When a computer can't boot, a boot floppy is often the only way to get access to the hard drive to troubleshoot and repair the system. Boot disks for 9x allow you only to get to DOS, but you'll have access to any FAT or FAT 32 hard drive on the system. Boot disks for XP/2000 can be used only to boot to Windows.

9x/DOS Boot Disks

When you install Windows 9x, you are prompted to create a boot floppy. If you don't have one, find a 9x computer that works and create one. With a blank floppy in the drive, go to Control Panel, Add/Remove Programs, and select Windows Setup tab. Then, click the boot disk tab. Follow the simple instructions for making a disk.

You can also make a disk using DOS, but it won't have all the features that a Windows boot disk has. For Windows 98SE and previous versions, you can format a floppy using the option to copy system files. Alternatively, from a DOS prompt you can use the command format a:/s. This is useful anytime you need a bootable floppy with extra room or more available memory.

You should have one for each version of 9x, but a different version's disk will often work in a pinch. The exception to this is that boot disks for 95 might not be able to access FAT 32 hard drives.

Although you will be able to start up any PC with a Windows 9x boot disk, you won't be able to access an NTFS-formatted hard drive partition. Therefore, unless you have a 2000 or XP computer with a FAT 16 or FAT 32 partition you need to access, a 9x boot disk isn't going to do you much good on these systems.

XP/2000 Boot Disks

Boot disks for XP and 2000 are different. There is no provision in 2000 or XP to create a boot disk. A boot disk will work only if Windows system files are intact. The most common reasons you might need to make a boot disk are if something happens to the MBR, or the disk configuration has been changed. In the latter situation, the problem is that one of the files, Boot.ini, points to the wrong partition for the boot files. In this case, you'll have to edit another boot.ini file to make the boot disk work, and then you'll need to edit the boot.ini file on the computer to correct the problem and enable Windows to boot normally. See the note after the tutorial for more information. You can make a boot disk on any XP or 2000 computer, or even a Windows NT 4.0 system. Tutorial 11.1 provides instructions for making an XP/2000 boot floppy.

TUTORIAL 11.1   **MAKING AN XP/2000 BOOT FLOPPY**

1. On any 2000, XP, or Windows NT 4.0 computer, format a floppy disk. Do this by inserting the disk, opening My Computer, right-clicking the floppy drive icon, and clicking Format from the menu that appears. Do not select the Quick Format check box.
2. Double-click to open the disk partition where the boot files are stored, the C: drive by default.
3. If hidden files aren't already showing, click the Tools menu and then Folder Options from the menu that appears. Click the View tab.
4. Look for and select the Show Hidden Files and Folders option button. In addition, make sure the "Hide protected operating system files (Recommended)" check box is cleared. It is also helpful to clear the "Hide file extensions for known file types" check box.
5. Locate the following files and copy them to the floppy disk: boot.ini, ntldr, and ntdetect.com. To copy the files, right-click each, click "Send to" from the menu that appears, and then 3-1/2 Floppy (A).

This boot disk will work only if the disk configuration of the computer you're making the boot disk on is the same as the computer you need to start; for example, if there is only one disk partition on each machine. If the disk configurations are different, you'll have to edit the boot.ini file in Notepad. That exercise is beyond the scope of this book. Search the Internet for editing boot.ini. A good selection of useful boot disk files can be found at bootdisk.com. *There is also a Web site,* http://www.nu2.nu/bootdisk/ntboot/index.php, *where you can copy or even download a boot.ini file that is purported to be all-purpose.*

BASIC REPAIRS THAT MIGHT HELP (AND COULDN'T HURT)

There are certain simple things to try with a malfunctioning computer that can save a great deal of time if they work:

- Check for power.
- Reboot (after removing the floppy).
- If the computer is locked up, you'll have to turn off the power, wait 30 seconds, and turn it back on. On ATX systems, which have a soft power switch, holding down the power button for at least four seconds will almost always shut the computer off.

- Boot from a boot floppy.
- Reinstall or roll back a device driver.
- Reseat expansion cards.
- Disconnect and reconnect connections.
- Clean adapter card contacts with a pencil eraser.
- Replace the power supply.
- Run ScanDisk and Defrag.
- Check Windows Device Manager.
- Check for a software patch or update, or update hardware's firmware.

DIAGNOSING SYSTEM CRASHES AND LOCKUPS

Virtually all PCs lock up at one time or another, 9x more than 2000 and XP. Also unpleasantly common is the "near lockup," in which the mouse pointer still moves, but nothing else works. If the mouse and keyboard are of the PS/2 variety, check to make sure they are connected to the correct ports and that no pins are bent. Make sure the heat sink and fan are properly mounted on the CPU. Check the air intake and other fans, and the operating temperature. Use a laser thermometer such as the Raytek to check the processor temperature, and/or a hard drive temperature-monitoring program such as SIGuardian (*siguardian.com*). Check the system resource use as discussed in Chapter 2. If there are too many programs running, close them and see if the system runs better. If it does, follow the instructions in Chapter 2 to resolve the problem. Also scan for viruses and malware. Run ScanDisk & Defrag. If Windows or applications have been recently upgraded, consider adding memory.

Shorted out parts can also cause lockups. If all other attempts fail, you can use a program such as Micro-Scope to diagnose the problem, or you might have to remove all expansion cards and then add one at a time until the computer locks up. Cables can also short, so check the cables and power supply. If you don't have a tester, you'll have to swap all the cables and power supply for known good units.

REMOTE TROUBLESHOOTING

You might find yourself in the position of having to troubleshoot a computer but traveling to it is impractical or impossible. Remote Desktop and Remote Assistance are two features that can make remote troubleshooting possible by actually placing another desktop on your own either through the Internet or a private network. PCAnywhere from *Symantec.com* is an excellent program for this purpose and is much more reliable than the Windows features. Another nice feature is that it can be configured to work from behind a firewall if one or both users have a router or firewall set up. Remote Desktop is a program that comes with XP. You can install it on other Windows computers by using the XP installation CD-ROM. When the main page appears, click Perform additional tasks, then Set up Remote Desktop connection, and follow the prompts.

Remote Assistance, which is basically the same, is available on Windows Messenger (XP only), or on NetMeeting (in any version with NetMeeting installed, type *conf* in the Run dialog). Search the Windows Help files for more information. NetMeeting, however, is often unreliable.

Some tips on troubleshooting:

- Any time troubleshooting becomes too time-consuming, or if the problem resists all efforts to solve it, it is best to back up the data, format the hard drive, reinstall Windows and the programs, and then restore the data.
- If you run a virus scan and find any Klez or Elkern viruses in the System and/or System32 folders, chances are the system is damaged beyond repair. Reinstall the system as described previously. However, Panda Software (*pandasoftware.com*) has repair utilities available that might help so the system can be repaired instead of redone.
- If you intend to format the hard drive and reinstall the system from scratch, and you don't have driver disks for all the hardware, it is a good idea to run an information-gathering utility that lists hardware, as discussed earlier in this chapter, and print a report. This way, if Windows doesn't recognize some of the installed hardware, you'll have a much easier time finding drivers.
- If you are upgrading Windows, instead of running the upgrade disc from within the previous version, it often is a better idea to back up the data, format the hard drive, and run a clean install from the upgrade disk. This is especially advisable if you're upgrading Windows Me. While installing Windows, you'll be prompted to insert the disk from the version of Windows that was previously installed on the computer. Make sure you have it handy.

TROUBLESHOOTING PRINTING PROBLEMS

Printing problems are very common, yet the fixes are usually not difficult. The main applet in Windows to configure a printer is called the Printers folder, except in XP where it's called "Printers and Faxes." Access the Printers folder by clicking it in My Computer, if it's there; in Start > Settings > Printers in most versions; in Control Panel in all versions; and in Start > Printers and Faxes in XP without the classic Start menu. You should see a folder containing an icon for each installed printer and fax program. Figure 11.3 shows a sample from Windows 2000.

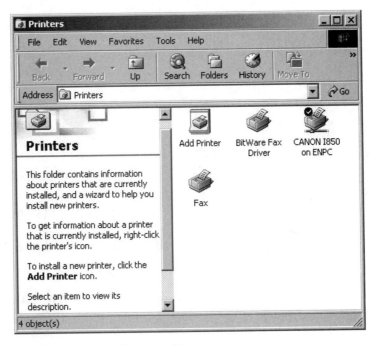

FIGURE 11.3   The Printers folder.

If you double-click the icon for a specific printer, you'll call up the print queue for that printer. A *print queue* is a queue of all documents waiting to be printed by that printer. Figure 11.4 shows a sample print queue.

The Printer and Document menus contain some useful commands, notably Pause Printing and Cancel All Documents in the Printer menu, and Pause, Resume, Restart, and Cancel in the Document menu. To use the Document menu commands, you must highlight the document in the print queue.

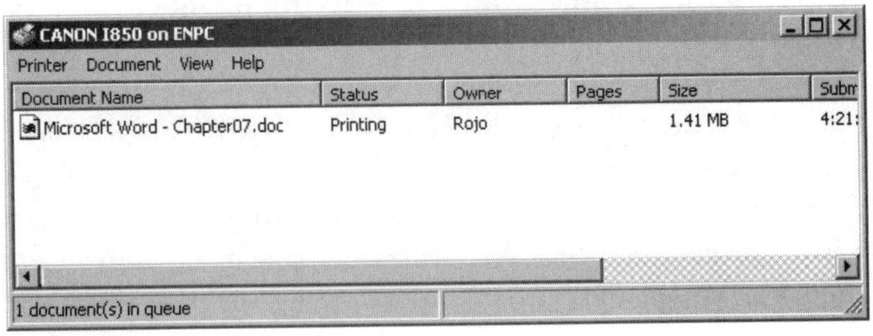

FIGURE 11.4   A print queue.

On 9x, attempts to pause or cancel printing usually take a long time to work, and are not worthwhile to use unless the document has many pages to go. If you try this and it says Deleting *in the Status column, but nothing changes, you'll just have to wait for it. Don't turn off the power to the printer; you'll just cause more problems.*

The other important location is Printer Properties, accessible by clicking the Properties command in the print queue's Printer menu, or by right-clicking the printer icon in the Printers folder and clicking Properties from the menu that appears. Use the Print Test Page button for a good test as to whether the printer is working. Other pages in the printer's properties vary based on the specific model of printer installed.

Here are some useful things to check if you are having printer problems:

- Make sure the printer is connected to power and turned on.
- If any error messages appear, and they are not obviously correct, search for them on the Internet.
- Reinstall the printer driver (see Tutorial 2.2). This is especially applicable if the computer prints nonsense characters and won't stop, or if the printer won't do anything.
- Check the cable. If it is a parallel cable, make sure it is IEEE 1284 compliant and that the pins are intact. The symptoms of a bad cable are often the same as those of a corrupted driver.
- Perhaps the problem is in the printer. Try installing another one. If that works, try installing the non-functioning printer in another computer. If it works, then the problem might be the printer driver.

Sometimes, a problem with another driver on the system causes the printer not to work. This seems to happen occasionally when USB devices are installed on certain laptops. Check to see if any new hardware devices have been installed. Try uninstalling the drivers of the new device and then attempting to print. Make sure that any program that is part of the new hardware is uninstalled, or at least not running. If printing resumes, you'll have to troubleshoot the problem related to the new hardware.

Printer inkjet cartridges should be replaced only if the printing becomes faint, if colors are missing, or the printer software reports low ink. Consider carefully whether you want to replace ink cartridges in old printers to get them to work. If the printer still doesn't work and you decide on a new one, you won't be able to return the open cartridges.

ACCESS DENIED (2000 AND XP ONLY)

If you are logged on to 2000 or XP with an administrator account (which should allow you to perform any task), but Windows prevents you from doing something that you ought to be able to do, or you need to configure the computer to allow another user to do something, the places to look are in the Group Policy Editor and Local Security Policy consoles (which are not available in XP Home), in addition to the security settings for users, groups, folders, and files. It often requires entire books or courses for users to learn these tools completely, but you should be able to view these and make basic changes without all that studying. Search the help files for these items, or consult an appropriate *Microsoft Certified Systems Engineer* (*MCSE*) certification book.

To open the Group Policy Editor, type gpedit.msc in the Run dialog. Access the Local Security Policy console from Administrative Tools in Control Panel.

If there is nothing in either local policy or group policy prohibiting an activity but the activity is still being prevented, you might have to consult Microsoft support. For example, after one laptop was upgraded from 98 to 2000, even the administrator was prevented from creating new Internet connections. None of the policies prevented this, but some arcane setting in the registry that only a Microsoft support technician could find, did.

THE WINDOWS REGISTRY

The *registry* is a database that stores every changeable piece of information related to Windows, including hardware and software configuration. In 9x, it is stored in two files, system.dat and user.dat. In 2000 and XP, the registry is stored in a series of files. Every change that a user or a program makes is stored in the registry. For this reason, the registry is delicate. Make one wrong move and your computer can become unbootable. Microsoft warns you over and over again that they bear no responsibility for a registry-editing mistake, even if they tell you what changes to make. They insist that every change can be made in a safer place, such as Control Panel. This is absolutely not true. If you search Microsoft's Web site for solutions to problems, you'll find that often, the registry is the only place to make certain changes and to correct certain problems. If the registry never needed to be modified directly, Microsoft wouldn't provide a registry editor with every installation, which, of course, they do.

Backing Up the Registry

It is highly advisable to back up the registry before editing so that incorrect changes can be undone. The registry is automatically backed up every time the system is booted, but you can't always depend on this being successful. Instructions are provided here and later in this chapter. It is possible to back up portions or the entire registry.

Windows 9x Registry Backups

There are a few different ways to back up the registry in 9x. One way starts with booting into DOS. You might recall that you can do this in 95/98 by selecting to re-boot into DOS in the shutdown menu. You can also use a boot floppy (this is the only way to do this in Me). The same procedure can also be done by booting into Safe Mode, Command Prompt Only, which you do by pressing F8 at the beginning of booting and making the appropriate selection. Once you get a command prompt, navigate to the Windows folder if you're not already there. (If you get a C:\> prompt, type "CD Windows" and then press <Enter>. If you get an A:\> prompt, type C:, press <Enter>, and then type "CD Windows" and then press <Enter> again.) Once you have reached the C:\>WINDOWS prompt, type the following, pressing <Enter> after each line:

```
attrib -r -h -s system.dat
attrib -r -h -s user.dat
copy system.dat *bu
copy user.dat *.bu
```

Then, restart the computer. See Appendix C, "Command-Line Tutorial," for a tutorial on using commands in MS-DOS. The attrib command changes the attributes of the file. The minus sign turns off each attribute; *r* represents the read only attribute; *h*, the hidden; and *s* means system. This is necessary in order to do anything with these files. The copy command is self-explanatory—these commands are making copies of the two files and naming them System.bu and User.bu.

Windows names the automatically backed up registry files System.da0 and User.da0. These final characters are zeros.

To restore these backups, get to the C:\>WINDOWS prompt as described in the backup instructions and type the following, again pressing <Enter> at the end of each line:

```
attrib -r -h -s system.dat
attrib -r -h -s system.da0
attrib -r -s -h user.dat
attrib -r -s -h user.da0
ren system.dat system.daa
ren system.da0 system.da1
ren user.dat user.daa
ren user.da0 user.da1
```

```
copy system.bu system.dat
copy user.bu user.dat
```

Then, restart the computer (*ren* is the rename command). If you need to restore the automatic backup in 95 (it *should* be handled automatically by 98 and Me), type the following, pressing <Enter> after each line:

```
attrib -h -r -s system.dat
attrib -h -r -s system.da0
attrib -h -r -s user.dat
attrib -h -r -s user.da0
copy system.da0 system.dat
copy user.da0 user.dat
```

Then, restart the computer.

There are utilities you can use to back up the registry. On the Windows 95 installation disc is a utility called ERU in the Other\Misc\ERU folder. Run the program from the CD-ROM and follow the prompts. For more information, search the Microsoft Knowledge Base for Article 139437 entitled *Windows 95 Emergency Recovery Utility.*

Windows 98 and Me have a utility called the Registry Checker. This is actually a combination of two program files. Scanreg.exe runs only in DOS, while Scanregw.exe runs in both DOS and Windows. Registry Checker runs automatically and, if it discovers no registry problems, makes a new backup of the registry every day in which the computer is successfully booted. If it finds problems, it will attempt to restore the backup automatically, and if that proves unsuccessful, Registry Checker will attempt to repair the registry. You can run scanregw in either the Run dialog or from a command prompt. For more information on Registry Checker and other information about the 9x registry, search the Microsoft Knowledge Base for "Chapter 31 - Windows 98 Registry."

Instructions on backing up and restoring the entire registry in 2000 and XP appear later in this chapter. Because backing up portions of the registry is done with the registry editor, we'll discuss partial backups with the editor next.

The Registry Editor: Regedit.exe (All Versions)

Regedit is available only by typing regedit in the Run dialog or at a Windows command prompt. Open the editor and take a look. You'll see that the registry has five keys: *HKEY_CLASSES_ROOT, HKEY_CURRENT_USER, HKEY_LOCAL_MACHINE, HKEY_USERS, and HKEY_CURRENT_CONFIG,* shown in Figure 11.5.

A *key* is like a *root folder* in Windows. It is the highest item in the hierarchy. Click the plus sign next to any of the keys and the next level of the hierarchy becomes visible (see Figure 11.5). These are called *subkeys,* just as folders inside other folders are

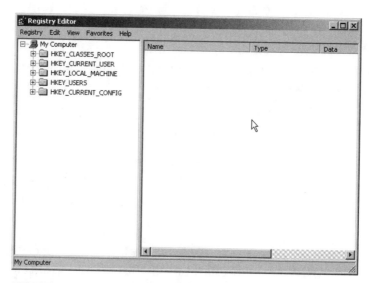

FIGURE 11.5.   The registry has five keys.

called subfolders. The last subkeys in the hierarchy have values (called *Name* in the editor), and some of the values have data, as you can see in Figure 11.6. The other column, labeled *Type*, refers to the type of data (REG_SZ,REG_DWORD, etc.). Data types aren't important for this discussion. Now, look at the bottom of Figure 11.6. This displays the full path to the last subkey you are on.

Editing the registry is very similar to editing any text document. The Edit menu contains straightforward commands, as shown in Figure 11.7. Especially helpful are

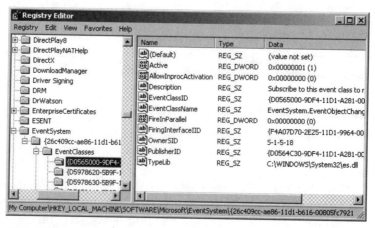

FIGURE 11.6   Keys, values, and data.

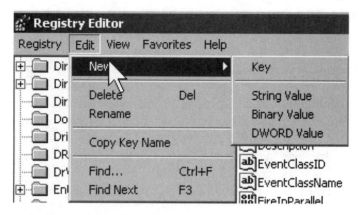

FIGURE 11.7 Regedit's Edit menu.

the Find and Find Next commands. In addition, the basic keyboard shortcuts such as <Ctrl> + <C> for copying the selected item work in the registry. For more information, search for "keyboard shortcuts" in Windows Help.

Backing Up and Restoring Registry Keys

Regedit's File menu has two commands for backing up and restoring keys and subkeys. These are the Import Registry File and Export Registry File commands. With a key selected, click the Export command. You can then give the file a name and save it anywhere on the system. Make sure to keep a record of the file's name and location. If you need to restore the file, click the Import command and browse for the file, and click Open when you find it. These commands also give you the opportunity to back up and save the entire registry by selecting the All option button at the bottom of the Export dialog box.

TIP

Unless and until you become experienced with editing the registry, it is recommended to limit editing to exact instructions by Microsoft support personnel and documents.

If you do make a serious mistake editing the registry in 2000 or XP, and you have not backed it up first, you can still restore the registry using the Last Known Good boot option, discussed later in this chapter.

Windows 2000 also has a registry editor called Regedt32.exe (type regedt32 *at the Run dialog or command prompt). This looks much like the Sysedit.exe program covered in Chapter 2. It has some important capabilities that regedit doesn't have, although it lacks a Find command. Microsoft recommends using Regedt32 for editing in Windows 2000. For more information on Regedt32, search Windows 2000 Help or the Microsoft Knowledge Base.*

WINDOWS REPAIR UTILITIES AND PROCEDURES

Windows comes with various programs and procedures to troubleshoot and repair problems. Some of these can be used at will, but others require a backup of one type or another to have been performed first. Now, if you are a technician who maintains computers, or if you maintain your own personal computers and their continued performance is important, you should perform regular backups. If you work in a repair shop, chances are very good that your customers didn't back up the OS before bringing the machine to you, although some make copies of their important user data. If they knew how to perform these OS backups, they would most likely know how to restore the OS themselves. Given that advice, you'll be able to determine which of the following procedures are most useful to you.

Safe Mode Boot (All Versions)

In the event that Windows is loading some program or device driver that is causing a problem, you can boot into Safe Mode (the system might force you to) and try to fix the problem. Safe Mode loads only essential drivers and programs. You won't be able to print, get on a network, hear sounds other than beeps, and so forth, but you will be able to make changes in Device Manager, .ini files, and other places. Press F8 as early in the boot process as possible to boot into Safe Mode.

System File Checker (98, 2000, and XP Only)

Microsoft developed this utility for Windows 98, put a different version in 2000 and XP, but inexplicably left it out of Windows Me. System File Checker scans the system files for corruption or unauthorized replacement by rogue programs, and retrieves a correct version from either a special system folder or the Windows installation CD-ROM.

System File Checker (SFC) in Windows 98

In the Run dialog from the Start menu, type "SFC." This invokes the program, as shown in Figure 11.8.

You can go into settings by clicking the button, but the default settings are generally the best. You'll want to be prompted to replace each corrupted file so that if the problem appears to be solved, you'll be able to tie the problem to the corruption. Figure 11.9 shows such a prompt.

It is a good idea to run SFC every time you install Windows 98, and any time you have a problem that is not easily corrected. One new Windows 98 computer had a sound problem. The sound either sounded terrible or it didn't work at all. Replacing the sound driver didn't help, but a run of SFC found nine corrupted files. Replacing these files solved the problem permanently.

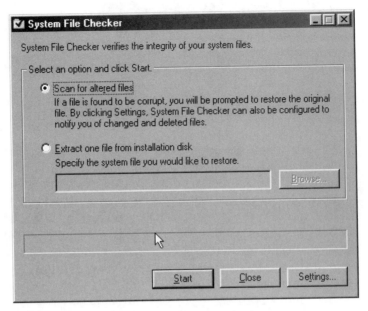

FIGURE 11.8 Windows 98 System File Checker.

In most installations of 98 (and 95 and Me, as well), there is a system folder whose default path is C:\Windows\Options\Cabs. These contain all of Windows' installation files in a highly compressed state. You might need to navigate to this folder using the Browse button to help SFC find the files to restore. If this folder doesn't exist, you'll have to browse to the Windows 98 folder on the Windows installation CD-ROM.

When SFC finds a corrupted file and prompts you to replace it, you will be prompted to make a backup of the original system file. Write down the location where SFC is going to place the backup of the file. You should also limit your folder names to eight characters or fewer here so you can find them in DOS in the event that you must restore the file in a no-boot situation. We suggest you accept the default path offered by SFC to keep things consistent.

Extraction of System Files (98 and Me)

Windows Me does have one of the functions of SFC: system file extraction. When you suspect that a particular system file is the cause of a problem, you can use Msconfig in Windows Me to extract the file. When you first open Msconfig (see Chapter 2) you will see the Extract File button near the lower right-hand corner of the window. By clicking here, you can follow the dialog boxes just as you would in

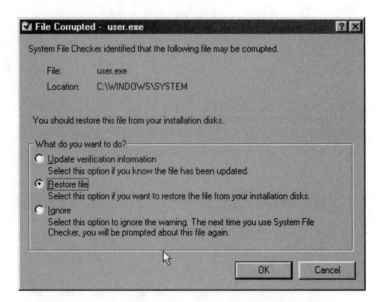

FIGURE 11.9   SFC prompts you to restore the corrupted file.

Windows 98 SFC. Be sure to make a backup and write down the location of the files just in case the system is unable to boot after you attempt to restart the system.

You can use SFC in Windows 98 without running the file check portion of the program if you know ahead of time just what file you need to replace. You might know this because of a message at boot, or if you get a dialog box or error message when Windows starts indicating that a particular file is not found or is corrupted. Or, you might have been told by a support representative from a component manufacturer to replace a particular file. If this is the case, do so and follow the same steps as you would if you had run SFC and it had found a corrupt file.

Windows 2000 and XP System File Checker

SFC in these versions is a command-line program. It is much less likely to be needed in these systems as compared to 98. Open a command prompt and type SFC. This will give you the list of command switches shown in Figure 11.10.

Let's say you want to run it now. At the following prompt, type the following:

```
SFC /scannow
```

If you are prompted for the installation CD-ROM, insert it. Then, wait for SFC to work.

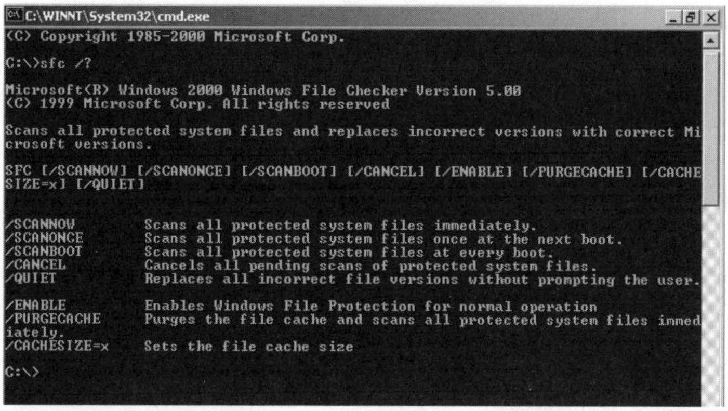

FIGURE 11.10 2000/XP SFC command switches.

Last Known Good Configuration (2000 and XP only)

Each time Windows 2000 and XP boots successfully, it stores a profile of the system in a system folder. If a computer won't boot or develops a serious problem after a change has been made, the next time you attempt to boot, press <F8> and select *Last Known Good Configuration (LKG)*. If the problem was caused by a change made since the last successful boot, LKG will undo it, along with all other changes made since then.

Any time the computer boots successfully, the LKG is reset to the system's current configuration. If you experience a problem after a change, try not to boot the computer again before you invoke LKG. In case the computer boots successfully but the problem is still not solved, the new LKG will include the problem, causing LKG to cease being an effective tool for that problem.

Windows 9x Registry Repairs

See the Windows 9x Registry section, earlier in this chapter.

Emergency Repair Process (2000 Only)

This process can be especially helpful if you can't boot your computer, as long as your hard drive hasn't failed, in which case the repair process is useless. It is much more useful if you have a very recent *Emergency Repair Disk (ERD)* made on the computer in question. Chances are excellent that if you are fixing someone else's computer, you will not have such a recent ERD to use. If you start the Windows

Backup program (Start > Programs > Accessories > System Tools > Backup, or by typing "ntbackup" in the Run dialog), and you start in the Welcome screen, you'll see an option for making an ERD. Simply follow the prompts.

To repair the system using the ERD, you'll have to boot either from the four Windows 2000 installation floppies, or from the installation CD-ROM. It is easier to boot from the CD-ROM, as long as the computer supports it. You might have to go into the BIOS to move CD-ROM up in the boot order. If you cannot boot from the CD-ROM and you don't have the installation floppies, you'll have to create the floppies from the CD-ROM. Tutorial 11.2 tells you how.

TUTORIAL 11.2   **CREATING 2000 SETUP BOOT FLOPPIES FROM THE CD-ROM**

1. Obtain four floppy disks and label each "Windows 2000 Setup Boot Disk." Number them from 1 through 4.
2. Insert the Windows 2000 installation CD-ROM in any Windows computer.
3. The disc will probably start up automatically. If it does, close it. Go to My Computer, right-click the disc, and click Explore from the menu that appears. A Windows Explorer window should appear.
4. Locate and open the Bootdisk folder, usually by double-clicking.
5. If the computer you're using is Windows 9x, run (usually by double-clicking) the MAKEBOOT program. If you are on 2000 or XP, run the MAKEBT32.exe program.
6. Follow the prompts.

Setup boot floppies do not exist for XP.

To use the ERD, boot the computer using either the CD-ROM or the floppies. Go through Setup as if you are installing Windows 2000. Eventually, you'll get to a prompt to set up or repair Windows. Choose R to repair, and follow the prompts, which will include one to insert the ERD. You will be prompted to select manual or fast repair. Manual repair gives you three options:

- **Inspect Startup Environment:** This applies only if the system is a *dual-*or *multiple-boot* system, meaning that you get a choice of different OSs when you boot the computer.
- **Verify Windows 2000 System Files:** Inspects files needed for Windows to boot and run and replaces them if necessary.
- **Inspect Boot Sector:** Inspects and repairs boot sector problems.

Manual repair doesn't give the option to repair the registry, but fast repair does.

Fast repair automatically performs all repair functions, including checking the registry for corruption. If it does find registry corruption, it copies portions from the %systemroot%\Repair\Regback folder (assuming that folder is accessible), where the system keeps the backup registry (*%systemroot%* refers to the main system folder, be it Winnt\System32, or Windows\System32). This registry backup is made automatically when the ERD is made.

If you don't have an ERD, instead of choosing to repair the system, choose to set up Windows. Follow the prompts and you will soon get another prompt to set up or repair. At this point, choose R to repair the system. This will reinstall Windows over the existing installation, hopefully fixing the problems in the process. Have the product key ready in the event you are prompted for it. Most existing settings, and all non-OS files should remain intact.

Reinstalling Windows 9x Over an Existing Installation

In the discussion about system file checker, we referred to the folder C:\Windows\Options\Cabs (C:\Windows\Options\Install in Me), which is present in most 9x installations. This folder has another purpose. If you are unable to fix a problem with 9x, navigate to it and locate Setup.exe. Note that the default setting for Windows is not to show known file extensions. You can change this setting by going to Tools > Folder Options in any Windows folder, clicking the View tab, and clearing the Hide extensions for known file types check box. If you don't want to change the setting, look for the word *Setup* followed by an icon that has a picture of a computer with an open box of disks in front of it (see Figure 11.11).

FIGURE 11.11   C:\Windows\Options\Cabs\Setup.exe from Windows 98.

It is important to know whether the system you are working on was ever upgraded from an earlier version of Windows. If that were the case, then the setup files found in the C:\Windows\Options\Cabs folder might attempt to install an older version of Windows and cause the installation to fail.

Once you have found Setup.exe, run it (usually by double-clicking) and follow the prompts. You might need to input the product key and other information, so have it ready. It can take anywhere from about 20 minutes to sometimes well over an hour to install Windows depending on the performance of the system. When you are finished, your settings and non-OS files should be intact.

Make sure the Windows CD-ROM that you use to reinstall windows is exactly the same version as what is installed in the system. Otherwise, you might get errors or Windows might not allow the installation to continue.

If your system doesn't have a Cabs or Install folder, you can still reinstall Windows from the installation disc. Insert the disc and follow the prompts to install, or open the disc in My Computer and run Setup.exe. When you are prompted to select the folder directory for the installation, selecting the original, usually C:\Windows, will install Windows over the old version, leaving all your settings intact. If you select a different directory, assuming you have enough disk space, you will cause the original Windows installation to be unusable, and your settings will not be kept. Then, you can delete the folder that contains the original installation.

It is a very good idea to back up important data files before reinstalling Windows, even when you use procedures that normally leave your files intact.

If reinstalling the system doesn't solve the problem, you might need to back up the data and downloaded program installation files (not actual program files), format the hard drive, reinstall Windows from scratch, reinstall the programs, and restore the data. If you get to a situation in which diagnosing and correcting problems will take an extraordinary amount of time, or when a computer has significant virus infection, this is usually your best bet. Just make certain not to restore any virus-infected data.

System Restore (Me and XP Only)

System Restore allows you to undo system changes made since the last restore point was created. A *restore point* is a point at which all of Windows' settings are recorded. Multiple restore points can be stored simultaneously. If System Restore is enabled, Windows sets restore points daily and when certain changes are made to the system. The user can also set restore points manually; it is a good idea to do this before installing new hardware or software, or making other significant changes. You would use System Restore to undo changes that you suspect caused problems. This can cause other problems. For example, if you restore to a point before a new program was installed, the program will probably not work correctly or at all afterward, even though all the program's files would be left intact. This is because System Restore removed all the registry entries related to the program. Of course, the new program might have been causing the problem you are using System Restore to fix. The best thing about System Restore is that you can undo a restore. The worst thing about it is that the folder System Restore uses to store the restore point data, entitled "_Restore," can be a receptacle for viruses. The folder is hidden by default, and it is very difficult to delete an individual file in this folder. It is for this reason that some users disable System Restore. See Chapter 2 for advice on deleting infected files from the _Restore folder.

Enabling/Disabling and Accessing System Restore

System Restore is enabled by default. To enable or disable it in Me, go to System Properties (right-click My Computer and select Properties or open the System applet in Control Panel), click the Performance tab, the File System button, and then the Advanced tab, and select or clear the Enable System Restore check box. In XP, go to System Properties and click the System Restore tab. Select or clear the check box. You can also use the slider on this page to set the maximum size of the _Restore folder on this page. Leave it at its maximum setting unless disk space is an issue.

   To access System Restore, go to Start > Programs (or All Programs) > Accessories > System Tools > System Restore. From here, you can set a restore point, restore the system, or undo a restore.

Recovery Console (2000 and XP Only)

The Recovery Console is a command-based system, similar to DOS, but has fewer commands. You can use it to access only the root folder, the Winnt or Windows folder, the Cmdcons folder, and removable media sources such as floppies or CD-ROMs. The Recovery Console is good for replacing missing files, stopping or starting services, formatting drives, and other tasks.

   There are two ways to run the Recovery Console.

   A. **Run Recovery Console from the Windows Installation CD-ROM:** Boot the computer from the Windows installation CD-ROM, or the 2000 setup boot floppies. At the "Welcome to Setup" screen, press <F10> or type <R>. In XP, you can start the console. In 2000, you'll have to type <C>. Make sure to have the administrator password handy (if one exists).

B. **Install Recovery Console so that it becomes a choice of OSs available at boot:** Insert the Windows Installation CD in the drive, click Start > Run, and type the following in the box (Substitute the CD-ROM drive letter for D if applicable):

```
D:\i386\winnt32.exe /cmdcons
```

Click OK, and then follow the prompts. Chances are good that installation will fail, but you'll be given a prompt to try it again. Do so, and it will probably work the second time. Reboot the computer and select the number for Recovery Console from the list of OSs.

Once you have started the Recovery Console, you'll be prompted to select the OS to which you want to boot, assuming you have a dual- or multi-boot system, and then you'll be prompted for the administrator password.

Using the Recovery Console

For a helpful tutorial on using Recovery Console commands, see the Recovery Console Commands section in Appendix C, "Command-Line Tutorial." You can also type HELP at the prompt and then press <Enter> for a complete list of commands. You can enter any individual command followed by a space and /? (such as DISABLE /?) to view a brief explanation plus the command's syntax and parameters. Additional helpful information is available in Windows' Help (search for Recovery Console Commands), and on the Microsoft Knowledge Base. The article numbers are 229716 for 2000 and 314058 for XP.

Restoration of System State Data (2000 and XP Only)

System state data consists of the registry files and many OS files. A recent System State data backup on a Windows 2000 machine created a 241MB file. Back up System State data by using Windows Backup (Start > Run > ntbackup, or Start > Programs (or All Programs) > Accessories > System Tools > Backup). If you use the Backup Wizard, you have the option of backing up the entire or parts of the system, or only the System State data.

Windows XP Home Edition does not have the Backup program; however, if you have a retail or OEM copy of XP Home (not a brand name recovery disk), you can install Backup from the disc. Navigate to the VALUEADD\MSFT\NTBACKUP folder on the CD-ROM and double-click the Ntbackup.msi file on the disc to install Backup.

If there is a recent backup of System State data, restoring it is the next step to take if using the ERD fails. If Windows is still running, open Backup and follow the instructions to restore the System State data. If not, you'll have to reinstall Windows, perhaps on a new hard drive, and then perform the restore.

Automated System Restore (XP Professional Only)

Automated System Restore (ASR) is XP Pro's system for backing up the entire OS, including the System State data. It is done through the Backup program, covered earlier.

If Backup is installed on XP Home Edition as described in the previous note, ASR appears to be available. However, it won't work.

The ASR Wizard recreates every disk partition on which there are Windows OS components. For this reason, ASR will back up user data on those partitions, even though Microsoft insists that ASR won't back up user data. In a system with one disk partition and XP Pro, ASR should be a valid method for backing up and restoring the entire computer. However, because of Microsoft's warnings, you will probably want to back up user data separately.

The ASR Wizard also creates a floppy that is needed for an ASR restore. An ASR backup includes System State data. Microsoft considers an ASR a last resort.

To create a backup for an ASR, open Backup as described earlier, make sure to be in the Advanced mode, not the Wizard mode, and select the ASR option button. You will need one blank floppy and media for the backup.

ASR Restore

To restore from an ASR backup, boot from an XP Pro CD-ROM as described in the section on the Emergency Repair procedure. When prompted, press <F2> to start the restore process, and follow the prompts. You will be prompted to insert the floppy made during the ASR backup, and the backup media.

Backup of All Information on the Computer (XP Pro Only)

If you run Backup in Wizard Mode and run through the wizard, there is a choice to back up "All information on this computer." This is actually a combination of ASR and a full data backup. Just follow the prompts in the wizard. Restore by running Setup from the Windows XP disc and following the prompts to do a restore.

Neither the "All information on this computer" nor the ASR backup will work on XP Home. To accomplish a backup and recovery in XP Home, you'll have to install Backup from the Windows disk and do a regular full backup. Then, you'll have to reinstall Windows anew and then restore the backup.

RESCUING A WET LAPTOP

It is unfortunately common for liquid to be spilled on laptops. Rescuing such a laptop is a dicey proposition. Success depends on a number of factors, such as the type and quantity of liquid spilled, the steps taken after the spill, and how fast those steps were taken. The proper steps to take are immediately disconnecting the power, removing the battery, and turning the machine over. Never try to power on the machine until it has been serviced—doing so will almost guarantee that the computer will be ruined.

To rescue the laptop, disassemble it. There are some instructions for doing this in Chapter 9, but because there is such variation in laptops, you'll probably want to consult the manufacturer's Web page for instructions. You'll find that some manufacturers provide better instructions than others do. IBM and Dell tend to provide detailed disassembly/reassembly instructions. Soak up any remaining liquid with an absorbent material such as paper towels, hold the computer at an angle, and spray liberally with an electronic contact cleaner that is safe for plastics, such as Blow Off Contact Cleaner (*blowoff.com*). Spray every nook and cranny in the machine except inside disk drives. Allow the unit to dry, and then reassemble. Then, reconnect power and attempt to boot. If it doesn't work, it is probably wise to give up, although you should try to connect the hard drive to another machine to back up the data (see Chapter 6, "Magnetic Disk Drives," for more information).

A FINAL COMMENT

Sometimes, all the hardware can be in working order and all the software configured correctly, yet something still doesn't work correctly. It is as if you've fixed everything but Windows doesn't quite realize it. Occasionally in these cases, the problem might go away spontaneously. The point here is that despite all the advancements, computers are still far from perfect. As we said earlier, if diagnosing and fixing a problem is taking more time than it's worth, it is usually best to back up the user data, format the hard drive, and start over again.

12 Things *Not* to Do with a Computer

Many of us have heard of how the PC user called in to say his cup holder was not working on his computer only to find out he was referring to his CD drive. Well, that's obviously a silly thing to do, but following are some less obvious but also not-so-wise things to do with your computer.

The switch on the back of the power supply that says *115/230* is not to be used to see if there is a problem with the power by switching it back and forth.

No matter how much you think you know, make it a rule never to plug in a new USB device until you read the manual. In most cases, the software has to be installed first or in a specific manner, and by skipping the proper steps, you might waste a lot of time trying to get the device to work correctly.

We are constantly getting laptop computers in the shop for repair due to all types of liquids spilling on the keyboard that were kept right next to it. Unlike a desktop computer where the keyboard is a separate and usually inexpensive peripheral, the notebook keyboard is directly over the circuitry of the computer, and the liquid will wick its way into every crevice and corrode and short out the system. Don't do as the user in Figure 12.1; keep your drinks and food away from electronics.

Speaking of spilling liquids on the laptop, customers often turn on their laptops after only wiping the outside of it right after the spill. Basic science tells us that will only ensure more, and most likely permanent and possibly fatal, damage. We try to tell all of our customers that if a spill ever occurs to immediately remove the battery, unplug the laptop, turn it upside down to minimize migration of the liquid into the components, and bring it to a qualified technician right away to be cleaned out. Never let your curiosity force you to turn it back on.

FIGURE 12.1 Don't try this at home.

A customer recently walked into the shop and asked if we could test his Pentium 4 processor. When asked if he had it with him, he retrieved it from his pocket and held it up proudly by the corners. It might have been working before he brought it in, but its chances started decreasing when he handled it that way. *Do not ever* handle a static-sensitive component (processors, memory, add-in cards, etc.) with your bare hands unless you are wearing a wrist strap and using precautions to ground yourself and prevent static discharge.

Another customer brought in his server because it was dead. We checked it out and discovered a 1/4-inch gap between the processor and its heat sink. We removed the heat sink and found globs of thermal transfer compound—so much that the heat sink didn't make good contact with the processor—and there was a thermal pad as well. Now, the ironic thing is that this customer is obsessed with cooling. There were two fans on the processor and various case fans. However, his failure to follow directions (see Chapter 3, "Motherboards and Their Components") caused his CPU to overheat and fail. The rule: use either a thermal pad or a small amount of thermal transfer compound, and make sure that the heat sink is flush against the processor.

One time a customer called and frantically explained that his video disappeared, and he needed his computer for business right away. He was willing to buy a new monitor. We told him to bring in his computer and monitor. When we checked out the monitor, we found that the brightness had been turned all the way down. The lesson here is to always check the simplest, most obvious things first.

Often, when a PC comes in to the shop it has loose wires hanging inside even though the original system builder took the time to tie the wires. The problem was that they used rubber bands, and the rubber bands had rotted away from age and the heat within a computer. Another thing we have seen is shorted wiring from twist ties. When the paper on a twist ties dries up and goes away, all that is left is a thin metal wire that can wear through insulation and short out connections. When you tie up all the wires inside your computer to make them look neat and to help increase the airflow for cooling, use nylon zip ties or nylon wire restraints and clips designed for the purpose. They are easier to work with and will last much longer.

Up in the cooler climates, we occasionally have PCs come in for freeze-ups or damage that cannot be immediately explained, until we find out that the computer is kept right next to a radiator or heating vent.

One of the frequent cause of problems in PCs we see is viruses. Most name brand computers come with some form of virus protection. Usually, it is good for one year or is a three-month trial version. When we ask the customers if they have virus protection, they say yes. When we ask them if it is up to date, they usually assume that you install it and forget it and you are protected forever. After they get the bill to clean out the virus and save the data on the computer, they rarely forget to stay up to date.

On that note, many people out there cannot believe they got a virus because they do not open attachments or open e-mails only from people they know. They forget or do not know that the virus can come from an e-mail sent from their friend's or family member's PC without their knowledge. Additionally, viruses can come over the Web, even if there is no browser open. In fact, my virus detection software detected and cleaned a virus while I was researching links on a Web site while writing this chapter.

Another less technical but important issue is the choice of cabinets for computers. While many computers are getting smaller all the time, we constantly see customers choosing a computer desk or cabinet that does not fit the case. I recently installed a pair of computer systems at a home and the new furniture had arrived and was installed. The so-called computer desks looked great, but the first thing I noticed was that the shelf for the PC had a door and only one small hole for the cables in the back. There was no consideration of ventilation, or cabling, and you had to open the door just to insert a CD, DVD, or floppy disk. Things worked out after I opened the backs and installed small bumpers on the doors so they would allow some ventilation. Often, the problem is size, and there is no room for the computer once it is in place with all the cables attached. It sometimes seems as if the designers of computer office furniture forget that they have to accommodate machines with cables attached and the need for ventilation.

Many times, I have been called upon to work with a small business that has two or more PCs they purchased at a big box store or online, and now they want to be able to take advantage of networking or need a server to accommodate their needs and growth. The assumption of many of these customers is that a computer is a computer, and one for home is the same as one for business, and the only difference is the work they are doing on them. That cannot be further from the truth. The difference between a professional versus home version of Windows when purchasing a new PC is usually $60 to $90 dollars versus approximately $180 dollars to upgrade later. Most home PCs come with a home suite of programs to keep the cost of the PC lower and more attractive to the buyers. However, Microsoft Office Professional or a similar office suite at the time of purchase will cost you about $300 now, or you can buy the full product later for about $600. The point here is that consulting an expert first will probably save you time and money in the long term.

A Practical Glossary

95   Microsoft Windows 95.

98   Microsoft Windows 98. Includes both the original and second editions unless otherwise noted.

98SE   Microsoft Windows 98 Second Edition.

2000   Microsoft Windows 2000 Professional.

%systemroot%   The Windows\System folder in 9x, and the Winnt\System32 folder or Windows\System32 folder in 2000 and XP. The actual folder used can vary. The percent marks indicate that the term is a variable.

AGP   The most common internal standard (as of this writing) for computer video. Uses SVGA connectors for monitors.

algorithm   A mathematical formula designed to solve a problem by accounting for expected occurrences.

applet   A small program within Windows that is used to configure certain aspects of hardware and software. The items in Control Panel are called applets—literally, "small applications."

application   A computer program.

AT   A discontinued form factor of case, motherboard, and power supply.

ATX   ATX and its variations are the most commonly used form factors of case, motherboard, and power supply as of this writing. Variations include MicroATX and others.

ATAPI   ATA Packet Interface. The standard for IDE optical drives.

base video   The minimum video Windows displays, usually 640x480 resolution with 16 colors. A PC can provide base video without any of the video drivers being loaded into memory, such as early in the boot process.

beta   Early version of a program that is not ready to be sold. Users often can obtain a free beta version of a program to test its performance and report bugs to the developer.

BIOS   Basic Input Output System. A program that works as soon as the computer is powered on to test hardware, locate the operating system (OS) startup files on the hard drive in order to start the OS, and support the transfer of data among hardware devices. The BIOS is usually stored on a *CMOS* (Complementary Metal Oxide Semiconductor) flash memory chip.

bitmap   A format of an image file that stores a map of each pixel along with the color information for each. Because of all this stored information, the files are rather large. In Windows, bitmap files have the extension .bmp. There are color, and black and white bitmaps.

blue screen of death   The nickname of a Windows 2000 or XP stop error. When Windows detects a serious problem with the system, it shuts down the computer and dumps the contents of the memory to a file. It also displays a blue screen with the error data.

broadband   High-speed Internet connection such as DSL or cable Internet, or faster business connections.

buffer underrun error   An error that happens when burning an optical disc that causes the media to become useful as a beverage coaster. This error was prevalent with old CD burners.

bug   A design flaw in a program.

burn-in test   A series of individual tests used to make sure a new computer is running properly. A computer that passes the burn-in test is ready to sell to the customer.

cache (pronounced "cash"):   1. High-speed memory that is used on various types of hardware components. It is designed to enhance the performance of these devices by storing data in such a way as to make sure that it is transmitted smoothly to and/or from the device. Generally, the more cache a device has, the better it performs. Disk drives and CPUs are examples of devices with caches. Synonym: *buffer*. 2. An area in memory or on a disk drive that holds frequently accessed data.

case   The cabinet that holds all parts of the computer. Most cases come with power supplies.

Cat5/Cat5e   A standard for Ethernet network cables. Cables that don't meet the standard might not work well in networks, but should be adequate for voice telephone connections.

CEE power cord   A three-conductor power cord used to connect computers, monitors, and many other devices to AC power. These are probably the most standard part of a computer, as almost every non-laptop computer power supply, CRT monitor, and many other devices use these.

check box   A small square box within a dialog box that enables an event when there is a checkmark inside. Add a checkmark by *selecting* the check box. Remove the checkmark by *clearing* it. You can normally have any combination of selected and cleared check boxes in a dialog box.

chipset   The set of integrated circuits used on a particular device.

coaster   A failed optical disc burn resulting in a useless disc.

COM port   See *serial port.*

composite video   An analog video signal that is carried through one cable. The same signal that is used by all standard VCRs and by many computer video capture and video output devices.

color depth   Number of different shades of color that can be reproduced by a monitor or imaging device. In computers discussed in this book, color depth ranges from 16 to 4,294,967,295 colors.

command-line interface   See *text-based interface.*

compressed file   A file that has been altered so that it takes up no unnecessary space. For example, a *bitmap* image file is one in which every picture element in the entire picture contains color or grayscale information. Because there are hundreds of thousands or millions of picture elements in various types of bitmap files, the files take up a lot of disk space. However, if you have a bitmap file containing an image that is mostly solid yellow with only a small drawing in one corner, the compression technique might use an *algorithm* that sets a range of all the picture elements that should be yellow and assigns yellow to all of them, rather than assigning yellow to each individual element. Such techniques make for a much smaller file. Some compressed files are self-extracting; that is, they open themselves when double-clicked. Others need some type of "unzip" program to open them. Still others are compressed and decompressed by Windows.

configure   Make changes to device, software, or firmware settings.

cookie   1. A small file placed on a computer when the user visits and/or enters data into a Web page. The cookie is used to customize the Web page for the next time the user visits the page, sometimes by identifying the user, sometimes by remembering the information the user entered into a Web form.   2. The magnetic disk inside a floppy disk case.

CPU   Central processing unit. The chip that performs all the calculations necessary for the computer to do its job. Intel's *Pentium* and *Celeron*, and AMD's *Athlon* and *Duron* are names of popular lines of CPUs. Synonym: *processor.*

CPU family   Set of processors of a similar design made by one company. *Pentium 4* and *Athlon* are examples of CPU families.

CRT monitor   A monitor with a television-type glass picture tube.

current folder   When using a command interpreter such as the MS-DOS prompt or the Windows 2000/XP command prompt, the *current folder* is the one that most commands will affect unless another folder is specified in the command's syntax.

cursor   The small image on the screen of a document that indicates the location where keyboard or other input will go. To illustrate the difference between a cursor and a pointer, note that the cursor in a document doesn't move along with the pointer until the pointing device is clicked, and that moving the cursor with any of the keyboard keys doesn't move the pointer. See also *pointer*.

Desktop   The Windows screen that opens when the computer is booted. Contains the Start menu, the Task Bar, the System Tray, and all the icons.

desktop computer   Originally meant to mean a computer in a horizontal case, it has come to mean any personal computer that is not portable.

developer   Company or individual who makes software.

dialog box   A rectangular window containing configuration controls.

DMA   Direct Memory Access. A system used by certain hardware devices such as hard drives, floppy drives, and sound cards to interact directly with system memory rather than burden the processor. Enable or disable DMA in a device's system property page.

DIN AT   The wide 5-pin plug/socket used to connect a keyboard to an AT motherboard.

DIP switch   A tiny switch used for configuring some hardware devices, especially older devices.

directory   See *folder*.

display   See *monitor*.

dongle   A small cable with a telephone or Ethernet jack on one end, the other end of which plugs into a PC Card network adapter or modem. Dongles are usually fragile, especially at the plug that plugs into the PC Card. Many newer PC Cards have built-in jacks, making dongles unnecessary. See *PC Card*.

drive cage   An assembly in a computer that holds disk drives.

driver, device   A piece of software that allows the OS and programs to communicate with a hardware device. Hardware devices can't work without some type of driver, even if Windows' Device Manager indicates that no driver is necessary.

driver, generic   .A device driver that is designed to work with most or all devices in a general category of hardware devices, such as a video adapter or modem. Generic drivers usually don't allow all of a device's features to work. An example of a generic driver is the video driver that provides minimum video resolution and color depth when a computer first starts to boot.

dual-boot   A computer with two separate OSs that are selectable at the time of boot.

DVI   Digital Video Interface. The standard interface for digital video on PCs. Digital monitors and video adapters have DVI connectors.

DVO   The digital video header connector on a motherboard for connection of a digital video adapter.

El Torito specification   A standard for CD-ROM drives that allows the computer to boot from a CD-ROM.

environment variable   In Windows and DOS, the setting of the path that enables the system to locate certain Windows program files and commands when entered into the command prompt or Run dialog. Although the term *environment variable* technically means anything that can be changed in a computer, the aforementioned definition represents the most important and common use of the term. See *path*.

Ethernet   The most common network system, usually making use of unshielded twisted-pair cables with RJ-45 connectors.

expansion slots   Slot connectors on the motherboard for attaching various components. Motherboards typically have several expansion slots.

extension, filename   Character(s) after the final period in a filename. The extension tells the OS what type of file it is, and Windows associates certain programs with each known file extension so that the file can be opened with minimum delay. For example, in the file chapter1.txt, "txt" is the extension, and it indicates a text file that would normally be opened by a text editor such as Notepad. Most file extensions are hidden by default in Windows; change this setting by going to Control Panel > Folder Options > View tab and clearing the "Hide file extensions for known file types" check box.

file system   System of storing data on a disk. File systems discussed in this book are FAT16, FAT32, NTFS, and various optical drive file systems. Not all versions of Windows can access all file systems.

firewall   A hardware- or software-based mechanism for blocking unwanted access to a computer over a network or the Internet.

FireWire   A high-throughput hardware interface standard that allows many devices to be connected to a single port with only the FireWire controller using any Device Manager resources. Synonym: *IEEE 1394*.

firmware   Flash memory that is used to manage the basic operation of hardware devices. The most well-known example of firmware is a computer's BIOS. Other devices, such as optical drives, have firmware. Firmware can be updated via a process called *flashing*.

flash memory   Expensive memory that holds its data indefinitely after the power has been disconnected, but the data can be changed in a process called *flashing*. Flash memory chips are used for devices such as digital cameras, data storage devices on computers, and BIOSs.

flat panel monitor   A physically thin monitor, such as a laptop monitor, that uses light-emitting semiconductors rather than a glass picture tube. Contrast with *CRT monitor*.

flat screen monitor   A CRT monitor in which the viewable portion of the glass picture tube is flat, not curved. Not to be confused with a *flat panel monitor*.

floppy disk drives   Devices that store data on removable magnetic disks. Virtually all floppy drives sold since the mid-1990s have been of the 3.5-inch variety. These floppy disks are enclosed in a thin, hard, plastic shell. Because of this, they are sometimes confused with hard drives. Because of their limited capacity, their susceptibility to data loss, and other reasons, floppy disks have become much less useful in recent years. However, floppy disks can be indispensable for certain repairs. Synonyms: *floppies, diskette drives, FDDs*.

folder   A virtual container used by Windows to organize files. Formerly called *directories*.

form factor   A standard of shapes, sizes, and mounting designs of hardware devices such as cases, power supplies, motherboards, hard drives, and others.

Front Side Bus (FSB)   The channel that connects the processor with main memory. The faster the FSB, the better the performance. As of this writing, this number will range between 33 and 800 MHz.

graphics adapter   See *video card*.

graphics card   See *video card*.

GUI (pronounced "*gooey*")   Graphical User Interface. The Windows interface that makes use of graphical elements for controls, using such objects as buttons to click and the procedure of clicking and dragging. Contrast to *text-based interface*.

hang   When a program or OS process gets stuck at a certain point and doesn't continue.

hard drive   A device that stores data on permanently enclosed magnetic disks. The vast majority of computers have at least one hard drive. Data stored on a hard drive remains after the power is disconnected. The OS (such as Windows), along with programs and data, are almost always stored on a hard drive. Synonyms: *hard disk drive*, HDD.

heat sink   A small metal radiator used to allow heat to dissipate from heat-producing electrical devices, especially processors. Fans are often mounted on heat sinks to facilitate dissipation of heat.

hex number See *hexadecimal number*.

hexadecimal number A base-16 number. With decimal numbers, after 9 comes 0, and the 1 is carried over into the next column. Hex numbers include the following digits: 0123456789ABCDEF. After F comes 0, and the 1 is carried over into the next column. For example, F *hex* equals 15 in decimal, and 10 *hex* equals 16 in decimal. The purpose of hex numbers is to shorten what would otherwise be very long decimal numbers when referring to random access memory addresses and input/output addresses on a computer.

hibernate Saving the desktop as it is with all open programs and applets the way they are to the hard drive, and then shutting off the power. When power is resumed, the desktop should appear exactly as it was when it was hibernated. Synonym: *suspend*.

hot-pluggable Capable of being connected or disconnected from the computer or peripheral without risk of damage. Synonym: *Hot-swappable*.

HTML HyperText Markup Language. The language in which most Web pages are written. E-mail messages using anything more than plain text use HTML.

IEEE 1284 A standard for parallel cables. IEEE 1284-certified cables are more likely than noncertified cables to work reliably.

IEEE 1394 See *FireWire*.

initialize To start a hardware device.

I/O address A location of a hardware device communication channel in a motherboard. Expressed in a hex number. I/O address ranges must be different for each hardware device installed in a computer.

IRQL or IRQ Interrupt ReQuest Line. A channel from a hardware device to the processor used to get the processor to respond to the device's request for attention. There are a limited number of IRQs on a computer, and two devices cannot use the same IRQ at the same time.

ISA Industry Standard Architecture. An expansion slot interface no longer included in new computers.

jumper A small connector used to connect two pins together on a circuit board for the purpose of configuration.

key 1. A notch or other physical feature that prevents a devices from being inserted into a slot the wrong way   2. The top level portions of the Windows registry.

knowledge base A collection of all technical information about a manufacturer's or developer's products. Almost always searchable on the Web.

laptop   A small portable computer. Although laptops are generally considered larger than *notebooks*, the two terms are often used interchangeably, including in this book.

legacy   Of or pertaining to any hardware using standards older than the computer on which they are to run. Also refers to versions of software that has been replaced by a newer version and data files created on such software.

load   Automatically copy files from disk into memory. When Windows or a program starts, it's actually loading into memory.

lockup   Situation in which the computer stops responding. The screen image and pointer freeze, keyboard lights get stuck, and hard drive activity stops.

malware   Programs that can cause various problems on a computer or can steal your personal data.

map a network drive   Assigning a drive letter to a folder or drive partition on a remote computer on the network.

MBR   Master boot record. The MBR is the first sector on a hard drive. A small program on the MBR contains information about the partitions, indicating which one is bootable, in case there are more than one.

Me   Microsoft Windows Millennium Edition. Microsoft uses the lower-case "e," so we do too.

media   Disks, flash memory, or other materials used for data storage.

memory   Chip assemblies that store data for very quick recall. The main memory in a computer requires constant power to be able to hold data. Every task performed by a computer requires the program and data to be loaded into memory. Synonym: *random access memory (RAM)*.

MicroATX   A small, commonly used (as of this writing) form factor of case, motherboard, and power supply. Based on *ATX*.

MIDI   Musical Instrument Digital Interface. A system of connecting electronic musical instruments to computers.

modem   A device that allows the computer to access a telephone line for the purpose of faxing, Internet access, data transfer between computers, or other tele-communications-related uses. Internal modems plug into expansion slots, while an external modem connects to a port on the computer.

monitor   A device resembling a television that displays the computer's video images. Synonyms: *screen, display*.

motherboard   The large printed-circuit board to which all other parts are connected. Synonyms: *system board, main board, desktop board*.

multimedia   The combination of sound and various forms of graphics including video and animation. Although the prefix "multi" indicates more than one, many people incorrectly use the term to refer to sound only.

multiple-boot   A computer with three or more OSs that can be selected when booting.

multitester   A device used to test various properties of electrical currents and circuits such as voltage, continuity, and resistance. Most commonly used in computer repair for testing power supplies.

network   A collection of two or more computers and other devices that can communicate with each other so that the users and computers can share information and hardware devices such as printers.

network card   A device that connects the computer to the network. Network cards come in the form of a separate card or are built in to the motherboard. Synonyms: *network adapter, network interface card, NIC.*

newsgroup   A group of subscribers who can post and reply to messages over the Internet using a newsreader program such as Outlook Express. Microsoft and other companies make use of newsgroups for professional and peer technical support. See *Usenet.*

NIC   network interface card. See *network adapter.*

notebook   A small portable computer. Although notebooks are supposed to be smaller than laptops, the two terms are often used interchangeably, including in this book.

OEM   Original Equipment Manufacturer. Refers to any product that is designed for manufacturers and retail computer builders to supply with their equipment. For example, Microsoft requires end users of OEM versions of Windows to get technical support from the manufacturer or computer builder rather than from Microsoft.

optical drives   Includes *CD-ROM, CD-RW, DVD-ROM*, and various writable DVD drives. Optical drives are devices that read, or read *and* write data from or onto discs using laser beams.

option button   One of at least two small round circles within a dialog box that can be *selected* (a dot placed inside) or *cleared* (the dot removed). With option buttons, normally only one in a group can be selected at a time. Originally referred to as "radio buttons," which came from old car radios with mechanical station preset buttons, in which only one button could be pushed in at a time.

page file   The file used by Windows for virtual memory. Synonym: *swap file.*

paging   When Windows moves data between memory and the page file for the use of virtual memory.

parallel   An interface used for external devices such as printers and scanners. Parallel devices communicate with the system by sending as many as eight electrical pulses simultaneously.

patch   Software designed to fix problems in other software.

path   1. The hierarchy of drives, folders, and subfolders that indicates the location of a file, folder, printer, or other element. For example, the path to this appendix could be C:\Documents and Settings\Rojo\My Documents\PCRepair\AppendixA.doc. In a network, the path can include the computer, usually in the form of the computer name preceded by two backslashes. Using the previous example on the computer named CRM, the network path could be \\CRM\C:\Documents and Settings\Rojo\My Documents\PCRepair\AppendixA.doc.   2. The indication of the location of commands in a command prompt or Run dialog. Usually called *the path*. When you change an *environment variable* related to the path to commands or Windows program files, you change the path to those commands or files.

PC Card   A credit card-sized hardware device that plugs into a slot in a laptop or the occasional desktop with a PC Card slot. The most common PC Card devices are modems and network adapters. The term *PC Card* replaced the term *PCMCIA* because nobody wanted to pronounce a six-syllable term.

PCI   Peripheral Component Interconnect. The most commonly used expansion card slot. New versions of PCI have been introduced that will be incompatible with current versions.

PCMCIA   See *PC Card*.

PDF   Portable Document Format. A type of text and image file that can be made only by programs developed by Adobe Software, Inc. The file extension is .pdf.

pins   Conductive metal pieces that are part of electrical connectors.

pixel   The smallest picture element in a video display or an image file.

pointer   The image on a computer screen that indicates the location of the pointing device control.

pointing device   A device that is used to move the on-screen pointer and choose or select screen elements. A mouse is the most common pointing device.

port   Connector on the outside of a computer to which peripheral devices can be connected. Examples are parallel, serial, PS/2, VGA, USB, and FireWire. Not to be confused with the networking term.

POST card   A card that can be plugged into an expansion slot and contains a small display to a show a problem code. A POST card is ideal for diagnosing computers that won't boot. It can be a great timesaver.

power supply   A box-shaped device that converts wall-outlet AC power to low-voltage DC used to power the devices in the computer.

processor   See *CPU*.

properties, property page   A dialog box that presents information about a device, folder, or file, usually allowing one or more configuration options.

protocol, network   A piece of software containing rules for a particular networking purpose. Every network connection requires all parties to be using the same protocol in order to communicate.

PS/2   Interface for keyboards and pointing devices on most ATX-based motherboards.

RAM   See *memory*.

read   Detect data from storage media. Technically, transfer data from a file into memory.

readme file   File that comes with software or hardware that contains useful information to the user.

rewritable   An optical disc that can be written to, erased, and written to again. Includes CD-RWs and recordable DVDs.

RJ11   A modular one-line telephone connector with two wires: red and green. An RJ11 connector has the same plastic shell as an RJ14 connector.

RJ14   A modular two-line telephone connector with four wires: red and green for line 1, and black and yellow for line 2. An RJ14 connector has the same plastic shell as an RJ11 connector.

RJ45   A modular telephone or network connector with eight wires. In order to be used with Ethernet networks, RJ45 connectors must adhere to the Cat5 or Cat5e standard.

root folder   The highest-level folder in a disk partition. If you open My Computer, and then any drive, you are looking at the root folder. For example, C:\ is the root directory of the C drive. Any files or folders you see with C:\ open are said to be in the root folder. Often called *root directory*.

SCSI   Small Computer System Interface. An interface known primarily for hard drives and optical drives (but is actually used with many other devices) that is used mostly for servers and other mission-critical systems.

serial port   A port through which electrical pulses are sent one at a time. Used for external modems and other devices. Original IBM PCs had four serial ports, with each assigned a logical address called a *COM port*.

server   A computer that provides services to other computers on a network, called *clients* or *workstations*. Servers tend to be high-powered machines.

service   A small program or part of a program whose purpose is supporting larger programs or OS components. In 2000 and XP, access Services in Administrative Tools from Control Panel, Start menu, or Manage.

setup   The installation of software, including Windows. Synonym: *installation* (only of software).

setup program   The BIOS configuration program.

shell   The system that gives the user control of the OS. In the case of Windows, the shell is the *GUI*.

slot   A horizontal multi-pin electrical connector that accepts a card-type connector. Expansion cards such as PCI, AGP, and ISA are slots. In addition, some processors, including many Pentium IIIs, plug into slots.

S.M.A.R.T. drive   Self-Monitoring Analysis and Reporting Technology drive. Technology incorporated into most modern IDE hard drives that can alert the user of possible impending hard drive failure and most likely allow for data backup before this happens. S.M.A.R.T. drive support should always be enabled in the setup program.

socket   A flat electrical connector with holes. A device such as a socket processor has pins that plug into the holes.

sound card   A device whose primary function is to allow a computer to play and record sound. A sound card can either be a separate card that plugs into an expansion slot, or a component built into the motherboard. Sometimes called a *multimedia device*.

standby   Saving the desktop as it is with all open programs and applets the way they are to memory, and then operating on low power. In most cases, you can resume from standby by moving or clicking the pointing device, or by pressing any keyboard key.

stop error   See *blue screen of death*.

surge suppressor   A device designed to absorb increases in voltage that can damage computers, peripherals, or other devices. Most very inexpensive models provide little or no protection.

suspend   See *hibernate*.

SVGA   Super Video Graphics Array. The standard for analog video on personal computers. Based on its predecessor, VGA, which uses the same connectors.

swap file   See *page file*.

syntax   The proper way to type commands with their parameters and switches.

tab   A graphical depiction of the tab on a paper file folder. Click a tab to select a different page in a dialog box or property sheet. Sometimes used to represent the entire page that a tab is on.

TCP/IP   The network protocol used on the Internet and in many other networks.

text-based interface   Interface that involves typing commands rather than using graphical elements. Contrast with *GUI*. Synonym: *command-line interface*.

throughput   Measurement of the speed of data transfer.

toggle   Turn a software or hardware element on or off. For example, pressing the <Caps Lock> key on the keyboard toggles uppercase letters on or off.

touchpad   A flat pointing device that works by sliding a fingertip across its surface. Software can provide additional features such as tapping to click. Synonym: *trackpad*.

trackpad   See *touchpad*.

trackball   A pointing device that has a partially enclosed ball that the user rolls to move the pointer.

UPS   Uninterruptible Power Supply. A UPS provides continuous power to a computer when there is a power failure. A UPS can protect the computer from the potentially harmful effects of power failures. It is indispensable when making changes to a computer's BIOS, because a power failure during a BIOS update will render a computer useless unless a replacement BIOS chip is obtained and installed, which isn't always possible. UPSs almost always include surge suppression. Synonym: *battery backup*.

USB   Universal Serial Bus. A hardware device interface that allows for up to 127 devices to be connected to a single USB port, given that the appropriate expansion hardware is used. Only the USB controller uses IRQs or other Device Manager resources; the connected devices don't.

Usenet   A system of communication on the Internet in which subscribers to newsgroups can post and reply to messages that all subscribers can see.

VGA   Video Graphics Array. See *SVGA*.

video card   A device whose primary function is to generate a video signal ("picture") to be shown on the monitor. A video card can either be a separate card that plugs into a slot on the motherboard, or a device built into the motherboard. Synonyms: *video adapter, graphics adapter, display adapter*.

virtual memory   System used by Windows that uses hard disk space to as additional memory in a process called *paging*. The file where Windows stores virtual memory data is called the *page file* or the *swap file*.

voltmeter   A device that tests only the voltage of a circuit.

write   Record data to a storage medium.

writable   Refers to a disc that can have data recorded on it.

XP   Microsoft Windows XP Home and Professional editions.

XP Home   Microsoft Windows XP Home Edition.

XP Pro   Microsoft Windows XP Professional Edition.

ZIF   Zero Insertion Force CPU socket. Allows a CPU to be inserted into a socket without applying much pressure. Uses a locking lever to hold the processor in place.

Zip file   A file compressed with the algorithm developed by the inventor of the Zip file. The file's extension is *.zip*. See *compressed file*.

B Practical Troubleshooting Table

Dead Computer

Symptom	Check and/or Try:
Dead computer (nothing happens when you press the power button).	• Check to make sure the power cable is connected, the outlet strip is plugged in and turned on, and the wall outlet is live. • If there is a UPS with a soft power switch, press it to turn the UPS on. • Check the rear power switch on the power supply if present. • Check the voltage switch on the power supply. Never attempt to power on the computer if the voltage switch is set incorrectly. • Check internal connections. • Check the computer's power switch to make sure it isn't broken.

System Powers On but Won't Boot Properly or at All

Boot Error Messages	Check and/or Try:
ntldr missing or *Non-system disk* or *disk error*, or similar message.	• Remove any removable disks from their drives and restart. • Use a POST card. • Run a diagnostic utility. • Check the BIOS for boot order. • 2000/XP only: In case of recent disk configuration changes, boot with the boot disk. The boot.ini file might need to be edited.

Boot Error Messages	Check and/or Try:
OS not found.	• Check the boot order in BIOS. • The hard drive might be bad. Test with diagnostic utility, hard drive utility, FDISK, Partition Magic Drive Information, Disk Management on a separate 2000 or XP computer or hardware-based hard drive tester.
Computer locks up while booting.	• Check the BIOS to see if Plug and Play is enabled. • A driver might be incompatible with the OS, especially 2000/XP. Boot to Safe Mode and check Device Manager for problems, or use Last Known Good configuration or System Restore. • A hardware device might be malfunctioning. Check with a POST card or diagnostic utility, or remove all peripherals and replace them one at a time.
Computer boots directly to Safe Mode.	• Attempt to boot to Normal Mode. It might work. • After boot to Safe Mode, check Device Manager for hardware problems and resource conflicts. • Use a POST card. • Run a diagnostic utility.

Bad Performance/Erratic Behavior

Symptom	Check and/or Try:
Windows won't shut down properly.	• Install Windows updates. • Search Microsoft Knowledge Base for shutdown problem, specifying the Windows version and using the "Any of the words" and 150 articles options. There are many articles for each version.
Compaq Presario won't shut down properly.	• Check the Startup tab of msconfig or the registry at HKEY_LOCAL_MACHINE\ SOFTWARE\Microsoft\Windows\CurrentVersion\ Run for the file SXGDSENU.exe. This file needs to start with Windows in order for Presarios to shut down.

Symptom	Check and/or Try:
Computer runs badly; might lock up, give random error messages, etc.	• Scan computer for viruses and malware. • Check temperatures, fan performance, and that the heat sink is properly seated on the CPU. • Run System File Checker. • Run a registry-cleaning program. • Use a diagnostic utility. • Run the 2000 emergency repair process or reinstall Windows over the existing installation. • You might have Windows Me. Back up and do a clean install of Windows XP.

Software Installation Problems

Symptom	Check and/or Try:
Windows won't install.	• Make sure the computer *exceeds* the system requirements of Windows version. • Search for an error message. • Test the hard drive. Use the hard drive manufacturer's utility to set up the drive. • Run EZ BIOS to see if it's installed; if it is, try uninstalling it.
2000 or XP installation hangs during hardware detection phase.	• Check for incompatible hardware. See Hardware Compatibility Lists (Microsoft Knowledge Base article 131303 for 2000, or 314062 for XP). Attempt to identify problem hardware. If non-essential, remove it or disable it in BIOS. Windows should install successfully. Then, search for an appropriate driver and reinstall device.
Windows 98 error message: *Windows Setup requires 'largest executable program size' to be at least 442368 bytes to run.*	• From a command prompt, run setup /im. This skips the memory check that allows the problem to occur.
Program won't install.	• Check the program documentation. • Make sure the program is compatible with Windows version; 16-bit programs (for DOS or Windows 3.x) that need to access hardware directly will not work in 2000 or XP. Newer versions of a program might not run on older versions of Windows.

Symptom	Check and/or Try:
Program won't install (cont.).	• Make sure the computer meets the system requirements of the program. • Copy setup files to the hard drive before running the installation program (usually setup.exe).
Driver installation unsuccessful.	• Make sure the driver being installed is designed for the installed Windows version. • Make sure the hardware is compatible with Windows version and with other hardware. See Hardware Compatibility Lists (Microsoft Knowledge Base article 131303 for 2000, or 314062 for XP). • Make sure the computer meets the system requirements of the hardware (usually printed on the box and in the documentation). • The device might be malfunctioning. Try the questionable device in another computer or another device in the same computer.
Hardware not detected when installation is attempted.	• Make sure the device is seated or otherwise connected properly. • Make sure Plug and Play is enabled in BIOS. • Test the device in another machine to make sure it's not defective or broken.

Heat Problems

Symptom	Check and/or Try:
Computer runs hot.	• Check the fan operation. • Vacuum and use air spray inside the computer. • Make sure the vents aren't blocked. • Cover openings such as unused expansion card slots and drive bays. • Make sure the computer isn't near a heat source. • Make sure the fan works. • Check for a BIOS update. Some BIOS updates allow a computer to run cooler, especially laptops.

Video Problems

Symptom	Check and/or Try:
No video.	• Make sure the monitor is powered on, connected to the computer, and that the brightness control is not turned all the way down. If the power indicator is blinking or glows orange, that means there is no video signal coming from the computer. Try another monitor, or connect the dark monitor to a different computer. • If there is no video at boot, listen for the POST beep code and/or use a POST card (see Chapter 11, "Troubleshooting," for more information on POST beep codes and POST cards). • Try removing the hard drive and scanning for viruses. • Try installing a known good video adapter.
Video at low resolution with splotchy colors.	• Try to adjust the settings from 640 x 480 resolution and 16 colors. • The video driver might be corrupted. Update or reinstall the driver. Try installing a known good video adapter.
Artifacts (parts or shapes of windows continue to appear on screen after the window is closed), other unwanted spots appear on screen.	• Reinstall or upgrade the video driver. • Scan for viruses.
Line appears on screen.	• Swap the monitor with a known good monitor. Reinstall or update the video driver.
One or more colors missing.	• Check the VGA connector pins. If the monitor cable is replaceable, swap with a known good cable. If not, swap with a known good monitor.
Problems with video and display settings. No choices in either resolution or color depth, or both.	• Certain LCD screens can display video at only one preset resolution. • Design limitation of the video adapter or monitor.

Symptom	Check and/or Try:
Problems with video and display settings (cont.).	• The computer is in Safe Mode. • There is a problem with the adapter or its driver.
One parameter decreases as the other one is increased.	• Lack of sufficient video memory to support high resolutions and large color palettes simultaneously.
The image is odd-shaped.	• The aspect ratio of the selected screen resolution does not match that of the screen (4x3 for standard computer monitors).
The page displays unusable or poor quality video.	• The settings exceed the capability of the video adapter or monitor.

Sound Problems

Symptom	Check and/or Try:
No sound.	• Make sure the speakers are connected, powered, and turned up. • Make sure the volume is up and not muted in the Windows volume control and Windows sound mixer. • Make sure sounds are enabled in the Multimedia/Sounds applet in Control Panel. • Check audio connectors. Make sure they are in the right jacks and free from damage. • Run SFC. • Check Device Manager for an installed sound card. • Install or reinstall the sound driver. • Try a known good sound card.
Bad sound.	• Check the audio connectors. Make sure they are in the right jacks and free from damage. • Run SFC. • Enable or disable digital sound playback in the sound card properties in Device Manager. • Check to see if the sound card is next to the video card. If so, try separating them. • Reinstall the sound driver.

Printing Problems

Symptom	Check and/or Try:
Printer won't print.	• Make sure the printer is connected to power and turned on. • If any error messages appear, and they are not obviously correct, search for them on the Internet. • Reinstall the printer driver. • Check the cable. If it is a parallel cable, make sure it is IEEE 1284 compliant and that the pins are intact. • Try a known good printer and/or cable. • Test the non-functioning printer in another computer. • If the computer is a laptop, uninstall any recently installed USB devices. • Try to print a test page in Printer Properties. • 2000/XP only: Check the print queue. If documents seem to be stuck in the queue, go to Services and stop and restart the spooler service.
Print quality is bad. Printer prints nonsense characters and/or prints on every page without stopping.	• Reinstall the printer driver. • Check the cable. If it is a parallel cable, make sure it is IEEE 1284 compliant and that the pins are intact.
One or more colors missing. Printed documents have streaks. Printer prints too light.	• Reinstall the printer driver. • Check the ink cartridges. • Follow the manufacturer's directions for cleaning the printer. • Check the ink cartridges.

Lost Data/I Can't Open My Files/I Can't Find My Files

Symptom	Check and/or Try:
Certain files won't open.	• Make sure you have a program that will open that type of file. • The file could be corrupted. Replace the file if possible. • Scan the system for viruses and malware.

Symptom	Check and/or Try:
Certain files won't open (cont.).	• On 2000 and XP, make sure you have permissions to open these files. • Check the hard drive for damage such as bad sectors.
Entire folders won't open.	• On 2000 and XP, make sure you have permission to open these files. • The folder could be corrupted. Replace the files in the folder if possible. • Scan the system for viruses and malware. • Check the hard drive for damage such as bad sectors.
Disk drive not recognized.	• Make sure the drive is connected properly. • Make sure the file format is recognized by Windows (9x won't recognize NTFS). • Check the drive with FDISK, Partition Magic, Windows Disk Management (2000 or XP only), or a diagnostic utility. • Run EZ BIOS; install or uninstall as needed.
Files open, but nonsense characters appear.	• The program used to open the file is not the correct program for that type of file. For example, a Microsoft Word file opened in Notepad will show nonsense characters. • The file could be corrupted. Check the hard drive for damage and scan the system for viruses and malware.
Entire partitions or drives don't open.	• Check the hard drive for damage. • Scan the system for viruses and malware. • Run hard drive restoration programs. If data is critical, send to data recovery company such as OnTrack.

Problems with Hardware Peripherals

Symptom	Check and/or Try:
Expansion cards don't work or work poorly.	• Check in Device Manager to see if there is a problem. If there is, reinstall the driver. • Reseat the card in its slot.

Symptom	Check and/or Try:
Expansion cards don't work or work poorly (cont.).	• Run a diagnostic utility. • Try a known good card with the same function.
External devices don't work or work poorly.	• Make sure the device is powered (unless power is provided through a USB or FireWire port). • Make sure all cables are intact—swap with known good cables. • Check in Device Manager for a problem with the device or the port. • Swap the device with a known good model. • If the device connects via infrared, make sure the infrared receiver/emitter is enabled in the BIOS.

Floppy Drives/Optical Drives Don't Work

Symptom	Check and/or Try:
Floppy drive can't open files.	• The disk might be bad. Check the floppy disk in a known good drive. • The drive might be the problem. Spray compressed air in the drive or replace the drive.
Floppy drive can't write files or format disk.	• The disk might have its write protect tab moved into place. Move the tab back to the other position or use another disk. • The disk might be bad. Try another disk. • The drive might be the problem. Spray with compressed air or replace the drive.
The A drive is not recognized on the system.	• Make sure the drive is enabled in the BIOS. • Check the drive cables and connections. Reattach the drive and/or replace the cable if necessary. • Replace the drive with a known good drive.
Optical drive can't read files.	• The disk might be in a format unrecognized by the drive, or it might have not been finalized after it was burned. Try a newer drive. • The disk might be damaged. Inspect the disk for damage and use a repair kit if necessary. • The drive might be broken. Try the disk in another drive.

Symptom	Check and/or Try:
Writable optical drive can't write files. You get a buffer underrun error message when attempting to burn a disk.	• The disk might not be writable, or it might have been writable but not rewritable and have already been written to. Try another disk. • The drive might be defective. Try another drive. • Copy the files to the hard drive before attempting to burn the disk.
Optical drive not recognized in system.	• Check in BIOS to make sure the drive is enabled. • Check all cables to the drive. Reattach and replace cables if necessary.

Hard Drive Problems

Symptom	Check and/or Try:
System reports bad sectors.	• Run a diagnostic utility. • Run thorough ScanDisk. • Copy data and replace the hard drive.
Hard drive crashes.	• If data is critical, send the drive to data recovery company such as OnTrack.

Unusual Noise

Symptom	Check and/or Try:
Change in fan noise.	• Check all fans in the system plus the power supply.
Strange noises coming from speakers.	• Follow the instructions in Sound Problems. • The system might be running badly. Reboot. • Scan the system for viruses and malware.

Internet and Modem Problems

Symptom	Check and/or Try:
You cannot connect to the ISP—dial-up or broadband.	• Check all the cables and connections. • Call the ISP to see if there is an outage. • Make sure the telephone line works (dial-up or DSL). Make sure the television cable is working (cable).

Symptom	**Check and/or Try:**
You cannot connect to the ISP—dial-up or broadband (cont.).	• Check the configuration of the computer and any other connection devices. • Check all the connection hardware devices for power and proper operation. • Reinstall the ISP software. • If you have Windows XP, stop using the ISP software and create a broadband connection in Windows. If dial-up, configure manually with any Windows version. • Make sure the correct modem or network adapter is selected. Detect the new device or delete and reinstall the connection. • Make sure the firewall, if used, is configured correctly. • Make sure there aren't multiple firewalls running on the system. • Make sure the username and password are correct and in the correct format. • Make sure Caps Lock isn't changing the case of the password. • Make sure the modem is dialing the correct telephone number with all necessary codes. • If the telephone line does not have Call Waiting, make sure the modem isn't dialing the code to disable it. • Scan for viruses and malware. • If the line has voicemail, make sure a pulsed dial tone isn't interfering with the modem. Either listen to the messages before connecting, or add three commas to the beginning of the dial-up telephone number.
You can connect to an ISP, but no Web pages appear.	• Call the ISP to see if there is an outage. • Make sure the firewall, if used, is configured correctly. • Make sure there aren't multiple firewalls running on the system. • Check the configuration in Internet Options. Make sure Security, Privacy, and Content settings aren't blocking Web pages. • Scan for viruses and malware.

Symptom	Check and/or Try:
Your home page changed.	• Change it back in the Internet Options, General page. • Scan for viruses and malware.
The wrong e-mail program or Web browser appears when you connect to the Internet.	• Change the settings in Internet Options, Programs page. • 2000 and XP: Change the settings in Set Program Access and Defaults from the Start menu.
Data transfer speed is slow.	• Try another ISP to see if the ISP's modems are slow. • Call your ISP to see if there's a slowdown in the system. • Upgrade to a 56Kbps modem. • If you're connecting through a hotel telephone line, this might be normal. • Check the quality of the telephone line. • Scan for viruses and malware.
The connection gets dropped frequently.	• Make sure to disable Call Waiting if you have it. • Check the quality of the telephone line. • Scan for viruses and malware.
You can't get your e-mail.	• Make sure the username and password are correct and in the required format. • Make sure all configuration information is the same as required by the ISP. • Make sure the computer is connected to the Internet.
You can't download attachments.	• Check your security settings.

C   Command-Line Tutorial: MS-DOS and 32-Bit Commands

A PRACTICAL TUTORIAL AND REFERENCE

In this appendix, we will discuss only those commands, switches, and parameters likely to be helpful to those repairing a computer. Because general networking is beyond the scope of this book, networking commands are excluded. In most command references, there is so much punctuation to indicate variables that until you become experienced with the commands, you might have trouble determining which punctuation is for variables and which is part of the syntax of the command. Therefore, we attempted to show these commands with a minimum of punctuation.

Selecting and Copying Text from a Command Prompt Window

1. Click the icon in the upper left-hand corner of the bar on top of the window, point to Edit in the menu that appears, and click Mark.
2. Click at the beginning of the text you want to copy.
3. Press and hold down the <SHIFT> key, and then click at the end of the text you want to copy.
4. Click the icon again, click Edit, and then click Copy.
5. Paste the text into a document by holding the <Ctrl> key and pressing <C>, or by selecting Paste from the Edit menu. If you want to paste the text back into the command prompt window, click the icon again, point to Edit, and click Paste.

Using Wildcard Characters

Wildcard characters can be used when using Windows Search or Find, and to represent multiple files or folders when using a command prompt. Wildcard characters are as follows:

Asterisk (*): Acts as a substitute for zero or more characters. For example, to search for or make a change to any .txt file that starts with *G*, enter *G*.txt*. If you want any file that has an extension starting with *.tif*, enter **.tif*. For all files in a particular folder, enter **.**.

Question mark (?): Acts as a substitute for any single character. For example, to search for or make changes to all .doc files that start with *Karen* followed by a single character, enter *karen?.doc*. This would find or change *karen1.doc*, *karen2.doc*, and so forth, but would ignore *karen10.doc* because the number *10* has two characters.

Notes

- For information on commands not listed here, 2000's and XP's Help files have lists of all available prompts. Search 2000's Help for "Command Reference Main Page," or XP's for "Command-Line Reference." For 9x's commands, search the Internet. You can also search Windows' Help for individual commands.
  - Not all commands are available in all versions. Additionally, certain MS-DOS commands won't be available in 2000 or XP if you access the 32-bit command prompt (Start > Programs (or All Programs) > Accessories > Command Prompt), or by typing "cmd" in the Run dialog. However, if you type "command" in the Run dialog, you'll be able to run some MS-DOS commands that would normally not be available in that version of Windows. Finally, not all commands work as described in Microsoft's documentation.
  - For a description and syntax of each command, plus a complete list of switches and parameters, enter the command followed by a space and "/?". For example, for information about the CD command, type:

  ```
  CD /?
  ```

  - Because folders were originally called *directories*, Microsoft uses the term whenever writing about commands. The two terms (*folders* and *directories*) are interchangeable.
  - Most of these commands can be used either by entering the full path of the file or folder being acted upon after the command name, or by navigating to that folder first. In our experience, it is usually easier to navigate to the folder first, eliminating any chance of typos invalidating the command and requiring the command to be retyped. For instructions on navigating to the correct folder, see the description of the CD (CHDIR) command.
  - In addition to the 8.3 limitation of file and folder names in MS-DOS (see Chapter 2, "System Configuration and Computer Hygiene"), there cannot be spaces in MS-DOS file and folder names. When referring to file and

folder names containing spaces when using an MS-DOS prompt on Windows, you might need to use quotation marks around the folder or filename. Otherwise, the system might interpret only the first word as the name and anything after that as invalid parameters or switches. This is however, by no means a universal rule, especially in 2000 and XP.

- Commands, parameters, and switches are not case sensitive.
- All switches must be preceded by a space character when typed as part of a single command line. The only time you would omit the space is when you are responding to a prompt, such as is possible in the CHKDSK command.
- Press <Enter> after each command to start it.
- A great trick that you can use with these commands is use of the < and > keys. < inputs the text from a text file into a command, and > sends the output from a command to a text file. For example, if you use the DIR command with the /p switch and want the output to go to a file in the current folder that you want to name output.txt, type DIR /p > output.txt

- If you want to import text from a file into a command, use the < key after the command and switches, followed by the name of the file.
- If you find that commands you want to use are not available, running the PATH command might help. This tells the system where to find commands.

ATTRIB

In Windows, files and folders have certain properties (called *attributes*) that can be configured. If you right-click on the file or folder's icon, you'll see some check boxes that allow you to change these attributes. The ATTRIB command allows you to do this when the Windows GUI is not available. The possible attributes, which vary based on Windows version and other factors, are as follows:

Read only: When set, this allows the file to be opened and viewed, but not changed or deleted.

Archive: This attribute affects whether the file will be backed up in certain backup schemes using a backup program, or whether running the XCOPY command will copy that particular file. For more information, see Windows Backup help files.

System: This indicates that the file is necessary for some Windows process.

Hidden: Windows hides certain files by default; however, any file can be hidden or displayed by changing this attribute. In 2000 and XP, when the user has enabled the showing of hidden files (in any Windows folder in Tools > Folder Options > View tab), icons for hidden folders and files appear translucent.

The most common repair use for the ATTRIB command is to replace corrupted registry files in 9x (see Chapter 11, "Troubleshooting," for more information).

When run without switches, ATTRIB shows the attributes of each file in the current folder.

ATTRIB displays, sets, or removes the read-only, archive, system, and hidden attributes assigned to files or folders. Used without parameters, ATTRIB displays attributes of all files in the current folder.

Use

ATTRIB uses the plus sign (+) to turn on an attribute, and the minus sign (-) to turn off an attribute. To use ATTRIB, navigate to the folder where the desired file is located (see the CD command description later in this appendix), and type the command followed by the filename (with or without wildcards) and the desired parameters and switches.

Parameters

+r: Sets the read-only file attribute.

-r: Clears the read-only file attribute.

+a: Sets the archive file attribute.

-a: Clears the archive file attribute.

+s: Sets the system file attribute.

-s: Clears the system file attribute.

+h: Sets the hidden file attribute.

-h: Clears the hidden file attribute.

Switches

/s: Applies the command to matching files in the current folder and all its subfolders.

/d: Applies the command to the entire folder.

Note

■ To apply a change to a group of files using wildcard characters, files with their system and/or hidden attributes will not be affected unless you turn off the hidden and system attributes first.

Examples

To display the attributes of a file named *chapter07.doc*, navigate to the folder and enter:

```
ATTRIB chapter07.doc
```

To assign the read-only attribute to the file, enter:

```
ATTRIB +r chapter07.doc
```

To remove the read-only, hidden, and system attributes from all .reg files on the C: drive, including in all subfolders, navigate to the C: drive and enter:

```
ATTRIB -r -h -s *.reg /s
```

CD OR CHDIR

This refers to *Change Directory*, and is used to change the current folder. When directions for another command say, "navigate to the xxx folder," this is the command that you would use to do that.

Use

When narrowing down to a subfolder within the current folder, type CD, followed by the subfolder name. For example, if the current folder is C:\WINDOWS, and you want to navigate to C:\WINDOWS\DESKTOP, type:

```
CD Desktop
```

To change the current folder to a root level (a drive letter without any additional folders) (e.g., C:\Documents and Settings to C:), make sure to enter the backslash (\) after the drive letter. For example, if the prompt says *C:\Documents and Settings>* and you want to navigate to the C drive, enter:

```
CD C:\.
```

Switch

.. : This navigates to the higher level folder. For example, if the current folder is C:\Documents and Settings\All Users, running CD with this switch will take you to C:\Documents and Settings. Note that there is a space before the two periods.

CHKDSK (PRESENT IN ALL VERSIONS, USEFUL IN 2000 AND XP ONLY)

CHKDSK is a program used for checking the status of magnetic drives/disks, fixing certain errors, and even recovering readable data from bad disk sectors. It isn't particularly useful in 9x, except for obtaining a report on files on the disk. To correct any disk errors on 9x, run ScanDisk. In 2000, and XP, CHKDSK replaces 9x's Scan-Disk. In 2000 and XP, it is easier to run CHKDSK from Windows, so you might as well save the command-line version for when the computer is booted into Safe Mode, Command prompt only. When invoked with the /f and/or /r switches to run on a disk in use, CHKDSK will prompt you to run at the next boot. See Chapter 2 for more information on CHKDSK and ScanDisk.

Use

Type CHKDSK followed by the drive letter and colon (:), followed by any switches (each switch must be preceded by a space character).

Switches

/c: Use with NTFS-formatted drives only. Skips folder structure cycle checking, resulting in a faster completion.

/f: Fixes file system errors on the disk. If run on a disk currently in use, /f causes CHKDSK to be run on the next boot.

/i: Use with NTFS-formatted drives only. Performs a less exhaustive check of index entries, resulting in a faster completion.

/r: Recovers readable information from bad disk sectors. If run on a disk currently in use, /r causes CHKDSK to be run on the next boot. See the listing for the RECOVER command for another tool that can recover lost data.

/v: Displays the name of each file in every folder as the disk is checked.

/x: Use with NTFS-formatted drives only. Makes all necessary changes to any network-mapped drives in order for CHKDSK to work on them. /x also includes the functionality of the /r switch.

Notes

- Running CHKDSK without the /f, /r, and/or /x switches is usually pointless and might report false disk errors.
- If you are prompted to convert lost chains (unidentified file fragments) to files, do so by typing <Y>. You can then find the files in the root folder (C:\ in

the C: drive). The files are named File****.chk (the asterisks stand for any character). If the files don't contain any data you need, you can delete them. If you type <N> (answer no) to the prompt, the fragments will be deleted automatically.

■ If you use the /f or /x switch on a very large disk such as 80GB, or one with huge numbers of files (e.g., millions of files), CHKDSK might take several days to complete. CHKDSK cannot be stopped while it is running, so the computer will not be available for this time.

CLS

CLS removes all text except the main heading and prompt from the command prompt window. CLS stands for *Clear Screen*.

Use

Type CLS.

CMD (2000 AND XP ONLY)

Although this command can be used in a command prompt window, its most common use is to be entered in the Run dialog for the purpose of opening a new 32-bit command prompt window in 2000 and XP.

Use

Type CMD in the Run dialog and click OK or press <Enter>.

COMMAND

Although this command can be used in a command prompt window, its most common use is to be entered in the Run dialog for opening a MS-DOS prompt window in all versions.

Use

Type COMMAND in the Run dialog and press <Enter>.

COMP (2000 AND XP ONLY)

Compares the data in two files or sets of files byte by byte. The two files or sets can be on the same or different drives or folders.

Use

Type COMP and press <Enter>. You'll be prompted for the first file to compare. Enter the full path and press <Enter>. You'll then be prompted for the second file to compare. Enter the full path and press <Enter>. You'll then be prompted for any switches. If you want to use no switches, press <Enter>. If you do want to use a switch, enter the first desired switch with any applicable parameters, if any, and press <Enter>. Every time you enter a switch, you'll be prompted to enter another after you press <Enter>. After you press <Enter> after having entered no switches, COMP will proceed to make the comparison.

Alternatively, you can type COMP followed by the first file path, the second file path, and any switches and other parameters desired. For example, using the 32-bit command prompt in 2000 or XP, compare two files designating the output to be noted in characters:

```
COMP C:\Documents and Settings\Rojo\My Documents\Chapter05.doc D:\Book
Chapters\Chapter05KJI.doc /a
```

Switches

/a: Displays differences as characters.

/c: Performs a comparison that is not case sensitive.

/d: Displays differences in decimal format. (The default format is hexadecimal.)

/l: Displays the number of the line on which a difference occurs, instead of displaying the byte offset.

/n=*number*: Compares the first *number* of lines of both files, even if the files are different sizes.

Notes

■ Use wildcard characters to compare groups of files.

■ COMP displays the results in memory addresses, so it's useful only to indicate that the files are different, not to display the differences.

■ Files must be the same size, or the only result will be that the files aren't the same size. The exception to this is if the /n=number switch is used. In place of the word *number*, enter the number of lines of data to be compared. If you enter, for example, 10, the first 10 lines of each file will be compared.

■ This command is extraordinarily particular; even a change in case somewhere in the path might cause COMP to report that it cannot open the file. Used in an MS-DOS prompt, you might have to convert folder names or filenames to the 8.3 standard. Look up 8.3 filename standard on the Internet if you need help.

CONVERT (XP AND 2000 ONLY)

Converts hard drive partitions formatted as FAT and FAT32 to NTFS. CONVERT cannot convert a partition to any file system other than NTFS.

Use

Type CONVERT followed by the drive letter and colon, and then /fs:ntfs followed by any switches. If you were converting drive C to NTFS in the verbose mode (see the switch listings), you would type:

```
CONVERT C: /fs:ntfs /v
```

and then press <Enter>.

Switches

/fs:ntfs: CONVERT won't work without this switch following the drive letter. fs means *file system*.

f/nosecurity: Specifies that files and folders already on the drive are accessible to everyone who uses the computer.

/v: Verbose mode. All possible information will be displayed while the conversion is taking place.

/x: Performs all changes to network-mapped drives necessary for the conversion to take place.

Note

■ Any drive in use will be converted at the next boot.

COPY

Copies one or more files. XCOPY provides much more flexibility than does COPY.

Use

Type COPY followed by general switches, then type the path of the file(s) to be copied followed by any switches that apply to the source files, then the path of the destination, if desired, followed by any switches that apply to the destination. The source can be a path to a drive, folder, or file. If it is a drive or folder, it will copy all the files in that folder to the destination, but it will not copy subfolders or any files within subfolders. Wildcards can be used in a source. Two or more files or folders can be specified in the source by using the plus sign (+) followed by a space character before each file after the first one listed, as in:

```
COPY /v D:\Backup\*.dll + D:\Backup\Example.txt C:\Windows\System32
```

This example would copy all .dll files in the Backup folder on the D drive, but no files in subfolders of Backup, plus the file Example.txt to the C:\Windows\System32 folder. The /v switch verifies that each file is copied properly.

The destination can also be a path to a drive, folder, or file. If the destination is a path to a drive or folder, the copy will keep the name of the original file. If the destination is a file with a name different from the original, the copy will have the new filename. If the destination is not specified, the copy will be placed in the current folder, as long as the current folder isn't the same as the source folder; in which case no copying will occur.

If two or more source files are specified but only one destination file is specified, the files will be combined into a single file, assuming the file formats are compatible with each other and can handle such a change. Text files (.txt), for example, can be combined.

Switches

/d: If any of the source files are encrypted, this switch removes the encryption attribute on the copies.

/n: Causes the filename to be converted to one that complies with the DOS 8.3 filename convention.

/v: Verifies that new files are copied correctly. It is advisable to use when copying critical files. It does cause the copying to take more time than without /v.

/y: By default, Windows prompts you to confirm that you want to overwrite an existing destination file of the same name in the same folder; /y stops these prompts.

/-y: Turns off the /y switch. Restores prompts to confirm that you want to overwrite an existing destination file of the same name in the same folder.

/z: In case copies are being made over a network and the network connection is lost, or one of the computers goes off line, /z sets the copy operation to automatically resume from where it left off after the connection is reestablished.

/a: Indicates an ASCII text file (see Windows' Help for more information).

/b: Indicates a binary file (see Windows' Help for more information).

Note

- You might have to surround folder names or filenames containing spaces with quotation marks, or use the 8.3 standard filenames when using this command.

DEL OR ERASE

Deletes specified files.

Use

Navigate to the folder that contains the file and type DEL or ERASE followed by the filename, and by any desired switches. You can also enter the entire path at the prompt rather than navigating to the folder. Multiple filenames can be entered separated by spaces, commas, or semicolons, or wildcards can be used. If only a folder name is entered, DEL or ERASE will delete only the files in the root of the folder. Subfolders and files within subfolders will not be affected unless the /s switch is used.

Switches

/f: Normally, files with the read-only attribute will not be deleted. /f overrides this and forces deletion.

/p: Prompts you to confirm that you want the file to be deleted.

/q: Prevents Windows from prompting you to confirm that you want the file to be deleted.

/s: Deletes specified files from the current folder and all subfolders. Displays each filename as the file is deleted.

Note

- Once you delete a file using the DEL or ERASE command, that file *does not* appear in the Recycle Bin and is considered irretrievable without some third-party recovery program.

DIR

Displays a list of the subfolders and files in a folder or drive with some information such as total file size, the last date and time each file was modified, and the amount of free disk space on the disk.

Use

Navigate to the desired folder and type DIR followed by any desired switches. Does not show hidden or system files unless you use the /a switch.

Switches

/p: Displays one screen at a time. To continue, press any key on the keyboard.

/q: Displays the owner of each file, if applicable.

/a: Displays all files, including files with the hidden and system attributes.

/a followed by attribute codes: displays only files or other items with attributes you specify.

Attribute Codes

a: Files ready for archiving only

d: Folders only

h: Hidden files and folders only

r: Read-only files only

s: System files and folders only

Each of these codes can be inversed by preceding it with a minus sign (-). For example, -r displays only files with the read-only attribute. In addition, using multiple attribute codes, Windows will display only files with *all* of the attributes indicated by the codes. Don't leave a space between codes when using multiple codes. For example, to display only files that are *both* read only and hidden, type:

```
DIR /arh
```

/s: Lists every occurrence, in the specified folder and all its subfolders, of the specified filename.

/x: Displays both long filenames and 8.3 filenames.

Note

■ DIR has several more switches. Consult Windows' Help or run DIR with the /? switch for more information.

EDIT (LIMITED USE IN 2000 AND XP)

Starts the MS-DOS Editor, which creates and changes ASCII text files. EDIT is an antiquated text editor that works without benefit of a mouse. It can be essential to use if you boot into DOS and need to edit a text file such as autoexec.bat or config.sys. Access menu commands by pressing and holding the <Alt> key while typing the first letter of the menu and the highlighted letter of each command. Once you have accessed a menu, the arrow keys can be used to navigate the menus. Another way to invoke a menu command is to highlight it by using the arrow keys, and then press <Enter>.

Use

Type EDIT followed by the full path to the file you want to open or create, followed by any desired switches.

EXIT

Closes a DOS prompt and many DOS programs. If you click the X to close the window in a DOS program, you'll get a message indicating that closing the program this way will cause any unsaved data to be lost. While you'll rarely have any unsaved data, it is probably easier to use this command to avoid the prompt.

Use

Type EXIT.

EXPAND (2000 AND XP ONLY)

Expands one or more compressed files. This command is used to retrieve compressed files from distribution disks such as Windows installation disks, often designated with an underscore as the final character in the file extension, or found in 9x in the \Windows\Options\Cabs or \Windows\Options\Install folder.

Use

Type EXPAND followed by the path of the source file and the path of the destination file. If you are expanding a file within a cabinet file, navigate to the cab file's folder and type EXPAND followed by the cab filename and then the -f: switch, followed, without a space, by the individual files within the cab file. For example, navigate to C:\Windows\Options\Cabs (found in many Windows 9x installations) and type:

```
EXPAND net10.cab -f:snip.vxd C:\Windows
```

This will expand the snip.vxd file into the C:\Windows folder.

Switch

-f: -f followed, without a space, by filenames of files within cab files.

FDISK (DOS AND 9X ONLY)

Opens a program that allows creation and deletion of partitions, and the viewing of partition information. Once the program is open, it is no longer a command-line program, but instead is menu based.

Use

While booted into DOS, type FDISK to open the program. Two switches will also perform functions without opening the menu-based program.

Switches

/mbr: This will replace the master boot record (MBR). The *MBR* is the first sector on the hard disk. There is a small program in the MBR that tells the system which partition is bootable. You cannot boot without the MBR being intact. Use this switch to replace a damaged MBR. This can occur if there is a boot-sector virus, or for other reasons. Try using this if you can't boot and you can't determine another cause. Using this switch does not open the menu-based program.

/status: This will display information about the partition. Using this switch does not open the menu-based program.

/x: Ignores extended disk partition support. If you receive a disk access or stack overflow error, use this switch; /x can be used with /status, but if used by itself, the menu-based program does open.

FORMAT

Formats magnetic disks and partitions in specified file formats (FAT, FAT32, NTFS). Works with floppy and hard disks.

Use

Type FORMAT followed by the drive letter and a colon, a space, then /fs: and the name of the file system (FAT, FAT32, or NTFS). For example, to format drive E: as FAT32, you would type:

```
FORMAT E: /fs:FAT32
```

Floppy disks can be formatted only as FAT. FAT is the designation for FAT16. If you omit the /fs switch, the system will use the default.

Switches

/fs: followed by the desired file system: This switch determines the file system, but if you leave it out, Windows will use the default. For example, floppies will automatically be formatted as FAT.

/q: Quick format. Skips a sector-by-sector surface scan of the disk. Use only with a disk known not to have any bad sectors.

/c: Compress newly added files. Works only with NTFS partitions.

/s: (95, 98, and DOS only) Formats a floppy and copies the three DOS files (Command.com, IO.sys, MSDOS.sys) onto it. This switch will work in 95 and 98, and any time the computer is booted into MS-DOS.

Note

■ Formatting a disk erases all data on the disk, regardless of the method used to format.

MD OR MKDIR

Stands for "Make Directory." Creates a folder or subfolder.

Use

Type MD followed by the full path of the new folder, including the name of the new folder. Alternatively, you can navigate to the drive or folder one level above that of the new folder, and type MD followed only by the desired name of the new folder.

MMC (2000 AND XP ONLY)

Opens Microsoft Management Console (MMC). Normally run from the Run dialog rather than the command prompt. If you have created or saved an MMC console, this command is an easy way to open it. MMC is beyond the scope of this book, but you might be instructed to use it by a Microsoft support technician. For more information on MMCs, search Windows 2000's or XP's Help for MMC.

Use

Type MMC in the Run dialog. If opening a saved console, navigate (browse) to the location of the saved console file, and then type MMC followed by a space and the filename.

Switch

/a: Opens a saved console in author mode. This switch is necessary to make changes to saved consoles.

MORE

Allows the viewing of files and the output of other commands one screen at a time. This command is commonly used to view long files. When the window is full, you will get the MORE prompt. There are several options for how you want to view the remaining output.

Use

To use MORE by itself, navigate to the folder that contains the files you want to view, type MORE followed by any desired switches, and then the path to the file. If you want to view multiple files, you can enter all the filenames separated by space characters. You can even view files in different folders by entering the full path for each. For example, to view files in 2000 or XP in the root folder of the C: drive, My Documents, and in a folder on a CD-ROM, clearing the screen before displaying the next page, navigate to My Documents, and type:

```
MORE /c test1.txt C:\test2.txt D:\"text files"\test3.txt
```

This will display one screen of test1.txt and allow you to view the remainder of the file using commands that will be described later. Once the entire test1 file has been displayed, test2 will be displayed, followed by test3.

To use MORE with another command, type the command followed by any desired switches for the command, a space, the pipe character (|) (see the note at the end of this listing), MORE, any desired switches pertaining to the MORE command, and then the path to the file or files you want to view. For example, to use the MEM /P command with MORE, clearing the screen after each page, type:

```
MEM /p | MORE /c
```

Switches

/c: Clears each screen before you use a command to view the next screen.

/s: Reduces a series of blank lines to a single blank line.

Responses to the — More — Prompt

<spacebar>: Displays next page.

<Enter>: Displays next line.

<F>: Skips to next file.

<Q>: Quits.

<?>: Displays available responses to — More – prompt.

<=>: Displays line number.

<P> followed by a space and a number: Displays the specified number of lines.

<S> followed by a space and a number: Skips the specified number of lines

Note

■   To type the pipe character, hold <Shift> and press the backslash (\) key.

MOVE

Moves files or folders from one drive or folder to another. Similar to COPY, except that MOVE deletes the source file.

Use

Type MOVE followed by a switch, if desired, then the source folder or file name, and then the destination folder or file name. If moving more than one file, the destination must be a folder.

Switches

/y: Normally, you would be prompted to confirm if you want to overwrite an existing destination file or folder of the same name; /y turns off this prompt. It is not necessary to use unless there actually is such a destination file or folder and you want to suppress the prompt.

/-y: Turns on the prompt to confirm that you want to overwrite a destination file or folder of the same name, if present.

Note

■ MOVE will not move encrypted files or folders to a drive that doesn't support the Encrypting File System (EFS). EFS is supported on NTFS drives in 2000, XP, or Windows Server 2003 only. Non-upgraded NTFS drives on systems that were upgraded from Windows NT do not support EFS, but that scenario is rare. To move these files, decrypt them first.

PATH

Although "path" has a more general meaning, "the path" refers to the path to all of these commands. In 9x, some of these are in the root folder of the boot drive (usually C:\), some are in the Windows folder (usually C:\Windows), and some are in the Command folder (usually C:\Windows\Command). In 2000 and XP, commands can be found in the Windows folder (usually C:\Windows or C:\Winnt), and in the System32 folder (usually C:\Windows\System32). There also might be a Command folder (usually C:\Windows\Command or C:\Winnt\Command). The PATH command sets the computer to recognize the locations of these commands. That is how Windows can find each command simply from the user entering commands at the command prompt or in the Run dialog. Run by itself, PATH displays the current path.

Use

Type PATH followed by the path that contains commands. You can enter multiple command paths by separating them with semicolons (;).

Parameter

;: Separates the different paths that are to make up "the path." If you use this by itself, the existing command path will be deleted.

Example

In 9x, if you find you don't have access to all commands that should be available, type:

```
PATH C:\;C:\Windows;C:\Windows\Command
```

You can add any other paths you want, separated by semicolons. This can be especially useful if you boot a 9x machine with a startup (MS-DOS) floppy.

RECOVER

Recovers readable data from a damaged bad or defective disk.

Use

Type RECOVER followed by the path to the file you want to rescue. RECOVER requires that the disk not be in use, so it cannot be used on the Windows boot partition while the computer is booted to Windows.

Note

■ RECOVER reads a file sector by sector and recovers data from the good sectors. Data in bad sectors is lost. It is common practice to open the file after recovery and attempt to re-enter missing data manually.

REN OR RENAME

Changes the name of a file or folder.

Use

Navigate to the folder that contains the file you want to rename, or to the parent folder of the subfolder you want to rename. Type REN followed by the existing file or folder name, a space, and then the new file or folder name. REN cannot be used to move files or folders, so you cannot enter a new path for the file.

Notes

■ You can use wildcards in either or both the existing and the new filenames, with the caveat that the wildcard characters will stand for the same real characters in both names. For example, let's say that the current folder has three files named test1.doc, test2.doc, and test3.doc. You enter test*.doc as the existing filename and sample*.doc as the new filename. Test1.doc will become sample1.doc, test2.doc will become sample2.doc, and so on.

■ If you try to rename a file to a filename in use in the same folder, you'll get an error message and the renaming operation will not proceed.

REPLACE

Replaces files in the destination folder with files in the source folder that have the same name. It also can be used to add files to the destination folder that don't already exist there. For example, if you need to make sure that all files on an optical disc have been copied to a folder on the hard drive, you could use another method to copy them again, and then get the prompt to overwrite existing files. Using REPLACE with the /a switch automatically copies only files that don't exist on the destination folder while ignoring those files that do exist there.

Use

To replace files or folders, type REPLACE followed by the path to the source files or folders, then the destination files or folders, followed by any appropriate switches. You can also navigate to the source folder before running the command. If you specify neither a source nor a destination folder, the current folder is used.

Switches

/a: Adds only files to the destination folder that aren't there already; /a cannot be used at the same time as the /s or /u switches.

/p: Prompts you for confirmation before replacing or adding a file or folder.

/r: Replaces read-only, hidden or system files or folders. Files or folders in the destination folder with these attributes normally would cause the operation to stop.

/w: Waits for you to insert a disk before searching for source files or folders. Without this switch, REPLACE attempts to replace or add files immediately after the user presses <ENTER>.

/s: Includes subfolders of the destination folder (not the source folder); /s cannot be used at the same time as the /a switch.

/u: Replaces only those files in the destination folder that are older than those with the same names in the source folder; /u cannot be used at the same time as the /a switch; /u cannot be used to update hidden or system files. You'll have to remove these attributes first, using the ATTRIB command or the Windows interface.

RD OR RMDIR

Deletes a folder. RD stands for "Remove Directory."

Use

Type RD followed by the path to the folder you want to delete, followed by any desired switches. Make sure to enter the full path, starting with the drive letter. Do not navigate first to the folder you want to delete; RD won't work if you do. Additionally, RD won't work if the folder to be deleted is a subfolder of the current folder.

Switches

/s: Includes all subfolders and their contents.

/q: Quiet mode. Normally, a confirmation is given after the deletion is complete; /q turns off this confirmation.

Note

■ You cannot delete a folder with hidden or system files without removing these attributes first. See DIR to locate these files and ATTRIB to remove these attributes.

SCANREG AND SCANREGW (9X ONLY)

See Chapter 11.

SFC (98, 2000 AND XP ONLY)

See Chapter 11.

SHUTDOWN (XP ONLY)

Allows you to shut down, restart, or log a user off the computer. Used without switches, SHUTDOWN will log off the current user.

Use

Type SHUTDOWN followed by any desired switches.

Switches

-s: Shuts down the computer.

-r: Reboots the computer.

-f: Forces any running programs to close.

-t followed by a space and a number of seconds: This sets the timer for system shutdown in the specified number of seconds. The default is 20 seconds.

-a: Aborts shutdown. If you run shutdown and then change your mind, during the timed interval before the machine shuts down you can abort the shutdown by running SHUTDOWN -a.

SYS (DOS AND 9X ONLY)

Copies the DOS system files, COMMAND.COM, IO.SYS, and MS DOS.SYS, to a disk.

Use

Navigate to the drive and folder you want to copy the DOS system files to and type SYS. *Never* run SYS on an NTFS drive.

SYSTEMINFO (XP ONLY)

Displays detailed configuration information about a computer and Windows, including operating system (OS) configuration, security information, product ID, and hardware properties, such as memory, disk space, and network adapters.

Use

Type SYSTEMINFO. If you want to configure the format of the output, use the /fo switch. SYSTEMINFO is an ideal command to be accompanied by the MORE command.

Switches

/fo followed by one of the three possibilities: TABLE, LIST, or CSV (Comma-Separated Values). LIST is the default.

Note

■ You might get the error message indicating that a required file, framedyn.dll, is missing. If this is the case, you'll need to find the file framedyn.dl_ on the XP installation disk in the I386 folder. Copy this file to Windows\System32. Then, use the EXPAND command to expand it and then REN or the Windows interface to rename it framedyn.dll.

TASKKILL (XP ONLY)

Terminates one or more programs or processes. Processes can be called by their process ID or by their name. View running processes by using the TASKLIST command.

Use

Run TASKLIST or Windows' Task Manager (type <Ctrl> + <Alt> + <Delete>). Once you've determined which processes to terminate, type TASKKILL followed by the appropriate switches and parameters.

Switches and Parameters

/pid followed by the process ID: Specifies the process ID of the process to be terminated.

/im followed by the process name: Specifies the process name (called *image name*) of the process to be terminated. TASKKILL will terminate all instances of a process.

/f: Terminates the process(es) by force, if necessary. Some processes will ordinarily not be terminated without this switch. Most of these are crucial to the operation of Windows, so don't be surprised if Windows shuts down if you end the wrong process.

/t: Terminates all "child processes" of the specified process.

TASKLIST (XP ONLY)

Displays a list of programs and processes with their Process ID (PID) for all tasks running on the computer. Useful to compile data for the TASKKILL command.

Use

Type TASKLIST followed by any desired switches.

Switches and Parameters

/fo followed by the type of output desired: Possible output types are TABLE, LIST, and CSV. CSV stands for *Comma Separated Value.* The default is TABLE.

/m followed by the module name: A module is a program that uses DLL files. *DLL* stands for *Dynamic Link Library.* Files with this extension are used by programs, and are often used by more than one program. For example, different card games might all use the same Cards.dll file to provide a deck of cards. If you run TASKLIST with this switch and specify a module, the output will show all the DLL files that could be used for that module. If you use the /m switch without a module name, all modules will be listed. The /m switch is incompatible with the /svc and /v switches.

/svc: Lists complete service information for each process. This switch will work only if the output is set to TABLE, the default (see the /fo switch); /svc is incompatible with the /m and /v switches.

/v: Verbose mode. All information will be displayed; /v is incompatible with the /svc and /m switches.

TYPE

Displays the text in a text file.

Use

Navigate to the text file's folder and type TYPE, or type TYPE followed by the path to the file or files to view. To view multiple files, separate them with spaces.

This is a command in which it is very helpful to use the MORE command.

VER

Displays the Windows version and number.

Use

Type VER.

WINNT32 (2000 AND XP ONLY)

Performs an installation of or upgrade to Windows 2000 or XP. WINNT32 is not in the usual command path. It is available when the current folder is an installation source such as a Windows 2000 or XP CD.

Use

Insert the 2000 or XP installation disk or connect to another installation source. Close the installation program after it opens. Open a command prompt and navigate to the installation folder, which will probably be I386. Type WINNT32 followed by any desired switches.

Switches

/checkupgradeonly: Checks your current version of Windows to determine if it's eligible to be upgraded to the new version, and checks your hardware to make sure its compatible with the new version. If you use this option with /unattend, you will not be prompted for any input. If you don't use /unattend, the output is displayed, and you are prompted to save it in a file. The default filename is Upgrade.txt, and its default location is in the System32 folder, usually C:\Windows\System32 or C:\Winnt\System32.

/cmdcons: Use this switch on a system that already has Windows 2000 or XP installed to install the Recovery Console as a startup option. For more information on the Recovery Console, see Chapter 11 and the last section in this appendix.

/unattend: Upgrades existing 98, Me, 2000, or XP in a mode that requires no user input. All information that is normally requested during setup is taken from the existing installation.

Note

■ There are a great many other switches for WINNT32 that are beyond the scope of this book. They are of use primarily to network administrators and others responsible for installing Windows on many machines simultaneously.

XCOPY

Copies files, folders, and subfolders. XCOPY offers great flexibility over any other way to copy, be it by command line or using the Windows graphical interface.

Use

Type XCOPY followed by the path to the source file or folder, then the destination file or folder, and then any desired switches.

Switches

/w: Prompts you to press a key before copying commences.

/p: Prompts you to confirm that you want to create each destination file.

/c: Continues copying regardless of errors.

/q: Quiet mode. XCOPY messages are not displayed.

/f: Displays filenames while copying.

/l: Displays the names of all the files that are set to be copied.

/g: Specifies that destination files not be encrypted (2000 and XP only).

/d followed by a colon and the date in the mm-dd-yyyy format: Copies only those source files that had been modified on or after the specified date. If you do not include a date, all source files newer than the existing destination files of the same name are copied. The purpose of this command is to update files with newer versions. For example, to copy only .doc files newer than March 5, 2006 from a CD to a folder, you would type:

```
XCOPY D:\*.doc c:\folder /d:03-05-2006
```

/u: Copies only those source files with the same names as those already in the destination folder.

/i: If you have specified a folder or a file name with wildcards as the source and the destination folder doesn't already exist, /i causes XCOPY to create the new folder. The default is for XCOPY to prompt you to specify whether the destination is a folder or file.

/s: Copies folders and subfolders as long as there are files inside them.

/e: Copies all subfolders, regardless of whether there are files inside them.

/t: Copies the entire folder tree, but none of the files. Add the /e switch to copy empty folders.

/k: (2000 and XP) Causes the copied files to retain the read-only attribute if the source files had it. By default, copied files do not have the read-only attribute.

/k: (9x) Causes all attributes to be copied with the files.

/r: Copies files with the read-only attribute, but is not supposed to copy the attribute. However, it might actually copy the attribute in some cases.

/h: Copies files with hidden and system attributes. The default is for system and hidden files not to be copied.

/a: Copies only files with the archive attributes.

/m: Copies only files with the archive attributes, but removes the archive attribute from the *source* file.

/n: Applies 8.3 file and/or folder names to the copies. Necessary when copying files with long filenames to systems that can handle only 8.3 filenames. See Chapter 2 for more information.

/y: Normally, XCOPY prompts you to confirm that you want to overwrite a destination file of the same name as the one being copied; /y turns off this prompting.

/-y: Restores prompting to overwrite existing files of the same name as the one being copied.

/z: (2000 and XP only) If you are copying over a network and the network connection is lost for whatever reason, if you used /z, copying can pick up where it left off once the connection is restored; /z saves you from having to start over again; /z also displays the copying progress for each file.

Notes

- If you attempt to copy encrypted files onto a drive that doesn't support the Encrypted File System (EFS), there will be an error and copying will not continue.
- If you don't specify a destination, XCOPY uses the current folder.
- By default, unless you use the /m switch, XCOPY's file copies all have the archive attribute set, regardless of whether it was set in the source files.

COMMENT INDICATORS

When directly editing the MS-DOS configuration files Autoexec.bat and Config.sys, or their XP/2000 counterparts, Config.nt and Autoexec.nt, the safest way to stop a line of text from being implemented is to "comment it out." In these files, you do this by typing REM at the beginning of a line. This tells the system to ignore that line. The advantage to using these indicators as opposed to simply deleting the line is that it's very easy to reverse if you discover that you erroneously commented out an important line.

For .ini files such as Win.ini and System.ini, comment out lines using a semicolon.

RECOVERY CONSOLE COMMANDS (2000 AND XP ONLY)

The Recovery Console is discussed in Chapter 11. The Recovery Console has a limited number of commands. Many of the commands are the same, but most of these have different switches and parameters. Additionally, there are other commands that are unique to the Recovery Console. Because the functions of the shared commands are very similar or the same as in the standard commands, only the differences, if any, will be noted. Moreover, only selected commands and switches will be presented here. For a complete list, search Windows' Help for "Recovery Console."

There are a few rules to be concerned with when using the Recovery Console:

- Except where indicated, wildcard characters don't work.
- Type quotation marks around folder and file names containing spaces.
- Only certain folders can be accessed:
    - The root folder of any hard drive partition.
    - The Windows or Winnt folder and its subfolders.
    - The Cmdcons folder, which is the folder, usually in the root folder of the C:\ drive, that contains the Recovery Console. It is hidden by default.
    - Removable media, but only to read and copy files. Files on removable media cannot be modified using the Recovery Console.
    - The Windows installation media.
- Attempts to access other folders will cause an "Access Denied" message.
- The /? switch for help works with all Recovery Console commands.

ATTRIB

Switches

+**r:** Sets the read-only attribute.

-**r:** Clears the read-only attribute.

+**s:** Sets the system attribute.

-**s:** Clears the system attribute.

+**h:** Sets the hidden attribute.

-**h:** Clears the hidden attribute.

+**c:** Sets the compressed attribute.

-**c:** Clears the compressed attribute.

CD OR CHDIR

This is the same as the command-prompt version, except that you always have to use quotation marks around folder names containing spaces.

CHKDSK

Switches

/p: Normally, a disk that doesn't indicate problems will not be checked exhaustively. Use /p to override this indication and run the exhaustive check anyway. CHKDSK does not make any changes to the drive when run only with /p.

/r: Locates bad sectors and recovers any readable data. /r automatically includes /p.

Note

- CHKDSK requires the file Autochk.exe in order to work. If it cannot find it in the system folder (usually \Winnt\System32 or \Windows\System32), it will look for it on the Windows Installation CD.

CLS

This command is the same as the command-prompt version.

COPY

Copies a single file only to another location. COPY will not copy a folder.

Note

- When copying a compressed file from the Windows installation CD, the file is automatically decompressed.

DEL OR DELETE

Deletes a single file only. DEL will not delete a folder.

DIR

Lists the volume (drive) label, serial number, and contents, along with codes indicating what each item is and what attributes are set in each.

Parameter

/ followed by a folder name, filename or group of filenames: DIR can limit itself to showing just those folder or file names you select, along with everything within a folder. *Wildcard characters can be used with this parameter.* Multiple filenames can be used by using wildcards or separating file names with spaces, commas, or semi-colons.

Notes

- The /p switch is not available with DIR in the Recovery Console because the command runs as if used with the MORE command prompt command.
- DIR's output includes the volume (drive) label, serial number, total number of files, the total size of all displayed items, and the amount of free disk space remaining (in bytes). Other information in the output includes time of last modification, file extension, individual file size, file attributes, and whether the item is a file or directory (folder). The last two items use the following codes:

Code	Meaning
d	Directory (folder)
h	Hidden
s	System
e	Encrypted
r	Read-only
a	Archive
c	Compressed
p	Reparse point

DISABLE

Disables a device driver or service. The opposite command is ENABLE.

Use

Type DISABLE followed by the service or driver name. You can use the LISTSVC command for a list of services and drivers on the computer.

Parameters

Service name: Type DISABLE followed by a service name, as shown:

```
DISABLE Messenger
```

This causes the messenger service to be disabled the next time the computer is booted to Windows. The previous state of the service is displayed as well.

Device driver name: Type DISABLE followed by the driver name. The driver will be disabled for the next boot to Windows. The previous state of the service is displayed as well.

DISKPART

Allows management of disk partitions.

Use

Type DISKPART followed by the appropriate switches and parameters. Run without switches and parameters, DISKPART starts the Windows Setup partitioning program. You'll recognize the program if you have installed NT 4.0, 2000 or XP.

Switches and Parameters

/add followed by the device name and the desired size, in MB, of the partition: Creates a new partition. For example, to add a 10-MB partition, type:

```
DISKPART /add \Device\HardDisk0 10
```

Device name is defined after the /delete switch.

/delete followed by the drive letter, partition name, or device name: Deletes an existing partition. *Partition name* and *device name* are defined here:

Device name: An identifier for the hard drive that uses a direct naming convention. This precludes the confusion that can come about due to drive letters than can change. To get this, run the MAP Recovery Console command with no switch and ignore the partition portion of the output. A typical device name is \Device\Harddisk0. The device name is valid only with both the /add and /delete switches.

Partition name: This uses the same naming convention as the device name, but has the added partition number at the end. A typical partition name is \Device\Harddisk0\Partition1. The partition name is valid only with the /delete switch.

Deletion Examples

```
DISKPART /delete \Device\HardDisk0\Partition2
DISKPART /delete E:
```

ENABLE

Enables a service or device driver.

Use

Type ENABLE followed by the service name or device driver name and the startup type. The possible startup types are SERVICE_BOOT_START, SERVICE_SYSTEM START, SERVICE_AUTO_START, SERVICE_DEMAND_START. For example, to enable the Messenger service to start automatically, type:

```
ENABLE Messenger SERVICE_AUTO_START
```

When the ENABLE is run with a device driver name or service name but no start type, the current start type is displayed. Write this down if you need to keep a record of it.

You can use the LISTSVC command for a list of services and drivers on the computer.

Parameter

Startup type: The possible startup types are defined here:

Startup Type	Definition	Applies Primarily To
SERVICE_BOOT_START	Starts with Windows	Device drivers
SERVICE_SYSTEM_START	Starts with the computer	Device drivers
SERVICE_AUTO_START	Starts with Windows	Services
SERVICE_DEMAND_START	Starts manually by a program or user	Services

EXIT

Exits the Recovery Console and restarts the computer.

EXPAND

Use

Type EXPAND followed by the source file and then the destination folder. If you want to select an individual file to extract from a cab file, type EXPAND followed by the cab filename, /F: followed without a space by the name of the file within the cab file, the destination folder, and then the /y switch if desired. The source cannot use wildcards, but the name of a file within a cab file can use wildcards. If you do not specify a destination folder, the current folder is used.

For example, to expand the Drvspace.bin file from within the C:\Windows\Options\Cabs\Base4.cab file to the root directory (realizing that this file is from Windows 98 and wouldn't actually be expanded using the Recovery Console), from the C:\ prompt type:

```
EXPAND \Windows\Options\Cabs\Base4.cab /F:drivespace.bin C:\
```

Entering the destination was optional because the command was run from the C:\ prompt. Recall that EXPAND uses the current folder if the destination folder isn't specified.

Switches and Parameters

/d: Lists the files within the cabinet file. Performs no action on the file. Not recommended for use on folders with large number of files.

/y: Normally, you are prompted to confirm that you want to overwrite files in the destination; /y turns off these prompts.

FIXBOOT

Creates a new boot sector on the system partition. Useful if the boot sector has been damaged.

Use

Type FIXBOOT. This will create a new boot sector on the partition that you are logged on to. If you want to create a boot sector on a different drive, enter the drive letter followed by a colon after FIXBOOT and a space. For example, to create a new boot sector on the E: drive, type:

```
FIXBOOT E:
```

FIXMBR

Creates a new MBR on a hard drive. The MBR is the first sector on a hard drive. A small program on the MBR contains information about the partitions, indicating which one is bootable, in case there are more than one.

Use

Type FIXMBR. This will create a new MBR on the existing boot disk drive. To select another drive, enter the device name after FIXMBR. Run the MAP command to find the device name. For example, to replace the MBR on the first drive on the system, you can type:

```
FIXMBR \Device\HardDisk\0
```

Note

■ Use FIXMBR with caution. *Never* run FIXMBR unless you are having trouble accessing the drive or trouble booting the computer and you cannot determine another reason. In certain cases, you can damage your partition. It is recommended not to use FIXMBR unless directed to do so by Microsoft support personnel or unless you are well versed in its use.

FORMAT

Use

Type FORMAT followed by the drive letter, fs:, the desired file system, and any desired switch. This version of FORMAT does not work with floppy disks, only hard drives.

Switches and Parameters

/q: Normally, FORMAT scans the disk for bad sectors. The /q switch causes FORMAT to skip this step, so it should be used only if the drive is known to be good and has been formatted before.

/fs: followed, without a space, by the name of the file system (NTFS, FAT, or FAT32): Specifies the file system. If you don't specify a file system, FORMAT uses the existing file system, if there is one.

LISTSVC

Lists the services and drivers available on the computer along with the startup type and description for each. The output appears one page at a time as if the MORE command prompt command were used.

LOGON

Logs you on to a particular installation of Windows. Useful on dual- or multi-boot systems when each OS is compatible with Recovery Console (NT 4.0, 2000, XP, Windows Server 2003). You will be able to select from a list of all Windows installations the Recovery Console can find. You will be prompted for the administrator password. If you get the password wrong three times, the Recovery Console will quit and the computer will automatically reboot.

MAP

Displays the assignment of drive letters to physical partitions. The output is useful if you want to run DISKPART, FIXBOOT, or FIXMBR.

Use

Type MAP, followed by the arc switch, if desired.

Switch

arc: Causes the output to use the ARC format rather than the device name format. The arc switch is preceded only by a space, not by a slash or any other punctuation mark, as shown:

```
MAP arc
```

Note

■   The ARC name looks like the following: multi(0)disk(0)rdisk(0)partition(1)

The device name for the same drive and partition is \Device\HardDisk0\Partition1. For more information on device names and the ARC naming convention, search the Web.

MD OR MKDIR

Wildcard characters will not work.

MORE

Displays the text in a text file.

Use

Type MORE followed by the path to the text file you want to read. Use quotation marks or asterisks around filenames with spaces. MORE displays one page at a time and prompts for input on how to view the next part of the text file.

Note

■   In the Recovery Console, MORE is identical to the TYPE command.

REN OR RENAME

Renames a single file. Wildcards will not work.

RD OR RMDIR

RD will not delete a folder unless it is empty.

SYSTEMROOT

Makes the system root folder (almost always \Windows or \Winnt) the current folder.

TYPE

See the MORE Recovery Console command.

D On the CD-ROM

VIDEOS

Title	Filename
Opening Different Types of Cases and Accessing Internal Parts	Opening_the_Case.mpg
Installing Memory	Installing_Memory.mpg
Removal and Replacement of Expansion Cards	Removal_and_Replacement_of_Expansion_Cards.mpg
Installing CPUs	Installing_CPUs.mpg
Motherboard Installation	Motherboard_Installation.mpg
Vacuuming	Vacuuming_and_Cleaning_Computers.mpg

Video System Requirements

- Sound card
- Windows 95 or later
- A media player such as Windows Media Player (Start > Programs or All Programs > Accessories > Entertainment > Windows Media Player), available free from *microsoft.com/windowsmedia* if you don't already have it), or QuickTime (*apple.com/quicktime/products/qt*)
- Pentium 1 or equivalent and higher
- 16MB RAM

DOCUMENTS AND DOCUMENT SYSTEM REQUIREMENTS

These two documents are available in two file formats: .doc, which can be opened by Microsoft Word, Microsoft Wordpad (Start > Programs (or All Programs) > Accessories > Wordpad), and many other word processing programs; and in PDF format, which can be opened by Adobe Acrobat and Acrobat Reader. (The reader is available free from *adobe.com*.)

Beep Codes

Beep Codes.doc, Beep Codes.pdf, Beep Codes.htm

Industry Contacts

Industry Contacts.doc, Industry Contacts.pdf, Industry Contacts.htm

Sample Material

Sample Chapter and Questions, A+ Adaptive Exams (*TestTaker's Guide Series* by Christopher A. Crayton)—AplusC.pdf. This document can be opened in Adobe Acrobat or Adobe Acrobat Reader only.

README

The README document is in .rtf, text, and .pdf formats. The text version (readme.txt) will open automatically in Microsoft Notepad. Any text editor or word processing program can open it. It can even be viewed by using the *Type* or *More* commands (see Appendix C, "Command-Line Tutorial," for instructions). The RTF file (readme.rtf) can be viewed in any word processing program, including Wordpad. The .pdf file can be opened in Adobe Acrobat and Adobe Reader. All of these documents are viewable on any PC with any of the aforementioned programs.

IMAGES AND IMAGE SYSTEM REQUIREMENTS

All of the images that appear elsewhere in this book are on the accompanying CD-ROM, in color. Any PC running Windows 95 and later with the default Windows component *Imaging* (Start > Programs or All Programs > Accessories > Imaging), or any other image-viewing program, and a minimum of 16MB of RAM can open the image files.

The CD-ROM should autostart and open to an HTML index with hyperlinks to all the files. If not, open My Computer, double-click the optical drive, and double-click on the index.html file icon. You can also double-click individual files to open them.

Index